TAGE & PALACE SQUARE ▲ 166

GW00374403

BOLSHAYA NEVKA

CARIES ND

FINLAND STATION

NEVA

ER AND PAUL FORTRESS
★

SUMMER GARDEN
★

SMOLNY MONASTERY

TAURIDE PALACE

ERMITAGE ND PALACE SQUARE
★

ARTS SQUARE
★

TATUE
I

NEVSKY PROSPEKT
★

MOSCOW STATION

ALEXANDER NEVSKY MONASTERY
★

SQUARE ▲ 224

A. NEVSKY MONASTERY ▲ 253

PETERHOF ▲ 256

how that attracts many devotees.
THEATER SQUARE
The Mariinsky Theater has made this square the city's artistic hub.
KOLOMNA DISTRICT
The four islands, fine embankments

and twenty bridges of this 19th-century district can be explored by boat.
NEVSKY PROSPEKT
The city's main thoroughfare is lined with shops, churches and various palaces. Malaya

Sadovaya Street is especially worth a visit.
ARTS SQUARE
Three museums, two theaters, the Philharmonia, and the crafts market nearby make up this historic area.

NEVSKY MONASTERY
It contains the Artists' Necropolis, where great Russian artists are buried.
PETERHOF
This great Baroque palace and its parks are the venue for popular festivities.

ST PETERSBURG

EVERYMAN GUIDES

● Encyclopedia section

■ **NATURE** The natural heritage: species and habitats characteristic to the area covered by the guide, annotated and illustrated by naturalist authors and artists.

HISTORY The impact of international historical events on local history, from the arrival of the first inhabitants to the present day, with key dates appearing in a timeline above the text.

ARTS AND TRADITIONS The region's local customs and traditions and their continuing role in contemporary life.

ARCHITECTURE The architectural heritage, focusing on style and topology, a look at rural and urban buildings, major civil, religious and military monuments.

AS SEEN BY PAINTERS A selection of paintings of the city or country by different artists and schools, arranged chronologically or thematically.

AS SEEN BY WRITERS An anthology of texts focusing on the city or country, taken from works of all periods and countries, arranged thematically.

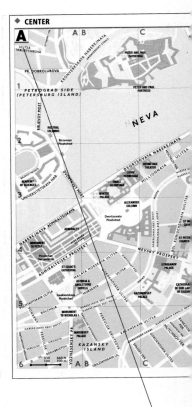

▲ Itineraries

Each itinerary begins with a map of the area to be explored.

✪ **SPECIAL INTEREST** These sites are not to be missed. They are highlighted in gray boxes in the margins.

★ **EDITOR'S CHOICE** Sites singled out by the editor for special attention.

INSETS On richly illustrated double pages, these insets turn the spotlight on subjects deserving more in-depth treatment.

◆ Practical information

All the travel information you will need before you go and when you get there.

USEFUL ADDRESSES A selection of the best hotels and restaurants compiled by an expert.

PLACES TO VISIT A handy table of addresses and opening hours.

APPENDICES Bibliography, list of illustrations and general index.

MAP SECTION Maps of all the areas covered by the guide, preceded by a street index; these maps are marked out with letters and figures making it easy for the reader to pinpoint a town, region or site.

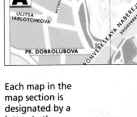

Each map in the map section is designated by a letter. In the practical information, each place can be pinpointed on the map (for example: ◆ **A** B1).

The itinerary map shows the main sites of interest.

■ ● ▲ ◆
The above symbols within the text provide cross-references to a place or a theme discussed elsewhere in the guide.

★ The star symbol signifies sites singled out by the editor for special attention.

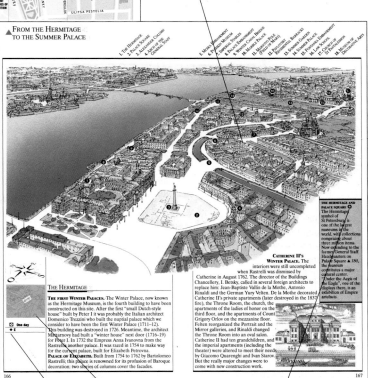

1. THE HERMITAGE
2. PALACE SQUARE
3. ALEXANDER COLUMN
4. ARCH OF THE GENERAL STAFF
5. MOIKA EMBANKMENT
6. PUSHKIN MUSEUM
7. IMPERIAL STABLES
8. PALACE EMBANKMENT
9. WINTER CANAL BRIDGE
10. MARBLE PALACE
11. MARSOVO POLE (FIELD OF MARS)
12. PAVLOVSKY REGIMENTAL BARRACKS
13. SUMMER GARDEN
14. SUMMER PALACE
15. FONTANKA EMBANKMENT
16. LAW SCHOOL
17. CHURCH OF ST PANTELEIMON
18. MUSEUM OF DECORATIVE ARTS

THE HERMITAGE AND PALACE SQUARE ✪
The Hermitage symbol of St Petersburg is one of the largest museums in the world, with collections comprising about three million items. Now extending to the former General Staff Headquarters on Palace Square ▲ 180, the museum constitutes a major cultural center. "Under the Aegis of the Eagle", one of the displays there, is an exhibition of Empire artefacts.

THE HERMITAGE

THE FIRST WINTER PALACES. The Winter Palace, now known as the Hermitage Museum, is the fourth building to have been constructed on this site. After the first "small Dutch-style house" built by Peter I it was probably the Italian architect Domenico Trezzini who built the nuptial palace which we consider to have been the first Winter Palace (1711–12). This building was destroyed in 1726. Meantime, the architect Mattarnovy had built a "winter house" next door (1716–19) for Peter I. In 1732 the Empress Anna Ivanovna from the Rastrellis another palace. It was razed in 1754 to make way for the current palace, built for Elizabeth Petrovna.
PALACE OF ELIZABETH. Built from 1754 to 1762 by Bartolomeo Rastrelli, this palace is renowned for its profusion of Baroque decoration: two stories of columns cover the facades.

CATHERINE II'S WINTER PALACE. The interiors were still uncompleted when Rastrelli was dismissed by Catherine in August 1762. The director of the Buildings Chancellery, I. Betsky, called in several foreign architects to replace him: Jean-Baptiste Vallin de la Mothe, Antonio Rinaldi and the German Yury Velten. De la Mothe decorated Catherine II's private apartments (later destroyed in the 1837 fire), the Throne Room, the church, the apartments of the ladies of honor on the third floor, and the apartments of Count Grigory Orlov on the mezzanine floor. Felten reorganized the Portrait and the Mirror galleries, and Rinaldi changed the Throne Room into an oval salon. Catherine II had ten grandchildren, and the imperial apartments (including the theater) were altered to meet their needs by Giacomo Quarenghi and Ivan Starov. But the really major changes were to come with new construction work.

⭘ One day
◆ E

166

167

At the beginning of each itinerary, the time it will take to cover the area is indicated beneath the mini-map, as are the grid references to the map section

The mini-map pinpoints the itinerary within the wider area covered by the guide.

✪ This symbol indicates places of special interest.

● <u>Encyclopedia section</u>

▲ Itineraries in St Petersburg

◆ Practical information

FROM THE FORTRESS TO THE ISLANDS OF THE DELTA ▲ 143
A historic place from which to explore the city, the Fortress contains the Peter and Paul Cathedral, the History Museum and the Old Arsenal. The Petrograd Side, a district on the right bank of the Neva, has buildings in the Art Nouveau style. To the west lie the islands of the delta, which, with their parks and gardens, are a favorite place of relaxation for St Petersburgers.

VASILYEVSKY ISLAND ▲ 155
The part of the island known as the Point (Strelka) has a large population of students and academics, and many monuments, museums, colleges and research institutes connected to the university or the Russian Navy. Menshikov Palace, with splendid apartments, and the Kunstkammer, Peter the Great's gallery of curiosities, both on University Embankment, are open to visitors.

FROM THE HERMITAGE TO THE SUMMER PALACE ▲ 165
Oppposite the Fortress, on the left bank of the Neva, stand palaces, gardens and major monuments, all of them examples of the Peter-the-Great style. They include the Hermitage, one of the largest museums in the world, Palace Square and, between the Marble Palace and the Summer Palace, the huge Field of Mars. Fine 18th-century statues grace the Summer Garden.

FROM THE ADMIRALTY TO THE HAYMARKET ▲ 189
Highlights include the Admiralty and New Holland districts, built on the site of former shipyards; the beautiful St Isaac's Cathedral, the largest church in St Petersburg; Theater Square, hub of the city's artistic life and home of the acclaimed Mariinsky Theater; St Nicholas' Cathedral, a fine example of Baroque elegance in blue, white and gold; and the 19th-century Dostoevsky District.

AROUND NEVSKY PROSPEKT ▲ 211
Nevsky Prospekt is the city's main thoroughfare and its finest commercial street. On Arts Square and Ostrovsky Square stand major artistic institutions: among them are the Russian Museum in Mikhail Palace, Engineers' Castle, the Shostakovich Philarmonia and the Alexandrinsky Theater. The Church of the Resurrection, with its famous twisted onion domes, is also not to be missed.

FROM THE FONTANKA TO INSURRECTION SQUARE ▲ 235
Running from Fountains House to the Rimsky-Korsakov Museum and Dostoevsky Museum, and taking in the Samoilov Museum and Pushkin Street, this literary and musical itinerary follows in the footsteps of great Russian writers and composers. An additional highlight is Beloselsky-Belozersky Palace, now used as a cultural center that also features a waxworks museum.

FROM SMOLNY TO ALEXANDER NEVSKY MONASTERY ▲ 245
Smolny Monastery and Cathedral, masterpieces of Russian Baroque architecture, contrast with the restrained style of the Smolny Institute , which played a prominent role in the 1917 Revolution. This historical itinerary takes in Kikin Palace, Tauride Palace and the Alexander Nevsky Monastery, where major figures in Russian intellectual life are buried.

PALACES ON THE OUTSKIRTS OF ST PETERSBURG ▲ 255
Major festivities takes place at Peterhof, a palace set in grounds with elaborate fountains. Oranienbaum, which has been open to visitors for several years now, contains some remarkable examples of marquetry. Also open to the public are Tsarskoe Selo, whose well-known façade is 985 feet wide, and Pavlovsk, by far the most sophisticated of all Russian summer palaces.

Numerous specialists and academics have contributed to this guide.
All the information that it contains has been approved by them.

● Encyclopedia section

NATURE
Vladimir Leftchenko,
Alexey Nekrassov, Jean-Pierre Verdet,
Philippe Dubois
LANGUAGE
Annette Lefebvre
HISTORY
Tamara Kondratieva
ARTS AND TRADITIONS
Antoine Nivière, Alexandra Schouwaloff,
Emmanuel Ducamp, Béatrice Picon-Vallin,
Natalia Metelitsa, Igor Dimitriev,
Prascovie de Saint-Hippolyte
ARCHITECTURE
Brigitte de Montclos, Ewa Bérard,
Andrey Punin, Vladimir Rivline
ST PETERSBURG AS SEEN BY PAINTERS
Alexandra Schouwaloff
THE RUSSIAN AVANT-GARDE
Andrey Nakov
ST PETERSBURG AS SEEN BY WRITERS
Lucinda Gane
ALEXANDER PUSHKIN
Anne Klimoff

▲ Itineraries in St Petersburg

Anne Nercessian, Alexander Noskov,
Brigitte de Montclos, Natalya Brodskaya,
Vera Biron, Vitaly Sychev, Natalya Metelitsa,
Vladimir Leon, Alexandra Schouwaloff,
Tamara Kondratieva, Emmanuel Ducamp

◆ Practical information

Olga Yartseva
Hotels and restaurants: Olga Yartseva,
Robert Cottrell of the *Financial Times*
and Catherine Sharpe

Everyman Guides
Published by Alfred A. Knopf, New York

Completely revised and
updated in 2007

Originally published in France by Nouveaux-
Loisirs, a subsidiary of Editions Gallimard,
Paris, 1993. Copyright © 1993 by Editions
Nouveaux-Loisirs

isbn 13: 978-1-84159-272-5
isbn 10: 1-84159-272-2

Series editors
Shelley Wanger and Clémence Jacquinet

Translated by
Anthony Roberts and Yvonne Worth

Edited and typeset by
Book Creation Services, London

Printed and bound in Italy by
Zanardi Group

ST PETERSBURG
Original French-language edition

Editors
Sophie Mastelinck and Agnès Baubault,
with Odile Simon (Nature)
Layout
Yann Le Duc assisted by Annie Civard
and Carole Gaborit
Picture research
Catherine Boncenne
Updating
Olga Yartseva and Sophie Besançon
(editing)

ILLUSTRATIONS
Nature: Jean Chevallier, François
Desbordes, Claire Felloni,
Catherine Lachaux, Dominique Mansion,
Pascale Robin, John Wilkinson
Architecture: Michel Aubois, Jean-François
Binet, Vincent Brunot, François Desbordes,
Jean-Marie Guillou, Jean-Michel Kacedan,
Maurice Pommier, Sylvain Roueri, Amato
Soro, Catherine Totems
Itineraries: Jean-Michel Kacedan,
Maurice Pommier, Laure Massin (coloring),
Jean-Philippe Chabot, Frédéric Bony
Maps: Vincent Brunot, Éric Gillion,
Marc Lagarde (coloring)
Computer graphics: Édigraphie, Paul
Coulbois, Xavier Garnerin (Latitude), Patrick
Merienne

PHOTOGRAPHY
V. Baranovsky, V. Buss, Roger Gain,
Koncharov, V. Savik, V. Terebenin

SPECIAL THANKS TO
Anne Nercessian, Vera Biron (Dostoevsky
Museum, St Petersburg), Véronique Schiltz,
Galina Vassiliev (Historic Archives of St
Petersburg), Georges Willembachov
(Hermitage Museum), Martine Kahane
(Opéra Garnier-Bastille), Alexandre Illinsky,
Vladimir Terebebin, Helena Asséeva,
Isabelle Haas and Stéphanie François

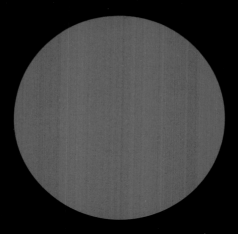

Encyclopedia section

"The quays of St Petersburg are among the loveliest things in Europe: why? Because they embody both luxury and solidity."
Astolphe de Custine

Photograph: bicentary celebrations of the founding of St Petersburg, May 1900

"The aspect of St Petersburg is more conducive of astonishment than admiration . . . if it is not quite perfectly beautiful, it is none the less completely strange."
Olympe Audovard

Photograph: The Fontanka from Anichkov Bridge, 1900

"On the left was a little
black canal, which lay
against the colossus of the
Admiralty . . . gilded at
every edge, and adorned
by a glinting statue of
Fame, all in gold . . ."

Louis-Ferdinand Céline

*Photograph: entrance to
the Admiralty, c. 1900*

"There is nothing finer than Nevsky Prospekt,
not in St Petersburg at any rate; for in
St Petersburg it is everything. And, indeed,
is there anything more gay, more brilliant,
more resplendent than this beautiful
street of our capital?"
Nikolai Gogol

Photograph: Nevsky Prospekt, 1906

Nature

■ THE SITE

F. Desbordes

The St Petersburg region extends 280 miles west to east and between 65 and 200 miles north to south. Its southeast extremity is washed by the waters of the Gulf of Finland; and to the north of it is Lake Ladoga. The region lies to the northwest of the Russian plateau, the substratum of which is crystalline rock. The various ice ages produced morainic elevations and lakes, which in general give the land its undulating aspect. The climate is one of strong contrasts, being conditioned on the one hand by the movement of air masses off the Atlantic and on the other by polar continental air, which is dry and very cold in winter. St Petersburg itself is situated more or less where the northern and temperate climatic regions meet.

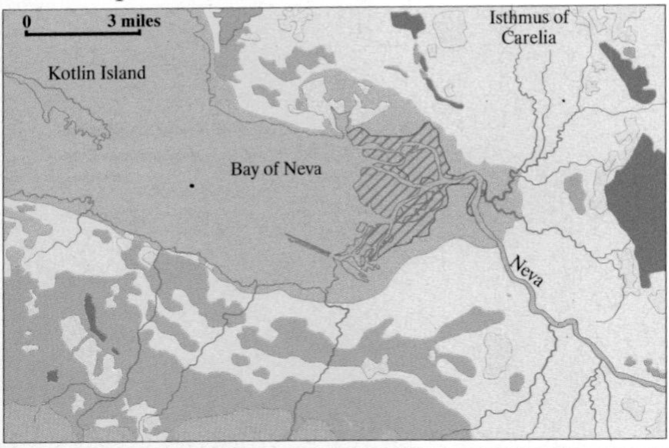

Map legend:

- Sandy banks along the seaboard
- Argillaceous plains, with forests and marshes in sandy soil areas
- Plains and plateaux with glacial moraines (mixed and coniferous forests)
- Marshes and peat-bogs
- Arable land and conifer forests (foothills)
- Calcareous plateau with deciduous or coniferous forests and grassland
- Prone to flooding

Map labels: 0 — 3 miles · Kotlin Island · Bay of Neva · Isthmus of Carelia · Neva

Autumn weather is characterized by frequent depressions, with strong winds causing occasional floods.

In December Atlantic depressions bring rain and snow; in January and February the arrival of dry air from the Arctic makes for cloudless skies.

18

The black tern lives in noisy colonies among the marshes skirting the Bay of the Neva.

On the island of Kotlin the construction of a dyke was begun in the 1980's as a measure to protect the city from flooding. The dyke is still unfinished, because it has been shown to disturb the Neva estuary's ecosystem.

The marshy, island-strewn delta in which Peter the Great chose to build his capital ● 78 benefits from Atlantic weather, without which the region would probably be icebound for much of the year.

AVERAGE TEMPERATURES AT GROUND LEVEL (°C)

— 16 —   July isotherm (61°F)

— -8 —   January isotherm (18°F)

33   Maximum temperatures (91°F)

-40   Minimum temperatures (-40°F)

AVERAGE PRECIPITATION (mm)

less   more

———   Isohyet

PREVAILING WINDS

———▶   July

———▶   January

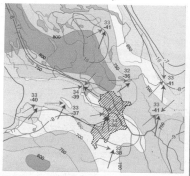

In the spring the weather changes frequently on account of the continual confrontation of air masses.

In July the average temperature is 67°F. July is also a season of thunderstorms; cloudbursts can be very violent.

■ THE NEVA

SPARLING
Between March and May this deep-sea fish runs up the Neva to Lake Ladoga, where it spawns. At this time of year hundreds of fishermen stand on the Neva bridges, waiting for the *koriuchka* to come up river.

The Neva flows out of Lake Ladoga, then crosses the isthmus of Carelia to form a delta at its junction with the Gulf of Finland. The river's entire length is less than 50 miles, but it is some 500 yards across at its widest point and about 80 feet deep. The Neva's vast volume of water makes it the sixth largest river in Europe.

ROACH
The roach frequents the lower stretches of the Neva, as far as the mouth; here it seeks the sandy substratum of the river bed.

PERCH
The strong currents of the Neva are a perfect habitat for the perch, which lays its eggs on aquatic plants.

BREAM
Well-adapted to the Neva's waters, bream tend to frequent the muddier parts of the river bed.

PIKE PERCH
This voracious fish, very common in Eastern Europe, prefers still waters but may also be found where the current flows strongly.

RUFFE
A bottom-dwelling fish confined to lakes and big rivers, the ruff habitually moves in shoals.

Swift

House martin

SWIFT AND HOUSE MARTIN
These birds nest on the great riverfront
buildings of St Petersburg, notably the
Hermitage ▲ 168. They feed on insects,
skimming close to the water's surface.

During the winter
the Neva may be
impassable for a
period varying
between two and five
months. In the winter
of 1941–2 ● 50 the
Neva was covered by
ice over 3 feet thick.
The river's powerful
current sometimes
brings very high water.

The worst flooding on record took place in
1824 ● 35. Dykes have been constructed in
the bay of the Neva to protect the city.

Following the thaw the Neva may still
remain impassable to ships for over a month.
Every spring great blocks of ice sweep down
the river from Lake Ladoga to the open sea.

BLACK-HEADED GULL
Present on the river all year round, this
half-tame gull will often eat from the
hand during the winter.

The Summer Garden ▲ *186* is a combination of rigorous landscaping and exuberant animal life.

The building of the city of St Petersburg led inevitably to a significant change in the vegetation of the surrounding region. The new artificial plantations brought with them a number of foreign exotic plant species to live alongside the indigenous varieties. Nowadays St Petersburg still remains a "green city", with historic spaces – such as the Summer Garden and the enormous parks of Krestovsky and Elagin islands – which serve as urban reminders of the great forests that lie further afield.

RED SQUIRREL
The shy, agile rodent is widespread throughout the parks and cemeteries of St Petersburg.

PINE MARTEN
A carnivorous member of the weasel family, which habitually feeds on birds as well as small mammals, beetles and carrion.

HOODED CROW
Omnipresent in the city, this crow is especially numerous in the smaller parks and around the Alexander Nevsky Monastery ▲ 253.

Male

Female

SISKIN
The siskin is common in the mountain and forest regions of Europe – and in the parks of St Petersburg.

SCARLET ROSEFINCH
This oriental species is currently expanding its range deep into Western Europe.

FIELDFARE
The fieldfare nests in noisy colonies, especially in the Summer Garden.

THRUSH NIGHTINGALE
A legendary songbird, the eastern European version of our common nightingale.

Tourists may be surprised by the sight of men scything the grass by hand in Elagin Park ▲ 154.

ALDER
The berries of this small tree, which favors cool, humid soils, attracts birds like the siskin during the winter months.

LIME TREE
The lime is very common in and around St Petersburg. In June and July the gardens are richly scented with its blooms.

HORNBEAM
Hornbeams, widely planted in Russia during the 19th century, supply generous shade and easily worked wood.

■ THE CARELIAN FOREST

WILLOW WARBLER
This long-distance migrant nests in large numbers in the woods around St Petersburg, where willows, rowans and birches predominate.

The forests of the St Petersburg region straddle a transitional zone between the northern taiga, where conifers proliferate, and the mixed woodlands of the temperate regions. The latter, a blend of deciduous trees and conifers, seem to have receded southward following a very cold, wet period over four thousand years ago. In the Carelian forest there are fewer deciduous trees, and rowans predominate. Numerous lakes, interspersed with marshes and heather-covered peat bogs, give this area a charm that is properly more Scandinavian than Russian, yet this is the quintessential "Russian forest" described by novelists.

CHAFFINCH
Large numbers of chaffinches populate the St Petersburg region in summer, migrating to southern Europe in the winter.

NORWAY PINE
Abundant on the sandy soils around the northern rim of the Gulf of the Neva.

BIRCH
One of the principal hardwood trees in the St Petersburg region; it often grows with conifers.

SPRUCE
Typical of the Carelian forest. Its fruits are a rich source of food for woodland birdlife.

BEARBERRY
The *toloknyanka* is very similar to the bilberry and is widely used in pharmacology.

MILITARY ORCHID
The military orchid flowers in May and June on calcareous sunny banks and along the margins of woods.

SWAMP-BERRY
The deep blue fruit of the swamp-berry is a common sight in marshy areas during the autumn.

COTTON GRASS
In June, when the *puchitsa* is in flower, its fluffy seedballs cover the ground like newly-fallen snow.

ELK (MOOSE)
In the 1970's elk were still present in large numbers up to the edge of the city. Stocks have declined steeply in recent years.

GRAY WOLF
A small wolf population survives around St Petersburg, but is now under severe threat from hunters.

■ CEMETERIES

SPOTTED FLYCATCHER
A migrant bird with dull plumage, the spotted flycatcher favors the upper branches of trees; often the only sign of its presence is a high-pitched "tsic" call.

The cemeteries of St Petersburg come as a surprise to most visitors to the city. From the outside they appear impenetrable, but those who persevere will be rewarded with the sight of an unkempt riot of graves, bushes and sprawling wild plants. During the Soviet era the cemeteries were not maintained, with the result that the growth of lush vegetation remained unchecked; this in turn attracted abundant wild creatures which took advantage of the near-natural conditions that prevailed there.

The tangle of plants and ruined tombstones offers a quiet refuge from the din of the surrounding city.

RED FOX
The parks and cemeteries of St Petersburg have made it possible for the red fox to survive in the heart of the city. Foxes may often be glimpsed by daylight, hunting for mice, rats and voles.

26

PIED FLYCATCHER
Very numerous in temperate woodlands, this migrant nests in older trees.

ROBIN
Unlike robins in western Europe, those in Russia migrate southward in winter.

BLACKCAP
This warbler arrives in St Petersburg in May, migrating south in August.

TREE SPARROW
Very common in the open green spaces of St Petersburg, it is seldom seen in the built-up areas, unlike its cousin the house sparrow.

POPLAR
In the early summer the cotton-like seeds of the catkin carpet the surrounding vegetation in white.

RUSSIAN ELM
These elms are especially common in St Petersburg's cemeteries; they seem less vulnerable to disease than the western European variety.

IVY
Most of the older graves in the cemeteries are completely obscured by ivy.

RASPBERRIES
In the autumn wild raspberries are a delight to strollers and birds alike.

NORWAY MAPLE
St Petersburg lies roughly at the northernmost limit of the Norway maple.

LIGHT AT MIDNIGHT

"Across the sky, gilded
By the sun's perpetual rays
Dawn hurries to relieve
The unconsummated dusk
And night endures for barely an hour."
Pushkin, *The Bronze Horseman*

As St Petersburg is not within the Arctic Circle, there is no midnight sun, but its latitude is sufficiently high (almost 60°N) to bring some light throughout the night. The sun only just dips below the horizon and the earth's atmosphere continues to diffuse its beams. Most plants are in full bloom at this time of year.

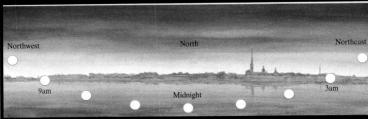

Northwest | North | Northeast
9am | Midnight | 3am

Toward the earth's poles, the sun rises less directly over the horizon, and the more the days vary in length over the year.

March 21
June 21
December 21
September 21

The earth describes its elliptical orbit around the sun in 365 days and 6 hours. During this revolution the inclination of the earth varies in relation to the sun, determining the lengths of the days and seasons.

▼ SUMMER SOLSTICE

On June 21 the night, or rather twilight, lasts only five hours at St Petersburg. At midnight the sun lies only 6° beneath the horizon. In London at the same time of year the night lasts for seven hours and the sun drops 23° below the horizon. In New York the night lasts for nine hours and twenty minutes and the sun drops 25° below the horizon.

▲ WINTER SOLSTICE

On December 21 at noon the sun stands at slightly over 6° above St Petersburg. In London it is at 26° and in New York at 27°. From mid-afternoon onward the Gulf of Finland is under cover of night.

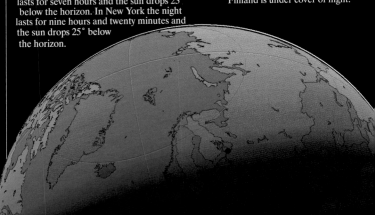

History
and language

1682–1725
Reign of Peter the Great, who
proclaimed himself Emperor

1700–21
Northern War: the Russians annex
Estonia, Latvia and Carelia

1703–25 "A WINDOW ON EUROPE"

A NEW ETERNAL CITY

On May 16, 1703 a village by the Neva, recently abandoned by its Finnish inhabitants, began to resound to the din of saws and axes. On June 29, the Feast of Saint Peter and Saint Paul, the foundations of a church were laid within the precinct of the future fortress of the same name: Sankt-Piter-Bourkh (pronounced in the Dutch manner) identified the Czar with the names of the two saints. In doing so, Peter the Great sought to endow Russia with an imperial, messianic destiny, of which Rome was the paramount model.

The arms of the city of St Petersburg borrow from the emblems of Rome and the Vatican: thus the crossed anchors refer both to the papal keys, which symbolize faith, and to the fleet created by Peter the Great, which could also "open the gates of Paradise". From the first years of its construction, the city of St Petersburg was known to Russians as "paradise".

THE CONQUEST OF NATURE FOR REASONS OF STATE

Peter's city gradually grew out of the marshes. In September 1703 the wooden fortress was completed, along with the Czar's house. But soon stone was brought in as the principal construction material. The richest families were obliged by law to build their mansions of stone, and were heavily fined if they failed to do so. According to an *ukaze* (edict) of 1714, which remained in force for sixty-five years, every boat, vessel or waggon entering the city had to bring with it a certain amount of cut stone. On the building sites labored vast numbers of convicts and serfs (40,000 on average between 1709 and 1716), adventurers, soldiers, Russian craftsmen and foreign specialists. The foreigners came in the hope of gain and were sometimes detained by force. Hunger and cold killed nearly 100,000 people during the first years of building, sacrificed to the will and ambition of the Czar. Strategic and commercial considerations justified the choice of his apparently unpromising site. By May 1703 Peter was promising substantial grants to the first three merchant vessels to drop anchor in the new port.

1795
Third partition of Poland between Austria,
Prussia and Russia

1800

1809
Annexation
of Finland

1812
Napoleon in
Moscow

June 18, 1815
Battle of Waterloo

September 26, 1815
Foundation of the Holy
Alliance

1853–6:
Crimean War

1725–1856: ORIGINALITY AND IMITATION

THE "PALMYRA OF THE NORTH"

In a letter dated September 28, 1704, Czar Peter referred to the city under construction as his "new capital". The inauguration took place in 1712, at which time the Russian court, the Senate and the foreign embassies all moved to St Petersburg from Moscow; Peter was subsequently married there, to a Lithuanian peasant girl. The first museums, a library, a theater, an observatory and the Academy of Sciences were quickly opened. In the vicinity of St Petersburg were built the palaces of Oranienbaum and Peterhof, while a road was built to Tsarskoe Selo, the future summer residence of the Czars.

THE DISAPPEARING CITY

After the death of Peter the Great, half the Russian court and at least half of the population of St Petersburg fled the city. The *ukaze* of 1729, which threatened fugitives with exile and the confiscation of their property, had little effect. New, harsher measures sparked a revolt, and in 1737 the city was burned down. Nevertheless the Empress Elizabeth I (right), Peter the Great's daughter, pressed on with the construction of the Winter and Anichkov palaces and the Gostiny Dvor, so realizing her father's dream. Catherine II ● *40* lifted the restrictions, enticed the population back with perquisites, and initiated major construction projects such as the Tauride Palace and Marble Palace, the Hermitage, the Smolny Institute, the bridges and the granite river embankment. Toward the mid-19th century, thanks to the talents of both Russian and foreign-born artists, St Petersburg ". . . became distinct from the other cities of Europe, precisely because it so nearly resembled each one of them". Travelers called it the "London", "Venice", "Rome", "Berlin" or "Paris" of Russia, as it struck them. But the city's new attractions obliged its inhabitants to adapt: some social groups to luxury and extravagance, the rest to the behavior of their superiors in the hierarchy. Poets and writers, meanwhile, became intrigued by the mystery of this seductive but far from traditional city.

| February 19, 1861 | December 1865 | | 1889–92 |
| Abolition of serfdom in Russia | Abolition of slavery in the USA | | Counter-reforms |

1861   **1880**

| 1863–5 | 1864–76 | March 1, 1881 | 1883 |
| Liberal reforms of Alexander II | Marx and Engels: the First International | Assassination of Czar Alexander | Marxist propaganda appears in Russia |

1856–1914 ST PETERSBURG IN THE FOREFRONT OF MODERNISM

THE INDUSTRIAL CENTER OF THE EMPIRE

The first steamships and the Moscow–St Petersburg railway line (1851) opened a new era in the city's history. By 1868 the Putilov factory was already a major producer of rails, locomotives and carriages. In 1900, 13,000 workers were employed there, with about a hundred more metallurgical factories developing in related sectors. Other factories, using modern British and German equipment (Nobel, Nevsky, Lessner) built ships and typographical machines and (in competition with Obukhov) supplied the needs of the Army. There was also a number of textile mills in and around St Petersburg. A new port, constructed in 1885, was added to that of Kronstadt, expanding the city's potential for international trade: corn and wood were exported in vast quantities, balancing imports of steel and machine tools. Banks, many of whose shareholders were foreigners, proliferated during the boom of the 1890's.

THE ST PETERSBURG CIVIL SERVANT

According to the poet Grigoriev, Russian civil servants – whose uniforms varied from one ministry to the next – were the "alpha and omega" of St Petersburg. Schoolboys, university students, soldiers, sailors, policemen and ecclesiastics completed the picture. Right from the time of its foundation, St Petersburg was a heavily regulated city: the aspect of the roofs and chimneys, the construction materials, the color and height of all buildings (which might on no account be taller than the Winter Palace), the width of the streets, the hours by which the gates had to be closed, and the arrangements for street cleaning were all carefully ordained by bureaucratic rules.

A CENTER FOR FREE THOUGHT

Paradoxically, it was in this tightly controlled environment that free thought blossomed – thanks to the culture of an intellectual elite, naturally, but also thanks to the special receptiveness of St Petersburgers. Seventy percent of the workers in the capital knew how to read and write, as opposed to an average of 21 percent in the rest of the Russian Empire. St Petersburgers spread the word on avant-garde art, along with technical innovation (airplanes) and new diversions (cinema, football).

| 1904–5 | 1912–13 | June 28, 1914 | 1924 |
| Russo-Japanese War | Balkan Wars | Assassination of Franz-Ferdinand of Austria at Sarajevo | England, France, Sweden and other European nations recognize the USSR |

900   **1920**

| 2 March 1918 | 1918–20 | March 2–6, 1919 | December 30, 1922 |
| Moscow replaces t Petersburg as capital | Civil War and foreign intervention | First Congress of the Third International (Komintern) in Moscow | The USSR is officially inaugurated |

1914–24: PETROGRAD: WAR AND REVOLUTION

THE COMING OF THE REVOLUTION

On July 20, 1914, from a balcony of the Winter Palace, Nicholas II read the declaration which brought Russia into the Great War. On August 18 the German name of the capital was changed to the more Russian-sounding Petrograd – much closer to "Pieter", as ordinary people had always called it. For the writer Solzhenitsyn, who described the war years practically from day to day (*The Red Wheel*, 4,000 pages), the declaration of war was the beginning of the greatest drama of the century, whilst for Lenin it represented a great gift offered by the Czar to the nascent Revolution.

According to Lenin, in an underdeveloped nation revolution could come about only as a consequence of war: while Karl Marx thought revolution improbable anywhere but within the most advanced capitalist systems. History began to prove Lenin right in February 1917.

On the night of October 24–5, 1917 insurgents attacked the Winter Palace, seat of the provisional government. With a roar that drowned the stutter of machine-gun fire, a wave of humanity swirled around the great building. The October Revolution was under way.

THE DESTRUCTION OF ST PETERSBURG

he October evolution – so orified for seventy-x years thereafter – d to many reparable losses for Petersburgers. The ty was transformed two ways. On the lge of the central ea quantities of lapidated buildings in which tens of thousands of workers lived were emptied and destroyed. Meantime the historic capital began to fall apart from the very first months of Soviet supremacy. Spacious apartments were divided up among working families, and the original décor, of two-headed eagles, crowns and statues, removed; a decree abolishing private ownership deprived houses and shops, fountains and gardens of ordinary maintenance; and railings, stained glass, stair carpets, bas-reliefs and weathercocks simply vanished. The campaigns against religion brought about the destruction or conversion into offices of a large number of churches. Much-needed capital was raised by the sale of works of art abroad. At the same time the names of streets and squares were altered, short-circuiting the collective memory: about 500 names were changed, including that of the Nevsky Prospekt, which became Avenue 25 October. About 400 names vanished altogether, along with the things they referred to. Finally, on Lenin's death in January 1924, the Soviet Congress, "at the request of the workers", abolished the name of the capital altogether.

1938	**1939**	**1940**	**1941**
Munich Agreements (September)	The Russo-German Pact (August). Partition of Poland (September)	Pact with Finland (March) Annexation of the Baltic States and Bessarabia (June)	The Germans invade Russ (June). They are halted ou Moscow (December)

1924		**1940**	

1929	**1936**	**April 8–11, 1940**	**1949**
First attempts at collectivization	The Anti-Komintern Pact (Germany and Russia)	Massacre of 1,400 Polish prisoners at Katyn by Russian security services	Creation of NATO (April)

1924–91: LENINGRAD, GLORY AND CALAMITY

A NEW IMAGE OF THE CITY

The houses of one and a half million emigrants and victims of war and revolution were occupied by workers and peasants fleeing collectivization (1928–33). These people became city workers and were distinct from the native St Petersburgers in their language and way of life. The atmosphere of the city, in which before the revolution the cream of the aristocracy and the intelligentsia had flourished, became envenomed as Leningrad found itself increasingly sidelined and provincialized. Nevertheless, the Soviet government in Moscow continued to regard Leningrad as a free-thinking potential rival. The Party's purges and wholesale arrests uprooted many recently arrived families, adding to the prevailing loss of identity in the city.

A new image was to emerge later, in consequence of the heroic resistance during the siege of Leningrad (1941–4), although the city's troubles did not come to an end until the 1960's and 1970's, with the stabilization of the population and an improvement in living conditions.

THE OPENING OF LENINGRAD TO TOURISM

The work of restoration which had continued ever since the end of the siege had taken on a different character by the end of the 1970's, the purpose of which was to recreate the city's former charm. After the opening of an initial underground railway in 1955, new lines were built on a regular basis; the length of the Neva embankment was tripled (nearly 100 miles of it were reinforced with granite); park space in the city was increased to 22,500 acres, and the number of bridges was increased to 310 by 1989. Meantime cheap high-rise housing began to make its mark on the various islands (42 new projects were completed in 1970). Soviet tourists arrive to visit the "glorious city", and with the new policy of detente toward the West eve foreign visitors began to appear.

March 5, 1953	August 1, 1975	November 1989	1993 September 21: Supreme Soviet is
Death of Stalin	Helsinki conference. Signature	Fall of the Berlin	dissolved. December 12: Election of the
	of the final act on Human	Wall	first Russian Duma; a new constitution
1960	Rights	1980	1990	is drawn up by referendum	2005

February 1956	March 11, 1985	1991 June 12: First democratic election in Russia:
Khrushchev denounces	Gorbachev is elected First Secretary	Yeltsin elected President. December 25: The USSR
Stalin's personality cult	of the Soviet Communist Party	becomes the Commonwealth of Independent States

THE PALACES AROUND LENINGRAD

The environs of Leningrad suffered terribly from the German occupation, and after the Allied victory in World War Two the towns in the region were so badly damaged that they had to be reconstructed rather than restored. With their 18th-century palaces and parks, these museum-towns are very much a part of Leningrad and are well worth visiting. They are also highly functional: Petrodvorets, with its university campus, is populated by students; Tsarskoe Selo trains farmers from all over the country at its Agricultural Institute; Gatchina is a scientific research center with a number of different institutes. Oranienbaum, Pavlosk and the isthmus of Carelia are now popular summer resorts. The latter is well-known for its beach, Duny; it has become an upmarket resort for the people of St Petersburg. A sports complex is also being built there.

ST PETERSBURG SINCE 1991

REBIRTH OF THE CITY

On June 12, 1991, 54 percent of the city's inhabitants voted to restore its historic name. "St Petersburg" has come back, but with more difficulty than the Kirov Ballet experienced in readopting the name of Mariinsky, or the University in jettisoning the name of Zhdanov. For the 300th anniversary celebrations in 2003, St Petersburg was spruced up to reflect its past splendors. Some important restoration work was undertaken in the historic districts. The façades of the houses along the Nevsky Prospekt were repainted in brilliant colors. Another sign of a renaissance has been the resumption of literary works on and about the city, including a major collection entitled *The Petersburg Metaphysic*.

A SOLUTION TO THE PROBLEM OF FLOODING

On several buildings in the city are plaques indicating the levels of the worst floods among the 253 which have afflicted St Petersburg since 1703. One of these recalls the catastrophe of November 7, 1824, when the water rose 12 feet. Today, the reformist administrators of St Petersburg and their Finnish neighbors are committed to renewing the city's flood protection facilities, while respecting the ecology of the region.

GEDENKE
DES HOHEN WASSERS
AM 7 NOVEMBER
1824

● THE ROMANOV DYNASTY

Czar Alexander I presents his army to Napoleon.

MIKHAIL FYODOROVICH (1613–45)*. The first of the Romanov Czars, son of Fyodor Nikitich, better known as Filaret, patriarch of Tuchino and descendant of the Riurik family (founder of the Kiev state, the first state of Russia).

ALEXEI I (1645–76)*. The son of Mikhail Fyodorovich. In the early years of his reign, the state was run by his tutor, the boyar B. Morozov. This reign was marked by a major social crisis and ecclesiastical reforms initiated by the Patriarch of Moscow, Nikon.

SOPHIA (1682–9)*. In 1689 Sophia Alexeyevna was assigned to the monastery of Novodyvichy (Moscow) and the regency passed to Natasha Naryshkin (second wife of Alexei I and mother of Peter I).

FYODOR III (1676–82)*. The son of Alexei I and Maria Ilinychna, Fyodor was bored by affairs of state and allowed his advisors to run the country. He died at 21.

CATHERINE (1691–1733)

ANNA YOANNOVNA (1730–40)*. Niece of Peter I, Anna was chosen by the supreme council (over her daughters Anna and Elizabeth) to succeed Peter II. Hers was an arbitrary regime.

ALEXEI (1690–1718). After joining the conspiracy against his father, Alexei was condemned by the Czar imprisoned and tortured.

PETER II (1727–30)*. Grandson of Peter I. Peter's brief reign was marked by the return of the court to Moscow and the eviction of Prince Menshikov.

IVAN VI (1740–1)*
Regency of Anna.

ALEXANDER I (1801–25)* (left). The adored grandson of Catherine II. Russia in his reign joined the coalition against Napoleon; later, Alexander instigated major reforms and founded many new institutions.

ALEXANDER III (1881–94)*. Son of Alexand The assassination of his father led him to bri a halt to the reform movement and re-establi conservative regime.

NICHOLAS II ● 44 (1894–1917)*. Son of Alexander III. The dynasty's last emperor. His reign ended in the upheaval of the Revolution in 1917, which cost Nicholas and his family their lives (July 17, 1918).

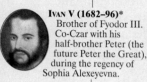

IVAN V (1682–96)*
Brother of Fyodor III. Co-Czar with his half-brother Peter (the future Peter the Great), during the regency of Sophia Alexeyevna.

PETER I (1682–1725)*. ● *38.* On the death of his mother, Peter the Great seized the reins of power. His second wife, **CATHERINE I (1725–7)*** was a Lithuanian peasant girl. On his death, she became the first Empress of Russia.

ANNA (1708–28)

ELIZABETH PETROVNA ● *31 (1741–61)**
Daughter of Peter the Great, she organized a coup d'etat in 1741, deposing Ivan IV, great-nephew of Anna Ivanovna.

PETER III (1761–2)*. Son of the Duke of Holstein-Gottorp. In 1745 he married Sophia of Anhalt-Zerbst (the future Catherine II).

CATHERINE II ● *40 (1762–96)**
Took power in a 1762 coup d'etat, supported by the officers who had assassinated her husband.

PAUL I (1796–1801)*. Son of Peter III and Catherine II, whom he loathed. Assassinated in the Engineer's Castle.

NICHOLAS I (1825–55)*. Brother of Alexander I. His reign was marked by the Decembrist uprising and the Crimean War.

ALEXANDER II (1855–81)*
Son of Nicholas I. From the end of the Crimean War, he undertook a reform program (abolition of serfdom in 1861) but was assassinated by terrorists.

* Dates of reign.

RASPUTIN ▲ *202 (1872–1916)*
Born a peasant (his real name was Grigor Novykh), Rasputin was introduced into the court of Nicholas II on account of his healing powers. Very quickly he gained huge influence over the Czar's political decisions. On December 16, 1916 he was assassinated by Prince Yusupov.

By inviting Western technicians and military officers to Russia, Peter the Great was able to form a regular Army and Navy capable of defending his country's interests. As Czar, his principal objective was to make Russia a great military power, not to transplant European civilization into it. But a century after his death, Russian intelligentsia was divided between the Slavophiles, who wished to eradicate Peter from Russian history, and the Occidentalists, who recognized his openness to progress while acknowledging that civilization was beaten into Russia "by blows of the knout".

> "He sought first to make Germans and Englishmen, when he should have been making Russians."
> J.-J. Rousseau

SAILOR, SOLDIER AND CRAFTSMAN . . .

At the age of ten, and on his own initiative, Peter formed an army. This "child's game" led to the founding of the three elite regiments which later spearheaded Russia's victory over Napoleon. The Czar grew up far from the sea but was forever dreaming of it. An abandoned English ship in one of his grandfather's dry-docks sparked his longing for a great Russian fleet. He learnt about naval construction at Saardam, in 1697: the first frigate of Russia's fleet was partly built by his hands.

A "NOBLE SAVAGE"

In the European vogue, Peter had an African prince called Ibrahim brought to his court. The man who organized the kidnapping was an ancestor of Tolstoy's. Ibrahim became a general (Hannibal) in the Russian Army, and was the great-grandfather of the poet Pushkin ● 114.

THE FOUNDER OF THE KUNSTKAMMER

A passionate collector, Peter was as interested in objects like this Scythian gold panther as in human foetuses, which horrified the Russians ▲ *160*. He was reduced to giving free meals as an enticement to whomever among his subjects would come and see his collections.

ECCENTRIC VALUES

Culturally, Peter was an innovator; but many of his changes were frankly viewed as sacrilege. Beards had to be shaved; clothes were "teutonized" in styles that had formerly been regarded in Russia as carnival costumes. The Czar also instituted a Council of Drunkenness as a parody of the Ecclesiastical Council, and arranged elaborate marriages and funerals for dwarves, whom he pilloried to amuse his court. Russian culture somehow remained in place, but with its values knocked topsy-turvy.

THE DESPOT

Peter, as Czar, pitied no man and respected nothing. During his reign the nobles were forced to educate themselves; if they did not, they were forbidden to marry. They also had to "divert themselves": in other words, frequent cafés and drink vodka, and serve vodka on all occasions, on pain of forfeiting all their possessions. The Czar's son Alexei ▲ *147* was accused of plotting against him, arrested, condemned to death – and tortured by Peter's own hand.

BRONZE GROTESQUE▲ *148*

In 1991 Chemiakin, a Russian-French-American sculptor, offered to the city of St Petersburg a symbol of the fallen empire, in the form of a statue of Peter fixed in his chair. The head, sculpted after a mask done by Rastrelli in 1719, is completely disproportionate to the body.

On her arrival in Russia Sophia of Anhalt-Zerbst, Princess of Pomerania and fiancée of Peter III, noted in her journal: "I will reign alone over Russia." Shortly after, while Russophobia and disdain for the orthodoxy of her husband were causing outrage in St Petersburg, she converted to the Orthodox religion. In 1762 she acceded to the throne as Catherine II, supported by the officers who had assassinated her husband.

A CIVILIZING INFLUENCE
When Catherine acceded, the state of academic faculties in the city was such that there might be only one student per class; police had to recruit pupils on the day schools opened.

A PHILOSOPHER ON THE THRONE
Catherine wished her reforms to answer the desires and interests of her subjects. Quoting Montesquieu, Quesnay and Beccaria, she put forward her ideas in a treatise, the *Nakaz*, whose triumph is depicted in the allegory at right. In 1767 Catherine formed a legislative committee, but came up against deputies who were ignorant of both government and the mechanics of the modern state, and unanimously defended the right to possess serfs.

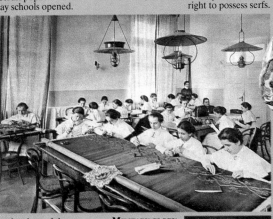

At the close of the 18th century Russia had nearly 300 schools, promoting the rise among ordinary Russians of an intelligentsia. The nobility was educated at home, but 200 of its daughters were taught at the Smolny Institute, which opened in 1764 ▲ *250*.

MILITARY GLORY
The victories of Marshal Alexander Suvarov over the Turks in 1790 and then over the French Army in the Alps in 1799 not only earned him the title of Prince of Italy but also gave Russia a decisive role on the European scene.

PUGACHOV'S REVOLT
In 1774, Pugachov, an illiterate cossack calling himself Peter III, threatened the throne of Catherine II.

People from the Volga regions, peasants working in the factories of the Urals and serfs flocked to Pugachov's banner.

"A WORSE REBEL THAN PUGACHOV"
This was Catherine's note on Radishchev's book *A Journey from St Petersburg to Moscow* (1790). Its author, a Russian noble who had studied at the University of Leipzig, was influenced by "half-baked scholars like Rousseau and Raynal". Observing the wretched state of the serfs in the two capitals, Radishchev condemned the regime of the "enthroned philosopher", who according to him was " . . . a deformed monster, impudent, obese, with a hundred yapping heads".

THE NOTES OF CATHERINE II
Kurakin, the Czar's best friend, secretly collected the only copy of the notes of Catherine II, sealed by Paul I. These notes did not appear until 1858, when they were published in French, in London, on the initiative of the revolutionary Herzen – who also published Radishchev.

MÉMOIRES
DE
L'IMPÉRATRICE CATHERINE

ÉCRITS PAR ELLE-MÊME,

ET PRÉCÉDÉS D'UNE PRÉFACE

PAR

A. HERZEN.

(ÉDITION DE N. TRÜBNER & CIE.)

LONDRES,
TRÜBNER & CIE, 60, PATERNOSTER R.
1859.

1825: THE DECEMBRISTS

During the military campaigns against Napoleon (1813–14) aristocratic Russian officers, educated from an early age by foreign tutors and (later) professors, saw at first hand constitutional regimes which had rid themselves of serfdom, and whose masses were moved by revolutionary ideals. On their return to Russia they formed secret societies with the aim of transforming their own country along the same lines. From 1822 onward these societies had polarized into two opposing groups, the Northern and the Southern.

CONSTITUTIONAL MONARCHY OR REPUBLIC?
Lively debates pitted Pestel, republican leader of the Southern Society, against Nikita Muraviev, the Northern leader, who proposed a constitutional monarchy. Some of the conspirators saw Pestel as a new Robespierre.

THE SENATE SQUARE
The conspirators decided to act on December 14, 1825, when the regiments of St Petersburg were scheduled to swear their oath of loyalty to Nicholas I. While some caused a diversion among the soldiers drawn up on the Senate Square ▲ *194*, others (including Prince Trubetskoy, the instigator of the coup) hesitated so long that the Czar's troops were able to foil the revolt, killing 1,271 people.

HANGED REBELS
The five leaders of the Decembrist insurrection were led to the gallows on July 14, 1826, with signs reading "Assassins of the Czar" hung around their necks. Three of the ropes broke, and the hangings had to be carried out again.

> "The public is right; in Russian writers it sees its only guides, its only defenders, and its only saviors against their country's autocracy, against orthodoxy, and against official nationalism."
>
> Bielinsky, Letter to Gogol, 1847

WOMEN OF COURAGE
"We, heroines? We are only such in the works of poets, for all we have done is follow our husbands . . ." wrote Alexandra Davidoff, wife of one of the Decembrist rebels condemned to exile in Siberia. With Alexandra went twenty-two other women, among them the princesses Trubetskoy, Volkonsky, and Shakhovskoy. All abandoned their children to go into voluntary exile.

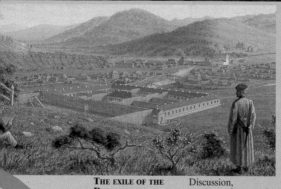

FOR POSTERITY
Lost in the crowd, the fourteen-year-old Alexander Herzen witnessed the religious service ordered by Nicholas I at the Kremlin following the hanging of the Decembrists, which impressed him with a lasting horror. In 1855 the five martyrs featured on the cover of the review *Pole Star*, which Herzen published in London and which was aimed at the Russian intelligentsia.

THE EXILE OF THE DECEMBRISTS
The women and their servants found lodgings in the vicinity of the prisons where their husbands were detained. The 120 men were condemned to hard labor in the salt mines. Their shackles were removed in 1830, and rings made out of them for the men's wives to wear.

Discussion, correspondence and clandestine visits helped the months to pass. Between 1832 and 1839, their sentences served, the Decembrists installed themselves in Siberia, where they contributed to cultural renewal and political debate.

The 1905 Revolution

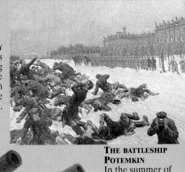

Following a wave of political reforms, after 1890 the Russian economy had to cope with the industrial revolution and the expansion of the cities, in which only 13 percent of the population lived. The agrarian sector remained stagnant: the peasants, who made up 85 percent of the Russian population, were kept in a state of abject serfdom by local aristocrats, despite their official enfranchisement. Two percent of the population owned nearly all of Russia's land, and the autocratic government proved incapable of changing a steadily worsening situation for the better. Finally, a disastrous war with Japan revealed the depth of the crisis.

BLOODY SUNDAY
On January 9, 1905, 140,000 demonstrators stood before the Winter Palace, brandishing icons and chanting their grievances. The response of the imperial troops was to open fire. The nationwide wave of outrage at the massacre turned into full-blown revolution.

THE BATTLESHIP POTEMKIN
In the summer of 1905 a spoiled meat broth served to the seamen aboard the battleship *Potemkin*, docked in a Black Sea port, provoked a violent uprising which left Odessa in ruins.

THE OPENING OF PARLIAMENT

Faced with a general strike, on October 17, 1905 the Czar approved a manifesto introducing a constitutional order. The inauguration of the Duma (parliament) took place on April 27, 1906 in the throne room of the Winter Palace.

TROTSKY
In St Petersburg the Menshevik Leon Trotsky took an active part in creating a form of direct democracy. Through the soviets workers were enabled to organize themselves independently of the government.

AFTERMATH OF 1905
After the crushing of the revolution, gallows – known as "Stolypin cravats" – became a common sight. Officially the Russian state was a constitutional monarchy, but in reality laws were applied arbitrarily and agrarian problems remained unsolved.

THE AGRARIAN REFORM OF 1906

This reform, arranged by Piotr Stolypin, consigned to oblivion the peasant communes which had hitherto regulated daily life in the countryside. Instead, it proposed the creation of a new social category of independent landowners.

THE 1917 REVOLUTION

Nicholas II and his family, prisoners at Tsarskoe Selo.

Russia's problems were compounded by World War One. The economy was unable to accelerate its rate of production to meet the new needs. Prices rose and inflation attained alarming proportions. Nicholas II was no longer a credible monarch, being perceived as the protector of Rasputin, a debauched charlatan who had cured his son Alexei; and as he was commander-in-chief of the Army a series of military defeats were sufficient to destroy the Czar altogether. The 4th Duma, which had remained loyal to him until 1915, finally stiffened in its opposition and resolved to depose him.

THE FALL OF THE CZARIST SYSTEM

The Czarist regime collapsed in five days, between February 23 and 27. Two plots, one in the Czar's immediate entourage, the other fomented by deputies in the Duma, projected the Czar's replacement by his brother. But the conspirators were forestalled by a spontaneous uprising by workers and soldiers in Petrograd, who seized the Arsenal and proclaimed a republic.

TWO POWERS

A power struggle ensued between the members of the provisional government, led by Prince Lvov, who wished to install a parliamentary regime and thereafter maintain the status quo, and the Petrograd Soviet, which advocated radical change.

FRATERNITY

While the streets of Petrograd resounded to the strains of the "Varsovienne" in honor of the martyrs of international revolution, the April Crisis suddenly struck. The Soviet offered the allies a "peace without annexations or reparations", which the provisional government affected to ignore.

ДА ЗДРАВСТВУЕТ III-ий ИНТЕРНАЦИОНАЛ!

Saluto, compagni!

Salut, camarades!

Grüße, Genossen

ПРИВЕТ

WELCOME, COMRADES!

ТОВАРИЩИ

SOCIALIST POWER
The socialist Kerensky, who became Prime Minister in July, was unable to control the radicalization of the masses.

ВСЯ ВЛАСТЬ СОВЕТАМ

"ALL POWER TO THE SOVIETS"
From April onward this was the rallying cry of the Bolsheviks. Their role in crushing a *putsch* led by General Kornilov, a monarchist rival of Kerensky, enabled them to attract both revolutionary socialists and Mensheviks to their cause during August. The bolshevization of the soviets was then quickly accomplished.

THE BOLSHEVIK TRIUMPH
This poster, which has since become an icon, was at first little understood. The failure of the Kornilov *putsch* drew Western attention away from Russia. In France and England the fall of Kerensky and the October Revolution ▲ 248 were passed over almost without comment, even in well-informed socialist circles. The bolshevization of the soviets likewise went unnoticed.

47

The Terror, or Purge, is often explained in terms of the personal motivations of Stalin himself, who was bent on revenge against the older Bolsheviks and on gaining absolute power. In fact, Stalin's ambitions were quickly outstripped by the sheer enormity of the phenomenon he had instigated. After the assassination of Kirov the Purge reached a paroxysm, with over two million political prisoners between 1934 and 1938. The State-Party system never succeeded in overcoming the socio-economic difficulties stemming from violent collectivization and accelerated industrialization. Confronted with social tensions, officials at every level of Soviet society promoted the fear of Stalin, along with his virtual deification.

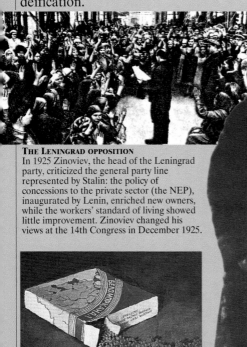

THE LENINGRAD OPPOSITION
In 1925 Zinoviev, the head of the Leningrad party, criticized the general party line represented by Stalin: the policy of concessions to the private sector (the NEP), inaugurated by Lenin, enriched new owners, while the workers' standard of living showed little improvement. Zinoviev changed his views at the 14th Congress in December 1925.

THE WHITE SEA–LAKE ONEGA CANAL
The canal linking the White Sea with Lake Onega, a giant construction project 140 miles long, was completed as part of the first Five Year Plan (1928–32). Mostly built by political prisoners, the canal gave its name to the tobacco brand Belomorkanal. The painting above illustrates the tribute in human lives which the Soviets had to pay to Stalin's planners.

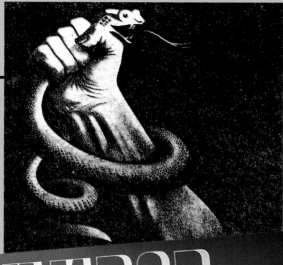

THE ASSASSINATION OF KIROV

Kirov (below), the party chief, was very popular in Leningrad on account of his attempts to raise the workers' standard of living. On December 1, 1934 Kirov's assassination allowed those responsible for Russia's economic chaos to direct the popular fury against "spies", "saboteurs" and other "turncoats".

М. КИРОВ

ИСКОРЕНИМ ШПИОНОВ и ДИВЕРСАНТОВ!

"NIGHT TERROR"

The great show trials held in Moscow unleashed a widespread sense of insecurity, the "night terror". Arrests were invariably carried out at dawn.

THE PURGE OF COSMOPOLITANS

Leningrad artists and intellectuals were the first victims of a campaign led by Zhdanov, the ideological head of the Central Committee, who demanded "proletarian science and art".

1948: THE LENINGRAD AFFAIR

Popov, the party chief (below), was shot along with a number of other officials on a charge of seeking to turn Leningrad into the capital of a federal Russia.

 БРЬСКОЙ

THE SIEGE OF LENINGRAD

CONDEMNED TO DEATH
The three million inhabitants under siege by the Wehrmacht had fuel and provisions for only two months: their water and electricity supplies were cut by the bombardments. Only a quarter of the sixty-eight armaments factories supplying the defenders of Leningrad were operational.

Soviet agents and diplomats rapidly informed Stalin of alarming German troop movements along the frontier. Having underestimated the threat, Stalin found himself obliged to intervene personally when Nazi troops flooded into the USSR. The ensuing battle, as sudden as it was catastrophic, took a huge toll in Russian lives. The siege of Leningrad, which was to last nine hundred days, was one of the most tragic consequences of Stalin's giant error. On September 8, 1941 the front had come within 4 miles of the city's southwestern edge, and Leningrad was linked to the rest of the country only by air and by way of the frozen waters of Lake Ladoga.

FAMINE IN LENINGRAD
Famine took hold from the autumn of 1941 onward, and was sharpened by the loss by fire of most of the warehouses containing the city's meager reserves of food. By December over 53,000 people had died, and the daily bread ration was down to 9 oz for workers and 4½ oz for the unemployed and for children. During the siege over 800,000 people died of hunger, 17,000 were killed, and 35,000 were wounded in the fighting.

THE LIFELINE
One of the few ways out of besieged Leningrad lay across the frozen waters of Lake Ladoga. From November 1942 a track was made across the ice which allowed the city to be supplied with bread. In the summer a network of pipes and cables running across the bed of the lake carried electricity and gasoline to the beleaguered citizens.

"We have no fear of bullets
Nor do we grieve for our houses,
But we are resolved to preserve our mother tongue
In all its truth and force."   Anna Akhmatova, Feb. 23, 1942

HOPE RETURNS
By the end of 1942 Leningrad was gradually coming back to life: factories reopened and the nightmare of famine faded. In January 1943 the Red Army succeeded in breaking the German blockade along the lake shore: a railway was constructed via Schlisselburg, known as the "Victory Line".

A SYMBOL OF LIFE
The composer Dmitry Shostakovich, who volunteered for military service, was assigned for his own safety to sentry duty on the roof of the Conservatoire and ordered to compose a special work for the People's Theater. Evacuated from Moscow at the age of 35, he completed his work in the Urals: the *7th ("Leningrad") Symphony* ▲ 228 was performed at Kubichev and Leningrad in 1942.

IMPERISHABLE GLORY
The celebratory fireworks of January 27, 1944 clothed the city in a lasting aura of heroism. After the war a million citizens were decorated for their part in the siege. At the coming of *perestroika*, the Museum of the Defense of Leningrad (instituted 1946–9) reopened its doors; an association of survivors was founded, and September 8 was declared a day of national mourning.

Russian belongs to the Eastern Slavic family of languages. This family is further subdivided into three main groups: the Occidental Slavic languages (Sorb, Czech and Slovak), the southern Slavic languages (Serbian, Macedonian and Bulgarian), and the oriental Slavic languages (Ukrainian, Byelorussian and Russian). The second and third groups are all written with the cyrillic alphabet, with very slight variations.

THE CYRILLIC ALPHABET

The monk Cyril and his brother Methodus perfected the glagolitic alphabet in 863. This alphabet was soon supplanted by a simplified equivalent, the cyrillic. The cyrillic alphabet includes several characters taken from both the Greek and Roman alphabets. In 1710 Peter the Great, with his *grajdnka* (civil alphabet), suppressed the graphic survivals of nasal vowels, and simplified the forms of certain letters. The orthographic reform of 1917 replaced the Ѣ by e, and almost did away with the use of the hard sign Ъ. The cyrillic alphabet in its present form contains thirty-two letters.

THE SLAVIC LANGUAGE

Common Slavic was the only language spoken in the plains of Northern Europe toward the middle of the first millennium AD. Old Slav as spoken in the 9th century (at the beginning of the differentiation between the Slavic languages and peoples) is still understood by most Slavs. From it came Slavonic, a literary and religious language still used in the liturgy of Orthodox Slavs.

FOREIGN CONTRIBUTIONS

Cyril and Methodus were sent to Moravia by the Byzantine Emperor Michael III to evangelize the Slavs. Their new alphabet allowed them to translate the New Testament into the old Slav language. For centuries thereafter the Psalter was to be the principal reading matter of Russians. Their many contacts with Byzantium, both peaceful and belligerent, eventually led to the conversion of the Kiev prince Vladimir in 988, followed by that of his people; this event marked the entry of the pagan Slavs into Christendom. Later Western influences contributed to the development of oral and folk art, in addition to an original and precocious body of literature, notably *The Sayings of Prince Igor*. After the 11th century, old Russian texts, such as the Ostromir New Testament, were written in a mixture of authentic Russian and Slavonic, the proportions of which varied from period to period and genre to genre. The interaction of these two languages eventually determined the form of what we know as literary Russian.

THE AWAKENING NATION

The Mongol invasion (13th century) and the domination of the "Golden Horde" (Tartar state) condemned the Russian language to centuries of isolation, which was eventually shaken off by a new religious and national awareness. This turning inward, at first forced but later deliberate, was generally damaging, but after a period of difficulty, in 1613 the Romanovs took over: intellectual inquiry again appeared along with literature. The Slavonic, Greek and Latin Academy, founded in Moscow in 1682, used a ponderous, artificial, heavily russified Slavonic language which stifled poetic creativity; yet it laid the groundwork for the blossoming of Russian literature in the following century, by bringing *belles-lettres* to the forefront of Russian life.

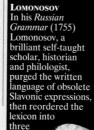

LOMONOSOV
In his *Russian Grammar* (1755) Lomonosov, a brilliant self-taught scholar, historian and philologist, purged the written language of obsolete Slavonic expressions, then reordered the lexicon into three categories: Slavonic, mixed and Russian terms. Three styles emerged from the combination of these elements: low, medium and high. This rigid classification had the merit of giving spoken Russian the place it deserved in literature (including song, epigram, private correspondence, comedy), the Slavonic terms being relegated to a more abstract, elevated linguistic register.

LITERATURE AND THE RUSSIAN LANGUAGE

THE LANGUAGE OF POETS

Even more than grammarians, writers like Sumarokov, Derzhavin and Karamzin (left) were the architects of the modern Russian language. At the turn of the 18th into the 19th century they prepared the ground for the great works of Pushkin. Under Catherine the Great intellectual and artistic life intensified in richness and was marked by a desire to imitate French classicism as well as scrupulously to respect the hierarchy of genres and styles established by Lomonosov. Karamzin rejected all distinctions between the spoken language and the written one: his ambition was to elevate spoken Russian to the status of a literary language.

MODERN RUSSIAN

Thus modern literary Russian emerged by stages, enriched by the language spoken by ordinary people. Russian songs and *bylines* (song epics) passed into print and, thanks to the discovery of *The Sayings of Prince Igor*, the master story-writer Ivan Krylov was able to contribute to a synthesis between popular and academic Russian. Nevertheless, it was Alexander Pushkin who perfected literary expression in the Russian language, with his motto: "When things are simple, say them simply."

THE SPREAD OF THE RUSSIAN LANGUAGE

With the creation of the Soviet Union and its fifteen republics, twelve of which were non-Slav, Russian became the official language of the Federation.

Learning the language was made compulsory, not only for Soviet youth but also for the youth of the other Eastern countries. Many Africans, Asians and Latin Americans went to study in the Soviet Union and learned to speak fluent Russian.

Under the cultural influence of the West the language has borrowed heavily (and sometimes inelegantly) from foreign tongues, absorbing words which have often supplanted Russian ones. Yet Russian is also acquiring new home-grown terms to describe the political, economic, social and moral upheavals of the era.

Today Russian is one of the five official languages of the United Nations, even though Russia's current difficulties impede its spread.

Arts and traditions

Today, as in the past, foreign visitors to Russia are amazed by the magnificence of the Orthodox liturgy, the gold of its icons and its polyphonic choral music. The Russians themselves cherish the beauty and symbolism of their Byzantine rite; a beauty which, according to the old chronicles, originally motivated their conversion to Christianity. Beyond their esthetic value these rites embody theological and spiritual teachings which remain unaltered since the 17th-century schism of the traditionalist "Old Believers". The Orthodox liturgy was the sole vehicle of faith permitted by the Soviet regime.

THE LITURGY
The length and the sheer splendor of Orthodox services tend to reinforce the idea of eternity and holiness, while its informality seems to welcome all comers.

The Orthodox year, with its round of feasts and fasts, is extremely rich and varied. The Russian Church still observes the Julian Calendar, which is thirteen days out of step with the Gregorian Calendar. The linchpin of church life is the Sunday Eucharist, during which clergy and congregation, including young children, take Communion.

RUSSIAN CLERGY
Parish priests (often married men) form the "white" clergy, while the "black" clergy are monks who have taken vows. Formerly the color of their vestments showed the difference between them. The bishops are appointed from among the monks and celibate or widowed priests; the principal of these bishops, the Patriarch of Moscow, is the titular head of the Russian Orthodox Church.

THE ICONOSTASIS
Covered with five rows of icons ● 58 and topped by a cross, the iconostasis is a central element in every Russian Orthodox church. It depicts the prophets, the feasts of the liturgical year and the dëesis (prayer) of the saints in company with Christ. The larger lower row is made up of the icons of Christ, the Virgin and the various saints. It has three doors, used by the clergy: the central one (the "royal door"), reserved for the most solemn rites of the Orthodox Church, symbolizes the entrance to the kingdom of God.

ORTHODOX CHURCHES
the meeting point of God and mankind, the church signifies heaven on earth. Orthodox churches can be square or cruciform, and have a central dome; important churches have five domes, symbolizing Christ and the four Evangelists.

THE SEVEN SACRAMENTS
The Orthodox rite of baptism is followed by Chrismation (or Confirmation). The other sacraments are the Eucharist, marriage, ordination of the clergy, penitence, and the anointing of the sick.

ORTHODOX EASTER
Called the "feast of feasts", Easter is the climax of the Orthodox year. After the forty-day Lenten fast and the ceremonies of Holy Week, the celebration rite begins with a candlelit procession, followed by the announcement of Christ's Resurrection. At Matins the victory of life over death is exalted; later, friends and relatives gather round the Easter table, with its Easter eggs and cakes blessed at church.

● ICONS

The Orthodox Church, which rejected the charge of idolatry made during the iconoclastic controversy in Byzantium (8th century), defines the icon as bearing witness to divine revelation, and thus justifiable in terms of the dogma of incarnation (God may not be represented in a picture but Christ, who was made man, can be). The icon is neither a work of art nor a pious image: it has a clear liturgical function, as well as a teaching role.

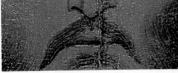

THE ORIGINS
Icons, which came to Russia with Christianity from Byzantium, reached a degree of perfection following the iconoclastic crisis. The Greek mosaic artists who decorated the churches of Kiev in the 11th century trained the first Russian iconographers. In the *Head of Christ* below the influence of mosaic is clearly discernible, notably in the golden lines traced through the hair.

A PAINTED SCRIPT
The technique of icon-making has not changed for centuries. It employs only natural materials. The wooden panel is first covered with a fine layer of plaster, and the image is painted on the wet surface; the powdered mineral colors are blended with an egg-based emulsion. The painting is then embellished with gold leaf and varnished, and the title is inscribed in vermilion lettering. In the Slavonic language a single word is used for the functions of writing and painting; therefore the artist does not merely paint his icon but he "writes" it too. Above: *Life of Saint Serge of Radonega* (16th century)

A WINDOW ON ETERNITY
This *Christ in Majesty* (16th century) shows all the symbolism and sanctity of the icon, through the use of concentric circles and inverted perspective to express a relationship between time and space which is very different to that of the world in which we live. In this way the icon becomes a kind of window on eternity. Such rules were codified in manuals, which also laid out guidelines for icon composition, the ordering of themes and use of color.

ANONYMOUS WORKS
Novgorod, Pskov, Suzdal and later Moscow succeeded one another as schools of iconography, each with its own tradition. The icon was never signed by an individual, but the fine rendering of the *Presentation of Christ* (right) is probably the work of Andrei Rublev, the great Muscovite icon-painter of the 15th century.

DECADENCE
From the 17th century onward the art of the icon was affected by excessive symbolism and borrowings from the West. The detailed and naturalistic *Trinity* (1671) by Simeon Ushakov, the official Kremlin painter, differs greatly from the icon by Rublev which inspired it.

REDISCOVERY OF THE ICON
In the 16th century a tradition arose of covering almost the entire work with precious metals. In the *Virgin of Kazan* (above, late 19th century) only the faces are visible. In the early 20th century the icon regained its original esthetic and theological aspects.

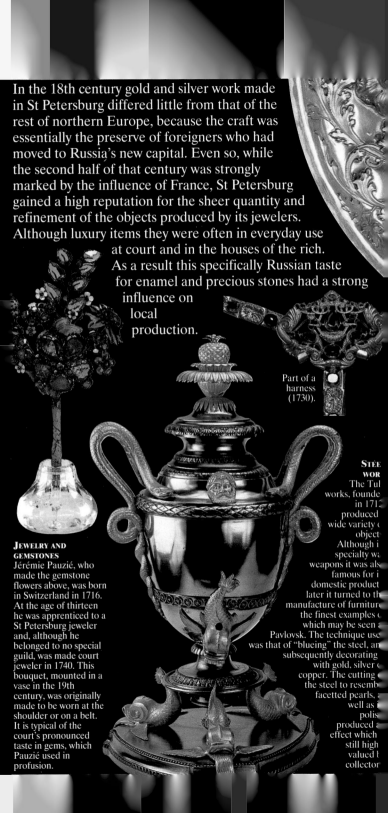

In the 18th century gold and silver work made in St Petersburg differed little from that of the rest of northern Europe, because the craft was essentially the preserve of foreigners who had moved to Russia's new capital. Even so, while the second half of that century was strongly marked by the influence of France, St Petersburg gained a high reputation for the sheer quantity and refinement of the objects produced by its jewelers. Although luxury items they were often in everyday use at court and in the houses of the rich. As a result this specifically Russian taste for enamel and precious stones had a strong influence on local production.

Part of a harness (1730).

JEWELRY AND GEMSTONES

Jérémie Pauzié, who made the gemstone flowers above, was born in Switzerland in 1716. At the age of thirteen he was apprenticed to a St Petersburg jeweler and, although he belonged to no special guild, was made court jeweler in 1740. This bouquet, mounted in a vase in the 19th century, was originally made to be worn at the shoulder or on a belt. It is typical of the court's pronounced taste in gems, which Pauzié used in profusion.

STEE WOR

The Tul works, founde in 171 produced wide variety o object Although i specialty wa weapons it was als famous for i domestic product later it turned to th manufacture of furnitur the finest examples o which may be seen a Pavlovsk. The technique use was that of "blueing" the steel, an subsequently decorating with gold, silver o copper. The cutting o the steel to resemb facetted pearls, well as polis produced a effect which still high valued b collector

MASTERWORKS
This gilded silver platter, decorated by the *repoussé* technique, resembles the work being done at the same period in Germany. There is no hallmark on the piece but the dedication to Peter the Great dates it to between 1721 and 1725.

Chessmen, Tula, late 18th century.

TOBACCO BOX
Tobacco boxes of this type were very much the fashion at the Russian court; they were frequently presented by monarchs as diplomatic gifts, and were also given as lovers' pledges. Pauzié made scores of them for the Empress Elizabeth I.

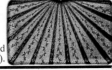

Cigarette box, gold
and enamel (1908).

"If you compare my creations to those
of Tiffany, Boucheron and Cartier you
will conclude that they are of lesser
value . . . but what, in fact, are these
companies? They are sellers of jewelry,
they are not artists. Hugely valuable
objects interest me little, if their value
resides in nothing more than an infinity of diamonds and
pearls." This remark by Fabergé neatly expresses
the spirit of his world-famous firm.

CARL FABERGÉ
Born in St Petersburg in 1846, the son of a
modest jeweler of Huguenot stock,
Peter Carl Fabergé took over the family
business in 1870 and began by
producing jewelry to conform with
the prevailing taste for all things
French. The arrival of his
brother Agathon, an
imaginative artist,
contributed to the
blossoming of the
business
after 1882.

THE FLOWERS
Fabergé's naturalist
compositions are
executed with
astonishing skill:
oatgrass and
cornflowers on
golden stalks rise
from a translucent
vase of rock crystal.

THE EGGS
Fabergé's eggs are
marvels of
inventiveness and
delicacy. They are still
copied today.

ENAMELS

Worked in *champlevé* or applied in successive layers on a checkered background, enamelwork was produced in over a hundred different hues.

PRECIOUS METALS

Fabergé's metals were also very finely worked: up to four shades of gold might be blended to produce the desired effect. Silver was deliberately left in its original state.

IMPERIAL COMMISSIONS

Under the aegis of the master Mikhail Perkhin, in the 1890's Fabergé's workshops produced large quantities of objects and gems, many of them commissioned by the Czar's family. Fabergé Easter eggs were given by Nicholas II to his mother and his wife.

SEMI-PRECIOUS STONES

Pink and black rhodonite, mouse-gray Kalkan jasper and pale green nephrite (mined in the Urals) gave Fabergé's designers all the imaginative scope they needed to create their confectionery dishes, figurines and quaint animal sculptures.

PORCELAIN

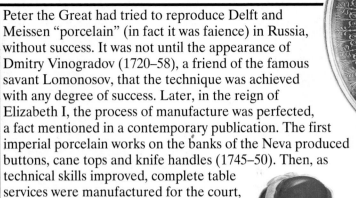

1749

Peter the Great had tried to reproduce Delft and Meissen "porcelain" (in fact it was faience) in Russia, without success. It was not until the appearance of Dmitry Vinogradov (1720–58), a friend of the famous savant Lomonosov, that the technique was achieved with any degree of success. Later, in the reign of Elizabeth I, the process of manufacture was perfected, a fact mentioned in a contemporary publication. The first imperial porcelain works on the banks of the Neva produced buttons, cane tops and knife handles (1745–50). Then, as technical skills improved, complete table services were manufactured for the court, along with statuettes whose imperfections were often masked by lavish gilding.

MADE-TO-ORDER TABLE SERVICES
Private factories soon made their appearance, competing directly with the imperial works; they created made-to-order table services, some commissioned by Catherine II. These services, which might include up to a thousand pieces, reflect the growing luxury of the imperial table, particularly in the 19th century.

FIGURINES
The production of figurines, typically Russian, has never ceased in St Petersburg. The only changes brought to it by the Revolution were in the types of figures portrayed.

GUREEV TABLE SERVICE (1807)
This service bears the name of the head of Alexander I's Imperial Cabinet. The various pieces are remarkably diverse, with beautifully defined figures.

109, 110

FROM REVIVED STYLES TO ART NOUVEAU
Following its approximation to the Sèvres style in the late 18th century, Russian porcelain went through a historicist period in the first quarter of the 19th century. Later it regressed into a multicolored, richly gilded Rococo style. At the close of the 19th century the imperial porcelain works came under the influence of Copenhagen, adopting modern simplified forms and new colors and designs in the Art Nouveau style.

CONSTRUCTIVIST PORCELAIN
Porcelain manufacture was a domain in which the modernization of designs and ideas could immediately be applied. This meant that propaganda themes coexisted with Constructivist work, often produced by such renowned artists as Malevich and Kandinsky, who in no way disdained this unusual medium. Above, a tea-service in porcelain designed by Malevich; the link with his paintings *109, 110* is evident.

As a rule the palaces of St Petersburg were decorated with furniture designed on French, English and German models, when these pieces were not directly imported from Western Europe. Furniture made in Russia remained simple and massive until the reign of Peter I, but its quality developed rapidly throughout the second half of the 18th century. The extensive building projects of Catherine II and her court stimulated a marked increase in demand, which eventually could be satisfied only by locally made products.

In the time of Peter the Great, the furniture trade specialized in marquetry as well as carved, painted and gilded pieces.

CARELIAN BIRCHWOOD
In the early 19th century new types of furniture – tiered consoles, serpent-shaped elbow rests and claw-foot armchairs – were introduced. Between 1820 and 1840 the use of natural woods became generalized, emphasizing the ornate aspect of Carelian birchwood.

FREEDOM OF MOVEMENT
In the 18th century the work of cabinet-making in Russia was shared between the master-craftsmen of St Petersburg and trained serfs on aristocratic estates. Their virtuosity proved the innate skills of Russian woodworkers: the materials they used were many and varied, and they did not hesitate to blend indigenous wood species, which had an undeserved reputation for poor quality, with more exotic ones.

NEW MATERIALS

An instinct for variety in materials is characteristic of this aspect of Russian decorative art. Already in the reigns of Elizabeth I and Catherine II steel-based furniture manufactured at the Tula works had made its appearance ● *60* near Moscow.

SCHOOL OF TALACHKINO

At the close of the 19th century the predominant furniture style still had its roots in Russian culture. Furniture of the Talachkino School reflected the carved geometrical shapes of the empire's Byzantine origins.

"RUSSIAN JACOB"

Another exclusive style of the late 18th century was "Russian Jacob" (strips of brass inlaid in mahogany, in geometrical patterns).

GILT AND SEMI-PRECIOUS STONES

In the 19th century Russia produced remarkable pieces of furniture (such as tables and monumental candelabra) incorporating colored crystal and stones mined in the Urals, which added to the exoticism of the new Italianate palaces then being built.

In their own way the theaters of St Petersburg bear witness to Russian political history, since their names invariably changed to reflect the party in power. As the custodians of Russia's great dramatic, lyrical and choreographical works the imperial Mariinsky and Alexandrinsky theaters mounted the masquerade of the early 20th century, which are evoked in Anna Akhmatova' "Poem without a Hero". These illustrated the dreams of a societ in crisis; they included Lermontov's legendary *Masked Ball*, with lavish décor by Alexander Golovine. With *perestroika*, new theate emerged; and innovative productions directed by Lev Dodin hav demonstrated the enduring vitality of the Russian theater.

ALEXANDRINSKY THEATER ▲ *230*. As the Academy of Drama in 1920, renamed the Pushkin Theater in 1937, the Alexandrinsky was, along with the Maly Theater in Moscow, one of the two great centers of 19th-century Russian culture. Between 1908 and 1918 it was profoundly influenced by the work of the great reformer Vsevolod Meyerhold (below).

MARIINSKY THEATER ▲ *202*
This great institution was inaugurated in 186 with the purpose of presenting the classica repertoire. Renamed the Kirov Theater in 19 it later became the mecca of the Russian Bal ▲ *200*. It reverted to its original name in 199

LITTLE THEATER OF OPERA AND BALLET ▲ *225*
Also known as the Maly or Mussorgsky Theater, at one time this was named the Mikhailovsky Theater. As the third of the former imperial playhouses it was the home of a French company from 1879 to 1917. Renamed the Little (*maly*) Theater, it was one of the few experimental institutions for opera and ballet in Russia during the 1930's.

В. Шекспир

BDT (Tovstonogov Theater)
Theater of tragedy, romantic drama and high comedy" – or so its original purpose was described.

The theater was known as the Gorky Theater between 1932 and 1993. For thirty years it mounted the classic plays of G.A. Tovstonogov (below right, during a rehearsal), after whom it was renamed in 1993.

BDT poster for Shakespeare's Henry IV (right)

Король Генрих IV

Theater of Musical Comedy (1929)
The director and satirical artist Nicholas Akimov (left) worked here from 1930 to 1950. This theater is known for its original repertoire.

Little (Maly) Dramatic Theater ▲ 238
This repertory theater, founded in 1944, acquired a wider reputation in the 1980's under its director Lev Dodin. The Maly Theater Company gained worldwide fame with new plays like *Brothers and Sisters* (1985, from a novel by F. Abramov) and *Gaudeamus* (1990, by Sergei Kaledin, left). In 1998 the Maly Theater won the accolade of Theater of Europe, the third to do so after the Odeon in Paris and the Piccolo Teatro in Milan.

St Petersburg, where the first school of Russian dance opened in 1738, well in advance of Moscow, is the cradle of ballet. The entire history of classical dance is marked by Russian emotion and poetry, which enriched a technique originally imported from Europe. This enabled Russian dancers, while mastering both Italian virtuosity and French academic rigor, to apply themselves to the expression of the inner life of their roles. From the *divertissements* and interludes devised by 18th-century ballet masters such as Landé and Fossano to the worldwide phenomenon of the Diaghilev ballets, Russia has raised this particular art to the highest level of her cultural heritage.

BALLETS RUSSES (1908–29)

The success of the Ballets Russes gave a new stimulus to European ballet, as dance in Russia became the focus of a wide variety of artistic movements and interests. The research of the choreographer Fokine and the painters Bakst and Benois resurrected images of antiquity, the Orient, Old Russia and traditional festivals.

LEON BAKST (1866–1924)

As a scene-painter and decorator working for Serge Diaghilev, Leon Bakst moved to Paris in 1909. Above, a costume design for *Narcisse*, Saisons Russes, Paris 1911.
Baskt's sketches are on show at the Theater Museum, Ostrovsky Square ▲ *231*.

SERGE DIAGHILEV (1872–1929)

As the founder of the World of Art association Diaghilev masterminded the successful Saisons Russes tours abroad. He brought together the most brilliant and innovative artistic talents of his time: Bakst and Picasso, Fokine and Nijinsky, Karsavina and Pavlova, Rimsky-Korsakov, Stravinsky, Prokofiev and many more.

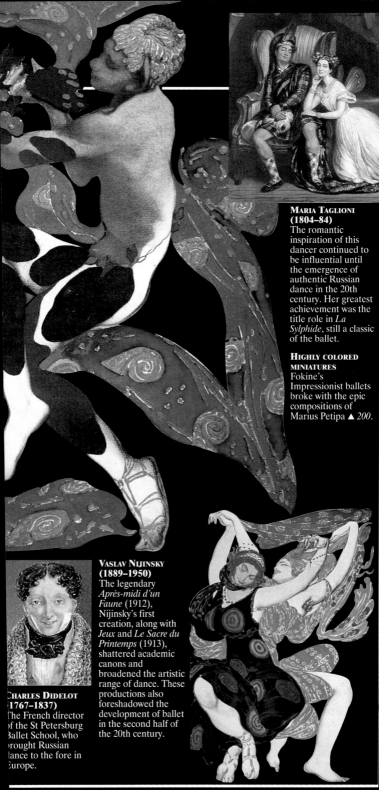

MARIA TAGLIONI (1804–84)
The romantic inspiration of this dancer continued to be influential until the emergence of authentic Russian dance in the 20th century. Her greatest achievement was the title role in *La Sylphide*, still a classic of the ballet.

HIGHLY COLORED MINIATURES
Fokine's Impressionist ballets broke with the epic compositions of Marius Petipa ▲ *200*.

VASLAV NIJINSKY (1889–1950)
The legendary *Après-midi d'un Faune* (1912), Nijinsky's first creation, along with *Jeux* and *Le Sacre du Printemps* (1913), shattered academic canons and broadened the artistic range of dance. These productions also foreshadowed the development of ballet in the second half of the 20th century.

CHARLES DIDELOT (1767–1837)
The French director of the St Petersburg Ballet School, who brought Russian dance to the fore in Europe.

The Capella, the Conservatoire and the Philharmonia, as the centers of St Petersburg's musical establishment, made it their business to encourage artistic creativity and the expression of musical talent. In the 20th century the musical traditions of the St Petersburg School are associated with the esthetic of the Group of Five, which included the composers Balakirev, Borodin, Cui, Mussorgsky and Rimsky-Korsakov. While the historic past and folktales of Russia were the main sources of inspiration, the music itself remained thoroughly European.

THE CAPELLA

Founded in 1479 in the reign of Ivan III, the original purpose of the Capella was to train church choirs. In the 18th century, at St Petersburg, it became an imperial chapel, with the most talented musicians serving as its directors. Later it offered a wide variety of musical training, from directing of choirs (1846) to folk music (1918). In 1920 the Capella introduced women's voices into Russian choirs for the first time.

THE CONSERVATOIRE

The fame of the Conservatoire, founded in 1862, rests on the extraordinary creative activity which at one time was centered upon it. The musicologist and art historian Stasov was the catalyst for the Group of Five composers, who were inspired by folktales and historical legend such as Boris Godunov; these were very different from the Moscow School, represented by Tchaikovsky and Rachmaninov, whose musical inspiration was more European in style.

E PHILHARMONIA
is institution
s named after
ostakovich in 1974.
nitry Shostakovich
06–75), although
uasi-official
viet composer,
out of favor
h the authorities
1947. Encouraged
Zhdanov, he
onged to the
dition of Bach
d Mussorgsky. His
rk includes fifteen
nphonies, among
m the famous
("*Leningrad*")
nphony ● 51.

SERGEI PROKOFIEV (1891–1953)
Trained as a pianist and composer
at the St Petersburg
Conservatoire, Prokofiev began
his career as a concert artist.
Between 1918 and 1932 he
lived outside Russia; on his
return to the Soviet Union he
suffered political persecution.
His work sums up the finest
achievements of Russian music,
from Glinka through to
Rachmaninov (*Romeo and Juliet*,
1938).

**OR
RAVINSKY
882–1971)**
pupil of
msky-Korsakov,
avinsky lived in
ssia until 1914.
was later a
rmanent
mber of the
sons Russes in
ris, where his
lets *The
ebird* (1910),
rushka (1911)
d *The Rite of
ring* (1913) were
rformed. The
emes of these
lets were
pired by
ssian folklore.

RECIPE: "BLINIS"

Blinis, made from one of the oldest of flour-based recipes, were originally eaten "in communion" with the souls of deceased loved ones in Russia: at Christmas with *koutia* (broth made with cracked wheat), at funerals and during Carnival. Following the 1917 Revolution *blinis* became everyday fare in Russia, unconnected with the Orthodox calendar.

PREPARING THE MIXTURE
Ingredients
(for six people):
2lb 3 oz/10 cups flour
1½ oz yeast
½ tsp salt
1 tsp caster sugar
10 fl. oz lukewarm water
1 pint lukewarm milk
3 tbsp oil
3 eggs

1. Prepare in advance: in a warm bowl dissolve the yeast, salt and sugar in the lukewarm water. Pour the mixture into a mixing bowl.

2. Mixing well with a whisk, add the flour, milk and egg yolks, working till smooth

3. Allow the mixture to rise in a warm place for 40 minutes. Cover the bowl. Then whip the egg whites until stiff.

4. Gently fold the egg whites into the mixture with a spatula.

6. Pour a little of the mixture into the heated frying pan, turning the pan to make the mixture spread as thinly as possible.

5. Lightly grease a 5-inch frying pan with a half-potato dipped in melted butter.

7. Cook at medium heat, as with pancakes (the first is often a disaster).

8. The *blinis* are then covered with melted butter and thick cream (*smetana*), and eaten with *zakuski* (hors d'oeuvres): smoked salmon, tarama, herring, salmon eggs, or similar tasty accompaniments. Traditionally, Russians serve *blinis* with an assortment of chilled red and black caviar and ice-cold vodka.

75

SHAWLS
Light and warm,
Russian shawls
come in many
colors, usually
with bright flower
patterns. They are
available in most
department stores
in St Petersburg.

ZEFIRS
Sweets
resembling
meringues
coated in
chocolate.

RUSSIAN VODKA
The best place to buy
good-quality vodka is
in shops specializing
in the national drink.
The most highly
recommended
brands are Sankt
Petersburg, Diplomat,
Piatizvezdnaya,
and Sinopskaya.

RUSSIAN VODKA MUSEUM
The displays here trace the history of
distilling in Russia from the 10th century.
Guided visits include the opportunity to
taste some of the best vodkas, along
with a suitable selection
of zakouski.

MATRYOSHKAS
These little dolls, usually made
by Muscovite craftsmen, are very
popular with tourists. The quality
of the painted design may vary
considerably.

CRAFTS
Handpainted wooden toys (above);
objects made of amber or semi-precious
stones (green malachite box, far right);
lacquered Palekh boxes (right) echo the
art of this former school of iconography.

Architecture

THE TOWN PLAN:
THE FOUNDING OF ST PETERSBURG

In May 1703 Peter I, then at war with the Swedes, captured a stronghold at the mouth of the Neva river. To consolidate his victory he began building a new fortress 4 miles downstream dedicated to saints Peter and Paul, later adding the Admiralty and shipyards on the left bank. The site was unhealthy and ill-protected; nevertheless, by 1712 the Czar was determined to build his new capital there. St Petersburg, ". . . the window through which Russia looked out on Europe", evolved into a huge experiment, whereby patterns borrowed from Western cities were assimilated into Russian tradition.

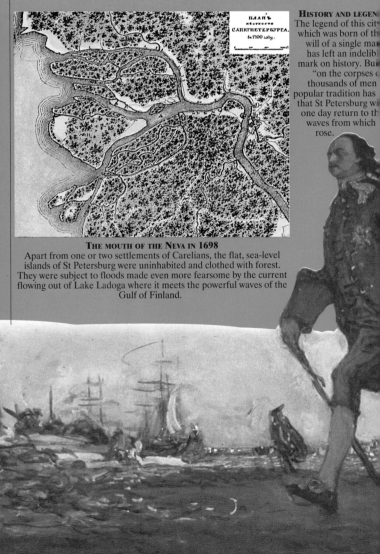

ПЛАНЪ
МѢСТНОСТИ
САНКТПЕТЕРБУРГА.
въ 1700 году.

THE MOUTH OF THE NEVA IN 1698
Apart from one or two settlements of Carelians, the flat, sea-level islands of St Petersburg were uninhabited and clothed with forest. They were subject to floods made even more fearsome by the current flowing out of Lake Ladoga where it meets the powerful waves of the Gulf of Finland.

HISTORY AND LEGEND
The legend of this city, which was born of the will of a single man, has left an indelible mark on history. Built "on the corpses of thousands of men", popular tradition has that St Petersburg will one day return to the waves from which it rose.

THE PETER AND PAUL FORTRESS (1703)

A symbol of autocratic military power, the Peter and Paul Fortress stands directly opposite the Imperial Palace. The gilded spires of the Peter and Paul Cathedral, the Admiralty and Mikhail Palace add bright verticals to the flat, gray urban landscape.

THE DEVELOPMENT OF THE CITY

The plans drawn up by Jean-Baptiste Leblond, the chief architect for St Petersburg, were remarkable for a system of Dutch-style canals, supposed to absorb the flood waters and facilitate communications. Other features were an arrangement of the various districts to suit different sections of the population, and an attempt (eventually abandoned) to surround the city with ramparts.

SПЕТРОПОЛІСъ 1703

St Petersburg in 1725

Although in 1725 St Petersburg was far from completed, the planning options governing its later construction were already fixed. There were two fortresses to guard the mouth of the Neva (Peter and Paul on the right bank and the Admiralty on the left); the Menshikov Palace and the Kunstkammer endowed Vasilyevsky Island with its first architectural features; the Summer Palace and the gardens bounded the city to eastward; the river's tributaries had been channeled; and the Nevsky Prospekt had been laid out.

WAREHOUSES
The first constructions in the city were of wood, always abundant in Russia.

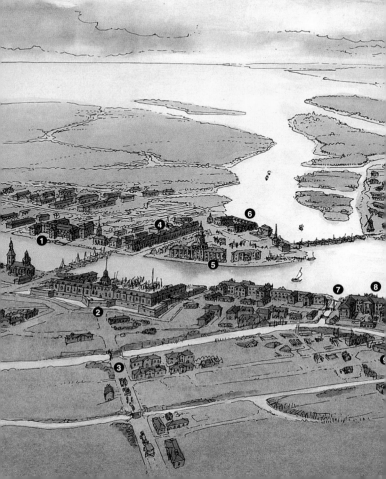

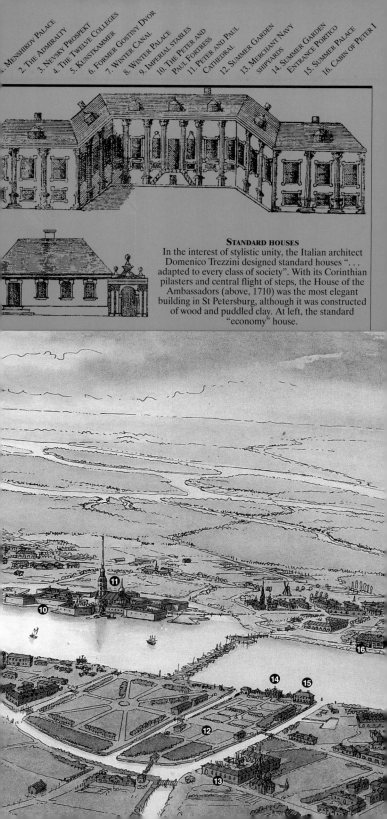

STANDARD HOUSES

In the interest of stylistic unity, the Italian architect Domenico Trezzini designed standard houses ". . . adapted to every class of society". With its Corinthian pilasters and central flight of steps, the House of the Ambassadors (above, 1710) was the most elegant building in St Petersburg, although it was constructed of wood and puddled clay. At left, the standard "economy" house.

In his haste to jettison Muscovite traditions Peter the Great engaged foreigners to build his modern city, naval installations and cultural center. Dutch engineers and Italian and German architects succeeded one another, until the arrival in 1716 of the French master builder Leblond. Leblond and his team were commissioned both to build, and to train the Russians in contemporary Western architectural concepts. "Naryshkin Baroque", characteristic of late 17th-century Moscow, gave way to Dutch pediments cheek by jowl with Italianate superimposed orders, German staircases and French curb-roofing.

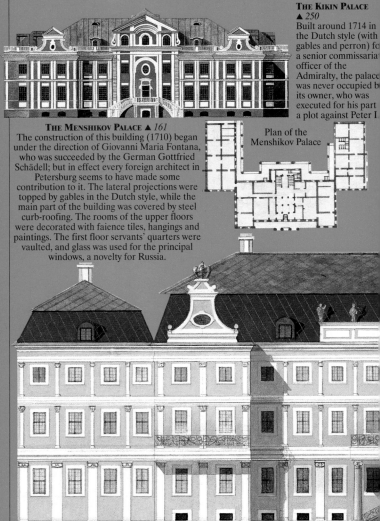

THE KIKIN PALACE
▲ 250
Built around 1714 in the Dutch style (with gables and perron) for a senior commissariat officer of the Admiralty, the palace was never occupied by its owner, who was executed for his part in a plot against Peter I

THE MENSHIKOV PALACE ▲ 161
The construction of this building (1710) began under the direction of Giovanni Maria Fontana, who was succeeded by the German Gottfried Schädell; but in effect every foreign architect in Petersburg seems to have made some contribution to it. The lateral projections were topped by gables in the Dutch style, while the main part of the building was covered by steel curb-roofing. The rooms of the upper floors were decorated with faience tiles, hangings and paintings. The first floor servants' quarters were vaulted, and glass was used for the principal windows, a novelty for Russia.

Plan of the Menshikov Palace

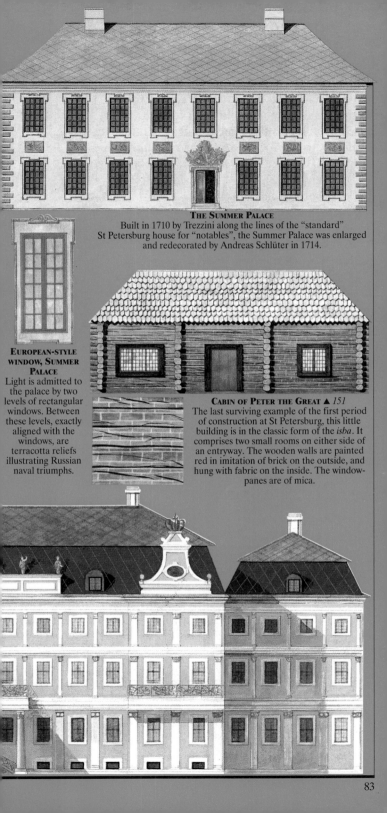

THE SUMMER PALACE
Built in 1710 by Trezzini along the lines of the "standard"
St Petersburg house for "notables", the Summer Palace was enlarged
and redecorated by Andreas Schlüter in 1714.

**EUROPEAN-STYLE
WINDOW, SUMMER
PALACE**
Light is admitted to
the palace by two
levels of rectangular
windows. Between
these levels, exactly
aligned with the
windows, are
terracotta reliefs
illustrating Russian
naval triumphs.

CABIN OF PETER THE GREAT ▲ 151
The last surviving example of the first period
of construction at St Petersburg, this little
building is in the classic form of the *isba*. It
comprises two small rooms on either side of
an entryway. The wooden walls are painted
red in imitation of brick on the outside, and
hung with fabric on the inside. The window-
panes are of mica.

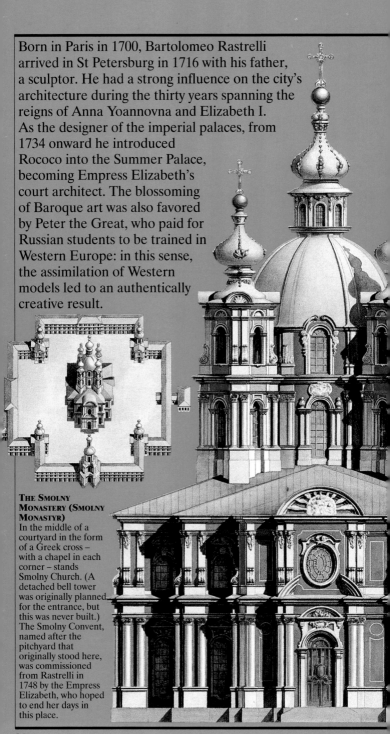

Born in Paris in 1700, Bartolomeo Rastrelli arrived in St Petersburg in 1716 with his father, a sculptor. He had a strong influence on the city's architecture during the thirty years spanning the reigns of Anna Yoannovna and Elizabeth I. As the designer of the imperial palaces, from 1734 onward he introduced Rococo into the Summer Palace, becoming Empress Elizabeth's court architect. The blossoming of Baroque art was also favored by Peter the Great, who paid for Russian students to be trained in Western Europe: in this sense, the assimilation of Western models led to an authentically creative result.

THE SMOLNY MONASTERY (SMOLNY MONASTYR)
In the middle of a courtyard in the form of a Greek cross – with a chapel in each corner – stands Smolny Church. (A detached bell tower was originally planned for the entrance, but this was never built.) The Smolny Convent, named after the pitchyard that originally stood here, was commissioned from Rastrelli in 1748 by the Empress Elizabeth, who hoped to end her days in this place.

ST NICHOLAS' CATHEDRAL ▲ 204
Isolated, Russian style, from the main church, Savva Chevakinsky's campanile (1756–8) is a model of elegant mid-18th-century Baroque. The concave façades of the lower floor contrast with the circular designs of the two upper ones, with their small dome and drum.

ATLAS FIGURES
The Atlas figures at Tsarskoe Selo ▲ 264 were covered with tin sulphate in the form of golden-colored leaves of crystal.

DECORATIVE STUCCOS
The stucco décor was made up of powdered marble, slaked lime and plaster, heightened with paint or gilt.

SMOLNY CATHEDRAL ▲ 247
The Church has five cupolas, in accordance with Russian tradition. The central one, supported by a windowed drum, is flanked by four smaller domes on towers. The rhythm of the projections, columns and pilasters framing pedimented bay windows lends the two lower levels originality and liveliness. This impression is strengthened by the blue color, of which Elizabeth was especially fond.

BAROQUE FAÇADES
Above the basement level the Winter Palace (above left) comprises a single Ionic order, followed by a double one, along with a balustrade. At Tsarskoe Selo (above right) the level of the galleries connecting the projections on the front of the building is handled like a stylobate, with Atlas figures supporting the two upper floors.

The New Holland Arch

On the accession of Catherine II, Bartolomeo Rastrelli was no longer in favor. The Czarina, wh[o] preferred sober lines, imposed a return to the canons of antiquity and the 17th century, surrounding herself wit[h] European architects such as Vallin de la Mothe, Antonio Rinald[i] the Scottish court architect Charles Cameron, Yuri Velten and Giacomo Quarenghi. Later, Alexander I brought the Empire sty[le] to St Petersburg (known in Russia, as the "classic" style), as a statement of imperial power. After the accession of Nicholas I in 1825 the major town planning review of the capital was entruste[d] to the Italian Carlo Rossi. It was Rossi who conceived the great colonnaded squares, so strong a feature of the city today.

THE TAURIDE PALACE ▲ 251
Built between 1783 and 1789 by Ivan Starov for Prince Potemkin, the Tauride Palace is austere to a fault, with smooth walls, rectangular unadorned bays, an upper level topped by a frieze of alternating triglyphs and bare metopes, and a Doric portico.

PLAN OF THE TAURIDE PALACE
The central axis leading to the main gallery is flanked by pavilions linked to the main body of the building by wings; one of these contains the theater, the other the private apartments.

A DECORATIVE PROJECT
Devised for the state bedroom of the Grand Duchess Maria Fyodorovna, the wife of the future Paul I, in the Catherine Palace of Tsarskoe Selo ▲ 264. The designer was Charles Cameron.

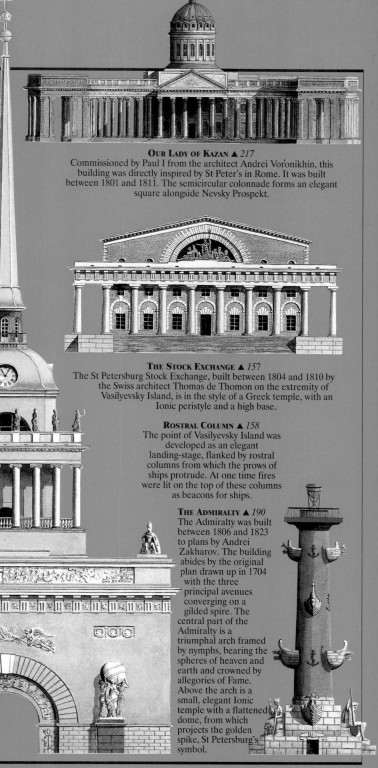

OUR LADY OF KAZAN ▲ 217

Commissioned by Paul I from the architect Andrei Voronikhin, this building was directly inspired by St Peter's in Rome. It was built between 1801 and 1811. The semicircular colonnade forms an elegant square alongside Nevsky Prospekt.

THE STOCK EXCHANGE ▲ 157

The St Petersburg Stock Exchange, built between 1804 and 1810 by the Swiss architect Thomas de Thomon on the extremity of Vasilyevsky Island, is in the style of a Greek temple, with an Ionic peristyle and a high base.

ROSTRAL COLUMN ▲ 158

The point of Vasilyevsky Island was developed as an elegant landing-stage, flanked by rostral columns from which the prows of ships protrude. At one time fires were lit on the top of these columns as beacons for ships.

THE ADMIRALTY ▲ 190

The Admiralty was built between 1806 and 1823 to plans by Andrei Zakharov. The building abides by the original plan drawn up in 1704 with the three principal avenues converging on a gilded spire. The central part of the Admiralty is a triumphal arch framed by nymphs, bearing the spheres of heaven and earth and crowned by allegories of Fame. Above the arch is a small, elegant Ionic temple with a flattened dome, from which projects the golden spike, St Petersburg's symbol.

● HISTORICISM AND ECLECTICISM

Western Europe's fascination with the past was reflected in St Petersburg, where neo-Baroque, neoclassicism, neo-Gothic and neo-Renaissance vied for precedence. The architecture of St Isaac's Cathedral is reminiscent of St Paul's in London, while the lavish décor of its interior borrows from every conceivable style. The Church of the Resurrection (also known as the Church of the Redeemer, or the Church of the Spilt Blood) is an example of a specifically Russian form of historicism, which had its origin in Moscow. It was built on the spot where Alexander II was assassinated, and has magnificent mosaics.

ATLAS AT THE BELOSELSKY-BELOZERSKY PALACE
This was the first palace in St Petersburg built with specific reference to the Russian Baroque style created by Rastrelli a century earlier.

THE CHESME CHURCH
Built between 1777 and 1780 by Yuri Velten, in honor of Orlov's 1770 naval victory against the Turks, this church and the palace in front of it are the earliest examples of neo-Gothic in Russia.

ECLECTIC DÉCOR
Behind the classical exterior of St Isaac's is a lavish interior: here painted frescos have been supplanted by mosaics (right) and marble wall-surfaces. The columns of the iconostasis are covered with lapis lazuli and malachite.

A HOMAGE TO TRADITIONAL RUSSIAN ART
Built between 1883 and 1907 by Alfred
Parland on the site of Alexander II's
assassination, this church was
intended as a celebration of Russian
art's enduring values. The aim was
not so much to imitate traditional
construction methods as to draw
on the decorative repertoire of
medieval Russia and 12th-century
mosaic techniques.

THE PEDIMENTS
The décor of the exterior pediments was
executed from cartoons by the greatest
Russian painters of the time, among them
V.M. Vaznetsov.

**CHURCH OF THE
RESURRECTION ▲** *228*
The building was
directly inspired by
St Basil's Cathedral
in Moscow (1555–60).
Its main features
include a variety of
onion domes,
central tower with
a pyramidal roof,
kokoshniki or
halo-like decorated
arches, and tall
drums supported
by columns. It is
now open to the
public and
contains some
magnificent
restored
mosaics.

The brick exterior
heightens the overall
impression of
lavishness.

THE PORCHES
With their stout balusters and
hanging arches the porches at
ground level are built to a pattern
common in Russia until the late
17th century.

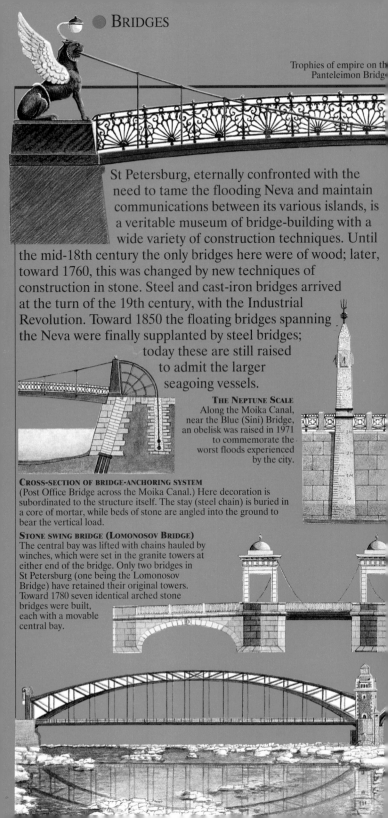

Trophies of empire on the
Panteleimon Bridge

St Petersburg, eternally confronted with the
need to tame the flooding Neva and maintain
communications between its various islands, is
a veritable museum of bridge-building with a
wide variety of construction techniques. Until
the mid-18th century the only bridges here were of wood; later,
toward 1760, this was changed by new techniques of
construction in stone. Steel and cast-iron bridges arrived
at the turn of the 19th century, with the Industrial
Revolution. Toward 1850 the floating bridges spanning
the Neva were finally supplanted by steel bridges;
today these are still raised
to admit the larger
seagoing vessels.

THE NEPTUNE SCALE
Along the Moika Canal,
near the Blue (Sini) Bridge,
an obelisk was raised in 1971
to commemorate the
worst floods experienced
by the city.

CROSS-SECTION OF BRIDGE-ANCHORING SYSTEM
(Post Office Bridge across the Moika Canal.) Here decoration is
subordinated to the structure itself. The stay (steel chain) is buried in
a core of mortar, while beds of stone are angled into the ground to
bear the vertical load.

STONE SWING BRIDGE (LOMONOSOV BRIDGE)
The central bay was lifted with chains hauled by
winches, which were set in the granite towers at
either end of the bridge. Only two bridges in
St Petersburg (one being the Lomonosov
Bridge) have retained their original towers.
Toward 1780 seven identical arched stone
bridges were built,
each with a movable
central bay.

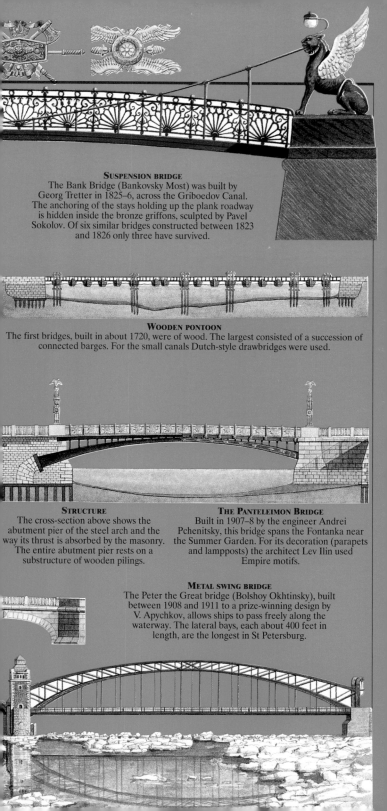

SUSPENSION BRIDGE
The Bank Bridge (Bankovsky Most) was built by
Georg Tretter in 1825–6, across the Griboedov Canal.
The anchoring of the stays holding up the plank roadway
is hidden inside the bronze griffons, sculpted by Pavel
Sokolov. Of six similar bridges constructed between 1823
and 1826 only three have survived.

WOODEN PONTOON
The first bridges, built in about 1720, were of wood. The largest consisted of a succession of
connected barges. For the small canals Dutch-style drawbridges were used.

STRUCTURE
The cross-section above shows the
abutment pier of the steel arch and the
way its thrust is absorbed by the masonry.
The entire abutment pier rests on a
substructure of wooden pilings.

THE PANTELEIMON BRIDGE
Built in 1907–8 by the engineer Andrei
Pchenitsky, this bridge spans the Fontanka near
the Summer Garden. For its decoration (parapets
and lampposts) the architect Lev Ilin used
Empire motifs.

METAL SWING BRIDGE
The Peter the Great bridge (Bolshoy Okhtinsky), built
between 1908 and 1911 to a prize-winning design by
V. Apychkov, allows ships to pass freely along the
waterway. The lateral bays, each about 400 feet in
length, are the longest in St Petersburg.

● ART NOUVEAU

Wrought-iron "entrelac" design.

In the early 20th century St Petersburg, like other European capitals, was affected by modernist trends. The Art Nouveau style, popular almost everywhere, seems to have acquired certain typically regional characteristic when it reached the banks of the Neva. The majestic architecture of the classical age, the exuberance of Baroque and the innovations of Art Nouveau in Europe and Scandinavia were metamorphosed in a highly original manner in St Petersburg.

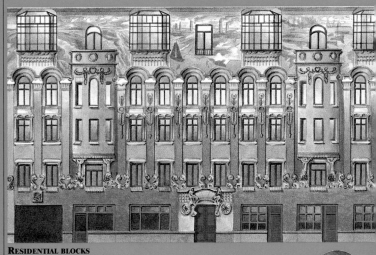

RESIDENTIAL BLOCKS

In the Petrograd district a number of Art Nouveau buildings were constructed, notably that of no. 28 Bolshaya Zelenina (19th century), which included both artists' studios and ordinary apartments. The façade is varied by two oriels, and crowned by an extensive mosaic.

THE PRIVATE TOWNHOUSE

The townhouse of the ballerina Mathilda Kshesinskaya, on Kronversky Avenue, is a typical example of a picturesque yet elegant European-style Art Nouveau structure. It was built (1904–6) by the architect A.I. Hogen.

THE COMMERCIAL BUILDING

The Azovsko-Donskoy bank was built (1908–9) by the architect F.I. Lidval and the sculptor V.V. Kuznetsov. Designed in every way to reflect the grand scale of the capital, this building was inspired by the classicism of Catherine II's reign.

BAS-RELIEFS

Neoclassical Art Nouveau also had its place, in the bas-reliefs, decorative friezes and medallions of the bank's façade.

MATERIALS OF ART NOUVEAU

The door of the Zimmerman building, built in 1906 in Avenue Kamennoostrovsky, shows the diversity of the materials and construction techniques used in Art Nouveau. Rough-hewn projecting stones, bricks and mortar surfaces combine for a colorful yet formal effect.

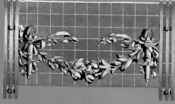

BLUE CERAMIC AND WROUGHT IRON

These supply the decorative motif for the cornice, which is handled in the classical manner. Note the foliated ribbon pattern on the flambeaux, with their pine-cone tops.

PROFILING

The profusion of glass, wrought iron, natural stone and vegetable ornamentation in the details of the surrounding balustrade and the projecting window show that the architect has fully mastered the new style without succumbing to eclecticism.

93

CONSTRUCTIVISM

The Revolution of October 1917 marked a turning point in the development of Russian architecture. Thereafter the vogue was for the "Soviet style", or Constructivism, which could suitably represent the new ideology and exonerate architects from the charge of Formalism. Soon enough, Russian architects accomplished a stylistic transition, assimilating their classical heritage into a relatively human brand of Constructivism. This style, which developed in the 1940's and 1950's, was later baptized "Stalinist Empire".

RATIONALISM AND FUNCTIONALISM
This 1929 project, with its extensive glass and its concrete-covered walls, is typical of Constructivism.

ABSENCE OF DECORATION
Constructivism sought to respond to the needs of society, and condemned all embellishments as "bourgeois" and superfluous. Nevertheless, the residential building above (Karpovka Embankment, 1930) displays an example of Constructivist sculpture.

THE REVIVAL OF DECORATION
Later attitudes changed and decoration became "useful" again. The frieze on the façade of the Moscow cinema (top) assimilated – and interpreted – the Russian classical heritage.

THE CLASSICAL MANNER
This building on Kamennoostrovsky Avenue was designed by the architect N. Lanser in 1936. The central part is flanked by slightly projecting wings, and the profiling is carefully worked, with faceted stonework, pilasters, arabesques and medallions.

MONUMENTALISM (THE KIROVSKY SOVIET)
This effect is achieved by emphasizing the horizontal lines in contrast to the vertical tower.

ART IN THE SERVICE OF THE STATE (KIROVSKY ZAVOD METRO STATION)
The building of the metro system, of the highest quality and very costly indeed, was meant to serve the Soviet ideal.

A MOVE TOWARD THE OUTSIDE WORLD
The Finland Station (Finlyandsky Vokzal), built in 1957, represented a timid gesture toward international modernism.

95

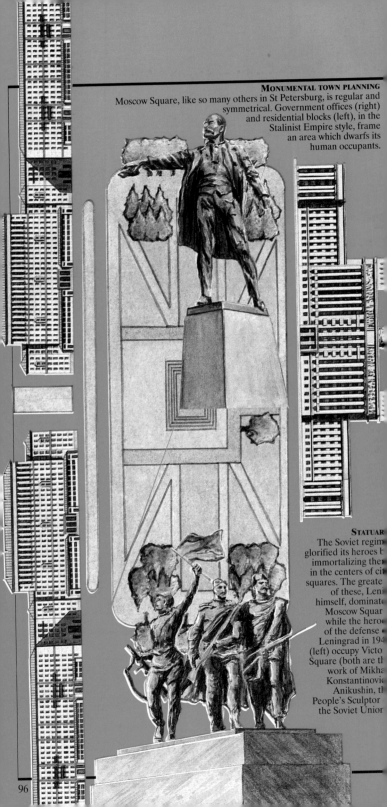

Moscow Square, like so many others in St Petersburg, is regular and symmetrical. Government offices (right) and residential blocks (left), in the Stalinist Empire style, frame an area which dwarfs its human occupants.

STATUAR
The Soviet regim
glorified its heroes b
immortalizing the
in the centers of cit
squares. The greate
of these, Leni
himself, dominate
Moscow Squar
while the heroe
of the defense
Leningrad in 194
(left) occupy Victo
Square (both are th
work of Mikha
Konstantinovic
Anikushin, th
People's Sculptor
the Soviet Unior

96

St Petersburg
as seen by painters

Like many of his Swedish compatriots Benjamin Patterssen (1750–1815) came to seek his fortune in St Petersburg. His arrival coincided with an important moment in the history of the city. The avenues were under construction and the people were impatient to see how their town would look once they were completed; above all, they had become acutely planning-conscious and were fascinated by major architectural ensembles. Profiting from this vogue, Patterssen began painting detailed views of St Petersburg in 1793; these were very popular on account of their refined technique and architectural exactitude. Patterssen also excelled as an engraver and draftsman; but his paintings of the city's monuments belong in the realm of poetry. His *View of the Kutuzov and Palace Embankment* (opposite) is remarkable for its rendering of the atmosphere and luminosity of springtime.

F yodor Alexeyev (1753–1824) was launched by the Fine Arts Academy as a painter of theater décors and a master of perspective. The result was that he was unable to give free rein to his own brand of classicism until 1790, at which time his views of St Petersburg had become so successful that Czar Paul I commissioned Alexeyev to paint several other cities in the empire, most notably Moscow. Below, his *View of the Palace Embankment from the Peter and Paul Fortress*.

Grigory Chernetsov (1801–65) shifted the artistic focus from topography to portraiture. As a former pupil at the Fine Arts Academy, he followed his master Maxim Vorobiov (1787–1855) on the path of Romanticism. His *Neva Embankment in Front of the Fine Arts Academy: Night* (2) (about 1830) is a subject also treated by Vorobiov. This picture is not so much a representation of the city but more a picture of the river itself, and of the dreamlike atmosphere investing it during the hours of darkness, while *Parade on the Marsovo Pole (Field of Mars)* (1831–7) (3), commissioned by Czar Nicholas I is a veritable portrait of St Petersburg society. The main interest of this huge painting lies in the figures that people it, which include, most notably, literary lions such as Krylov, Pushkin, Griboedov and Zhukovsky (1).

At the St Petersburg Fine Arts Academy the art of interior painting reached its apogee in the mid-19th century. The teaching of perspective was revived by the efforts of Maxim Vorobiov (1787–1855). One of his pupils, Constantin Ukhtomsky (1818–81), along with two St Petersburg-based foreign painters (Edward Hau, 1807–87, and Luigi Premazzi, 1814–91), were chosen to paint the Winter Palace and the rooms of the New Hermitage (Novy Ermitazh) designed for the imperial collections. The three artists faced an identical challenge: to paint as much space as possible with the maximum number of details, juggling angles of view from perspectives that were impossible in real life. The commission was brilliantly carried out, as attested by Ukhtomsky's *Cimmerian Bosphorus Antiquities Room* (**2**), Hau's *Italian School Gallery* (**3**) and *History of Painting Gallery* (**4**), and Premazzi's *Artist's Apartment, Winter Palace* (**1**). The three artists' talents as watercolorists and their mastery of trompe l'oeil were also much admired by contemporaries, who followed the Czar's example in having the interiors of their palaces and houses similarly recorded.

1	
2	4
3	

From the time of their arrival in Russia in the late 18th century until the October Revolution of 1917 the Benois family remained implacably French. Nevertheless the painter Alexander Benois (1870–1960) was able to make the connection between the culture of his origins and that of St Petersburg, which he always considered his home. An avid historian, he maintained that his feelings about the past were ". . . more tender and affectionate" than his feelings about the present. As leader of the World of Art movement Benois created a completely new genre, the historical landscape, which allowed him to bring the 18th century back to life. His city of St Petersburg, whose image he held so clearly in his mind that he tirelessly painted it from memory, is peopled by courtesans and more or less enlightened monarchs. In much of his work St Petersburg is the background for ballet and theater décors. Real landscapes, personal memories and Benois' own deep knowledge allowed him to fill these décors with childlike innocence and freshness, as in *Holy Week Fair on Admiralty Square*, *about 1830* (right).

A nna Ostrumova-Lebedeva (1871–1955) illustrated another aspect of the historical landscape, with St Petersburg as the central theme. For her the only significant epoch was that of classicism, whose architecture and ambiance she painted in preference to people, as seen in *Columns of Our Lady of Kazan* (1903) (**2**). Until her death, she continued to perfect her art, using watercolors and xylographs to depict the four elements and above all the waters of the Neva, which she viewed as the fountainhead of the city's poetry. *The Fontanka and the Summer Garden* (1922) (**1**).

The Russian Avant-Garde

In the early 20th century the intellectual and artistic catalyst of St Petersburg (renamed Petrograd in 1914 and Leningrad in 1924) produced several avant-garde movements, led by creative talents of the first rank. Russian ists felt themselves on a par with their European unterparts, notably the French Cubists and Italian Futurists. ey also expressed themselves within the context of various nds dominated by the new painting.

he Young Movement 0–14), which erated most of the nt-garde's atives, attracted sts as different as tiushin, Rozanova, levich, Tatlin and onov. Their links Parisian Cubists the Expressionists Munich ndinsky) ntually produced a ceptual structure ozanova, 1913) ch led to the ssoming of bo-Futurism and abstract art ociated with alevich. The vement which was reverberate through rest of the 20th tury came to the efront in December 15 with the "Last turist Exhibition: 0, ", at which Tatlin's ounter-reliefs" mly established the nd toward onstructivism. Thus e dialectic of the cades that followed s inaugurated in St tersburg. The 1917 evolution led many the most prominent tists to migrate to oscow, but after 21 the focus of odern art, now bordinated to oductivism, again ifted to Petrograd. rtists met at the stitute of Artistic ulture (GINHUK), whose agency their orks were assembled the Russian

Museum ▲ 226 and the Zubov Art History Institute. The latter, which was opened in 1912, was intended to give St Petersburg's art an international dimension. Formalist (or Abstract) art, as championed by the Institute, fell into disfavor in the later 1920's, and eventuall disappeared altogether.

MIKHAIL LARIONOV
Autumn (1912), a Primitivist wor

OLGA ROZANOVA, *Suprematist Composition* (1916–17)

In the years leading up to World War One, St Petersburg attracted artists who had a powerful influence on the development of plastic arts in the 20th century. Expression and Cubist exhibitions were held in the city, as were Futurist shows and other activities organized by Marinetti, Mayakovsky and oth

KASIMIR MALEVICH
Portrait of Ivan Klium (1913)

Goncharova (1881–1962) and Larionov (1881–1964), the leaders of Futurism in Moscow, featured strongly in the exhibitions of 1910–14.

NATALIA GONCHAROVA
Peasants Carrying Fruit (1911–12)

KASIMIR MALEVICH
Supremus no. 55 (1916)

The brilliant Cubo-Futurist theories of Matvejs (1877–1914) were championed by Olga Rozanova (1886–1918). This artist, whose notions of color emerged in the form of Futurist-Expressionist paintings between 1911 and 1913, went on to produce striking "trans-rational" compositions (1915) in which the figurative element was used as a metaphor rather than an object. The Cubist work of Pavel Filonov (1883–1941) was inspired by Russian folklore and mystical aspirations, while the Suprematism of Malevich (1879–1935) took its cue from European culture. With its intuitive, abstract construction, Malevich's work moved away from material reality to celebrate "pure sensibility" (Suprematism, or "pure non-objectivity" as he himself defined it). Malevich's approach, inspired by Cubism but refined by him, demonstrates a basic unity; and it was this above all which characterized his first Suprematist constructions.

KASIMIR MALEVICH
The Carpenter (1930–1)

PAVEL FILONOV
Orient and Occident
(1912–13)

MIKHAIL MATIUSHIN
Movement in Space
(1919–22)

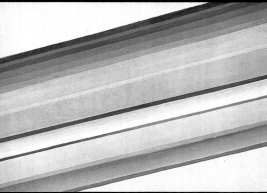

This passage to the "third dimension" led to a theorization of his thought and an individual approach to spatial reality, to which the artist applied himself in the 1920's. Mikhail Matiushin (1861–1934), a friend of Malevich, was one of the most original artists in the Futurist group. A musician, painter, sculptor and theorist of the plastic arts, he developed an original view of the multi-dimensional space revealed by supra-sensorial experience. According to his theory of "enlarged vision" our perception of the world can go beyond the real to a different level of subjective and intuitive experience. His work as a teacher and publisher established the literary and theoretical validity of the Russian Avant-Garde.

OLGA ROZANOVA
Office (1915)

THE RUSSIAN AVANT-GARDE

VLADIMIR TATLIN
*Project for the
Monument to the
Third International*
(1920)

It is also in
St Petersburg
that the most famous
work of Vladimir
Tatlin (1885–1953),
the model for his
monument to the
Third International,
was created in
1919–20. This
emblematic
Constructivist
piece, inspired by
the Eiffel Tower,
was supposed to
ally the "logic of
materials", which had
fascinated Tatlin
since 1914, with
the Functionalist
demands of the
dawning technical
age. The fame of
the monument
eclipsed the purely
pictorial decline
of this artist,
who embraced
the ideology of
"renunciation of
painting" in 1920–21.
After the brief
Formalist (Abstract)
period epitomized
by the work
of Altman and
Lebedev (now in
the Russian
Museum), the
Avant-Garde
period was
supplanted by
Socialist Realism,
which faithfully
reflected the new
"restrictive"
ideology.

Relief, 1914

● ALEXANDER PUSHKIN

"An extraordinary phemonemon and a unique expression of the Russian spirit," said Nikolai Gogol ● *122* of Alexander Sergeivich Pushkin (1799–1837). One of Russia's greatest poets, he was born into ancient Russian gentry on his father's side and, on his mother's, was descended from the Ethiopian Ibrahim Hannibal. After a rebellious childhood and the restrictive life of a courtier in St Petersburg, he lived through censorship, exile, close surveillance . . . and complete isolation. Revered as a national genius and a liberator of the Russian language, he is still considered to be a major figure in world literature. At his funeral a distraught elderly man, asked if he was close to the poet, replied "No, but I am a Russian."

A CLASSICAL EDUCATION
At an early age Pushkin discovered the major classical writers in the extensive family library. His taste for French writers (Voltaire especially) earned him the nickname of "Frenchman" at the Tsarskoe Selo Lyceum ▲ *267* (1811) where he was a pupil. It was here, at this famous school for the sons of nobility, that Pushkin first began writing poetry at the age of fifteen.

FIRST JOB, FIRST WRITING
In October 1817, Pushkin entered government service but was more interested in launching himself into a literary career and a rowdy lifestyle. He completed his first work, the Romantic epic poem *Ruslan and Ludmilla* (1817–20), which earned him a position at the forefront of the literary world.

"DEAR FRIEND HAVE FAITH . . . RUSSIA SHALL FROM HER AGE-OLD SLEEP ARISE"
In 1819, Pushkin belonged to a circle known as "The Green Lamp"; the Tsar's discovery of his revolutionary writings led to his exile (1820–4) in the south, followed by a period under close surveillance in Mikhailovskoe. The Decembrists' rising ● *42* changed his life. In a letter to the Tsar, he swore he had had nothing to do with this plot and requested permission to leave Mikhailovskoe. In exchange, Nicolas I offered his protection . . . and his own personal censorship.

AN UNHAPPY BUT CREATIVE EXILE

During his exile in the south of Russia, Pushkin was given subaltern duties under the governor of Bessarabia. He was allowed, however, to visit the Caucasus and the Crimea, where he was introduced to Eastern and Greek culture. Pushkin's *Southern Poems:* "The Prisoner of the Caucasus", "The Fountain of Bakhchisarai" (1823) and "The Gypsies" (1824) bear witness to these new and exotic influences and also demonstrate his admiration for the poetry of his contemporary, Lord Byron.

"EUGENE ONEGIN"

A mirror of 19th-century Russian society, *Eugene Onegin* (1823–30) is considered by some to be the first Russian novel worthy of that title. Its eponymous hero is a frivolous dandy based in St Petersburg, leading a life of excess. He eventually wearies of the tedious merry-go-round and retreats to the provinces, a reflection of Pushkin's own fate.

"...S GODUNOV"

...ing publication ...historical drama *...Godunov*, Nicolas I ...d to make Pushkin ... poet insisting ...ust write a novel ...style of Walter

Les Grands-Croix, Commandeurs et Chevaliers du Sérénissime Ordre des Cocus réunis en grand Chapitre sous la présidence du vénérable grand-Maître de l'Ordre, S. E. D. L. Narychkine, ont nommé à l'unanimité Mr Alexand. Pouchkine coadjuteur du grand M. de l'Ordre des Cocus et historiogra... l'Ordre.

Le sécrétaire perpétuel: Cte J. Bo...

"THE BRONZE HORSEMAN" AND "THE QUEEN OF SPADES"

"I earn money from my work and my work demands solitude . . ." Despite feeling oppressed by a difficult and turbulent life during his enforced stay at the family home of Boldino in 1833, Pushkin wrote two of his most celebrated works: "The Bronze Horseman" ● *118* and *The Queen of Spades*. The latter is the story of an obsession which turns into a nightmare: it tells of the secret of three cards the last of which, the Queen of Spades, brings about the downfall of the protagonist.

A LIBELOUS LETTER

On November 4, 1836, Pushkin received an unsigned letter dishonoring him and his wife. The writer was Baron Haeckeren, the adopted father of George d'Anthès, a French emigrant who was devoted to Pushkin's wife. The last thing that Pushkin wrote was a letter of reply to Baron Haeckeren.

СРЕДА. **ТОМ. I. №. 8.** ФЕВРАЛЯ 5.

ЛИТЕРАТУРНАЯ ГАЗЕТА.

1830 ГОДЪ.

LITERARY CRITICISM

Pushkin was one of the first Russian writers to make a living almost entirely from writing. Following his return from exile, he became involved with his friend Delvig's *Literary Gazette*. In 1836, he obtained permission to start his own literary review, *Contemporary Life*, a collection of articles and critical studies on contemporary Russian and foreign literature. Only four editions were published during Pushkin's lifetime.

СОВРЕМЕННИКЪ,

ЛИТТЕРАТУРНЫЙ ЖУРНАЛЪ,

издаваемый

АЛЕКСАНДРОМЪ ПУШКИНЫМЪ.

THE DUEL

On January 26, 1837, George d'Anthès challenged the poet to a duel. On January 27, on the banks of the Moika Canal, Pushkin was mortally wounded and carried back to his home at 12, Moika Quay ● *82*. He died on January 29. Several days later the young Lermontov hurled these vengeful lines: "All of your vile blood can never wash away/The fair blood of the poet!"

"VENUS AND THE VULCAN"

On February 18, 1831, Pushkin and Natalia Goncharova were married in Moscow. The poet was then caught up in a whirl of celebrations (and growing debts). 1831 at Tsarkoe Selo, Natalia was officially presented to the Empress . . . and was soon after courted by the Emperor.

MAJESTY

PETER'S CREATION

"The Bronze Horseman" (1833) is an epic poem in which Etienne-Maurice Falconet's statue of Peter the Great, erected by Catherine the Great, comes to life and chases a clerk through the city during the 1824 flood. In this poem Alexander Pushkin (1799–1837) ● 114 uses the contrast between the menacing equestrian statue and the hero Eugene to symbolize the destructive effect of Peter the Great's imperialist Russia upon the ordinary man.

❝I love you, Peter's creation, I love your stern
Harmonious look, the Neva's majestic flow,
Her granite banks, the iron tracery
Of your railings, the transparent twilight and
The moonless glitter of your pensive nights,
When in my room I write or read without
A lamp, and slumbering masses of deserted
Streets shine clearly, and the Admiralty spire
Is luminous, and, without letting in
The dark of night to golden skies, one dawn
Hastens to relieve another, granting
a mere half-hour to night. I love
The motionless air and frost of your harsh winter,
The sledges coursing along the solid Neva,
Girls' faces brighter than roses, and the sparkle
And noise and sound of voices at the balls,
And, at the hour of the bachelor's feast, the hiss
Of foaming goblets and the pale-blue flame
Of punch. I love the warlike energy
Of Mars' Field, the uniform beauty of the troops
Of infantry and of the horses, tattered
Remnants of those victorious banners in array
Harmoniously swaying, the gleam of those
Bronze helmets, shot through in battle. O martial
Capital, I love the smoke and thunder
Of your fortress, when the empress of the north
Presents a son to the royal house, or when
Russia celebrates another victory
Over the foe, or when the Neva, breaking
Her blue ice, bears it to the seas, exulting,
Scenting spring days.❞

"THE BRONZE HORSEMAN",
SELECTED POEMS OF ALEXANDER PUSHKIN,
TRANS. D.M. THOMAS, PUB. SECKER & WARBURG, LONDON 1982

ST PETERSBURG MORNING

Vladimir Nabokov (1899–1977) and his family left Russia for Germany in 1919, and he lived thereafter in Berlin, Paris, the US and finally Switzerland. He wrote mainly in Russian until he moved to the US in 1940.

❝How utterly foreign to the troubles of the night
were those exciting St. Petersburg mornings when
the fierce and tender, damp and dazzling arctic spring
bundled away broken ice down the sea-bright Neva!
It made the roofs shine. It painted the slush in the
streets a rich purplish-blue shade which I have never
seen anywhere since. On those glorious days *on aller se*

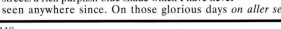

[handwritten notes in margin at top]

❝It was only this morning that at last I discovered the real cause of my unhappiness. Oh, so they are all running away from me to the country, are they? I'm afraid I must apologise for the use of this rather homely word, but I'm not in the mood now for the more exquisite refinements of style, for everybody in Petersburg has either left or is about to leave for the country; for every worthy gentleman of a solidly-prosperous and dignified position who hails a cab in the street is at once transformed in my mind into a worthy parent of a family who, after his usual office duties, immediately leaves town and, unencumbered by luggage, hastens to the bosom of his family – to the country; for every passer-by now wears quite a different look, a look which almost seems to say to every person he meets, 'As a matter of fact, sir, I'm here by sheer chance, just passing through, you understand, and in a few hours I shall be on the way to the country.' If a window is thrown open and a most ravishing young girl, who a moment ago had been drumming on it with her lovely white fingers, pokes out her pretty head and calls to the man selling pots of plants in the street, I immediately jump to the conclusion that the flowers are bought not for the purpose of enjoying the spring and the flowers in a stuffy old flat in town, for very soon everybody will anyway be leaving for the country and will take even the flowers with them. Why, I've got so far in my new discovery (quite a unique discovery, you must admit) that I can tell at once, just by looking at a man, in what sort of a cottage he lives in the country. The residents of the Stone and Apothecary Islands can be recognised by their studied exquisiteness of manners, their smart summer clothes, and their wonderful carriages in which they come to town. The inhabitants of Pargolov and places beyond 'inspire' your confidence at the first glance by their solidly prosperous position and their general air of sobriety and common sense; while the householder of Krestovsky Island is distinguished by his imperturbably cheerful look. Whether I happen to come across a long procession of carters, each walking leisurely, reins in hand, beside his cart, laden with whole mountains of furniture of every description – tables, chairs, Turkish and non-Turkish divans, and other household chattels – and, moreover, often presided over by a frail-looking cook who, perched on the

very top of the cart, guards the property of her master as though it were the apple of her eye; or whether I look at the barges, heavily laden with all sorts of domestic junk, sailing on the Neva or the Fontanka, as far as the Black River or the Islands – both carts and barges multiply tenfold, nay, a hundredfold in my eyes. It really seems as though everything had arisen and set off on a journey, as though everything were moving off in caravan after caravan into the country; it seems as though the whole of Petersburg were about to turn into a desert, and it is hardly surprising that in the end I am overwhelmed with shame, humiliation, and sadness.❞

DOSTOEVSKY, "WHITE NIGHTS",
FROM *THE BEST SHORT STORIES OF DOSTOEVSKY*,
TRANS. BY DAVID MAGARSHACK,
PUB. THE MODERN LIBRARY, NEW YORK, 1955

ENTRANCE TO A BALL

It took Count Lev Nikolaevich Tolstoy (1828–1910) almost seven years to write "War and Peace", an epic novel following the fortunes of three aristo-cratic families through the Napoleonic invasion.

❝Natasha had not had a moment free since early morning and had not once had time to think of what lay before her.

In the damp chill air and crowded closeness of the swaying carriage, she for the first time vividly imagined what was in store for her there at the ball, in the brightly lighted rooms – with music, flowers, dances, the Emperor, and all the brilliant young people of Petersburg. The prospect was so splendid that she hardly believed it would come true, so out of keeping was it with the chill darkness and closeness of the carriage. She understood all that awaited her only when, after stepping over the red baize at the entrance, she entered the hall, took off her fur cloak and, beside Sonya and in front of her mother, mounted the brightly illuminated stairs between the flowers. Only then did she remember how she must behave at a ball, and tried to assume the majestic air she considered indispensable for a girl on such an occasion. But, fortunately for her, she felt her eyes growing misty, she saw nothing clearly, her pulse beat a hundred to the minute and the blood throbbed at her heart. She could not assume that pose, which would have made her ridiculous, and she moved on almost fainting from excitement and trying with all her might to conceal it. And this was the very attitude that became her best. Before and behind them other visitors were entering, also talking in low tones and wearing ball-dresses. The mirrors on the landing reflected ladies in white, pale-blue, and pink dresses, with diamonds and pearls on their bare necks and arms.

Natasha looked in the mirrors and could not distinguish her reflection from the others. All was blent into one brilliant procession. On entering the ball-room the regular hum of voices, footsteps, and greetings deafened Natasha, and the light and glitter dazzled her still more. The host and hostess, who had already been standing at the door for half an hour repeating the same words to the various arrivals, 'Charmé de vous voir,' greeted the Rostovs and Peronskaya in the same manner. The two girls in their white dresses, each with a rose in her black hair, both curtsied in the same way, but the hostess's eye involuntarily rested longer on the slim Natasha. She looked at her and gave her alone a special smile, in addition to her usual smile as hostess. Looking at her she may have recalled the golden irrevocable days of her own girlhood and her own first ball. The host also followed Natasha with his eyes and asked the count which was his daughter.

'Charming!' said he, kissing the tips of his fingers.

In the ball-room guests stood crowding at the entrance doors awaiting the Emperor. The countess took up a position in one of the front rows of that crowd. Natasha heard and felt that several people were asking about her and looking at her. She realized that those noticing her liked her, and this observation helped to calm her.

'There are some like ourselves and some worse,' she thought.❞

LEO TOLSTOY, *WAR AND PEACE*,
TRANS. BY LOUISE AND AYLMER MAUDE,
PUB. EVERYMAN'S LIBRARY, LONDON,
AND ALFRED A. KNOPF, NEW YORK, 1992

BACKSTABBING

Anton Chekhov (1860–1904) deplored theatrical society in St Petersburg. The premiere of "The Sea Gull" at the State Theatre in 1896 was disastrous yet it was later a great success when staged at the Moscow Arts Theatre, and he took all his subsequent plays to the latter.

❝I am tired out, like a ballerina after five acts and eight tableaux. Banquets, letters which one is too lazy to answer, conversations and all sorts of bosh. Right now I've got to take a cab to Vasilievsky Island, to dine there, yet I am bored and I have to work. I will stay here for three days more and see: if this ballet continues I'll either go home or to Ivan in Sudoroga.

I am enveloped by a dense atmosphere of ill will, extremely vague, and to me inexplicable. They are tendering me dinners and chanting banal dithyrambs to me and at the same time are all set to devour me. Why? The devil knows. If I had shot myself I would have afforded great pleasure to nine-tenths of my friends and admirers. And in what petty ways people express their pettiness! Burenin berates me in a *feuilleton*, even though it is not customary for newpapers to berate their own contributors; Maslov (Bezhetsky) no longer goes to dine with the Suvorins; Shcheglov tells all the gossip current about me, and so on. All this is dreadfully foolish and boring. They're not people, but some sort of mold. **99**

> LETTER TO M.P. CHEKHOVA, ST PETERSBURG, JANUARY 14, 1891,
> IN *LETTERS OF ANTON CHEKHOV*, TRANS. BERNARD GUILBERT GUERNEY,
> PUB. VIKING PRESS, NEW YORK, 1968

66There is in Petersburg a species of men whose speciality it is to jeer at every aspect of life; they cannot even pass by a starving man or a suicide without saying something vulgar. But Orlov and his friends did not jeer or make jokes, they talked ironically. They used to say that there was no God, and personality was completely lost at death; the immortals only existed in the French Academy. Real good did not and could not possibly exist, as its existence was conditional upon human perfection, which was a logical absurdity. Russia was a country as poor and dull as Persia. The intellectual class was hopeless; in Pekarsky's opinion the overwhelming majority in it were incompetent persons, good for nothing. The people were drunken, lazy, thievish, and degenerate. We had no science, our literature was uncouth, our commerce rested on swindling – 'No selling without cheating.' And everything was in that style, and everything was a subject for laughter. **99**

> ANTON CHEKHOV, "AN ANONYMOUS STORY",
> FROM *THE LADY WITH THE DOG*, TRANS. CONSTANCE GARNETT,
> PUB. CHATTO & WINDUS, LONDON, 1919

LERMONTOV

The writings of Ivan Turgenev (1818–83) were the first by a major Russian author to find success in Europe. Here he describes a meeting with the Romantic poet and novelist Mikhail Lermontov (1814–41), just over a year before the latter was killed in a duel.

ST PETERSBURG
AS SEEN BY WRITERS

66Lermontov, too, I saw only twice: at the house of Princess Sh[akhovskoy], a Petersburg high society woman, and a few days later at a New Year's fancy dress ball at the Noblemen's Club on the eve of 1840. At Princess Sh[akhovskoy]'s I, a very rare and unaccustomed visitor at high society parties, saw him only from a distance, observing the poet, who had become famous in so short a time, from a corner where I had secreted myself. Lermontov sat down on a low stool in front of a sofa on which, wearing a black gown, was sitting one of the society beauties of those days, the fair-haired Countess [Emilia] Mussin-Pushkin, who die young and who really was a strikingly beautiful girl. Lermontov wore the uniform of the Life Guards Hussar Regiment. He had removed neither his sword nor h gloves and, frowning and hunching his shoulders, gazed sullenly at the Countes She only exchanged a few words with him, talking mostly to Count Sh[akhovskoy also a Hussar officer, who was sitting beside him. There was something ominou and tragic in Lermontov's appearance: his swarthy face and large, motionless da eyes exuded a sort of sombre and evil strength, a sort of pensive scornfulness an passion. His hard gaze was strangely out of keeping with the expression of h almost childishly tender, protruding lips. His whole figure, thick-set, bow-legge with a large head on broad, stooping shoulders, aroused an unpleasant feeling; b everyone had at once to acknowledge its immense inherent strength. It is, course, a well-known fact that he had to some extent portrayed himself in Pechori The words: 'His eyes did not laugh when he laughed,' from *A Hero of Our Tim* etc., could really have been applied to himself. I remember that Cou Sh[akhovskoy] and the young Countess suddenly burst out laughing at somethin and went on laughing for some time; Lermontov, too, laughed, but at the sam time he kept looking at them with a sort of offensive astonishment. For all that could not help feeling that he was fond of Count Sh[akhovskoy] as a fellow-offic and that he was also well-disposed towards the Countess. There could be no dou that, following the fashion of those days, he was trying to assume a Byronic a together with a number of other even worse eccentricities and whimsicalities. An he paid dearly for them! At heart Lermontov was probably terribly bored; he fe stifled in the airless atmosphere where fate had forced him to live.99

IVAN TURGENEV, *LITERARY REMINISCENCES AND AUTOBIOGRAPHICAL FRAGMENT*
TRANS. BY DAVID MAGARSHACK, PUB. FABER & FABER, LONDON, 19:

FASHION

Russian revolutionary Alexander Herzen (1812–70) combined his personal life and h opinions with political views in his autobiography published in 1885.

66The Petersburghers laugh at the costumes seen in Moscow; they are outraged the caps and Hungarian jackets, the long hair and civilian moustaches. Mosco certainly is a non-military city, rather careless and unaccustomed to discipline, b whether that is a good quality or a defect is a matter of opinion. The harmony uniformity, the absence of variety, of what is personal and whimsical, a tradition obligatory dress and external discipline are all found on the largest scale in t most inhuman condition in which men live – in barracks. The uniform and complete absence of variety are passionately loved by despotism. Nowhere a fashions followed so respectfully as in Petersburg, and that shows the immaturity our culture; our clothes are alien. In Europe people dress, but we dress up, and are terrified if a sleeve is too full, or a collar too narrow. In Paris all that people a afraid of is being dressed without taste; in London all that they are afraid of catching cold; in Italy every one dresses as he likes best. If one were to show Englishman the battalions of fops on the Nevsky Prospect, all wearing exac similar, tightly buttoned coats, he would take them for a squad of 'policemen'.99

ALEXANDER HERZEN, *MY PAST AND THOUGH*
TRANS. BY CONSTANCE GARNE
PUB. CHATTO & WINDUS, LONDON, 19

FESTIVITIES

English tutor William Coxe (1747–1828) witnessed an enormous and ultimately rather dangerous party in St Petersburg.

On the 6th of December we were witness to a very singular entertainment given to the public by a Russian, who had acquired a large fortune by farming, during four years only, the right of vending spirituous liquors. On surrendering his contract, he gave, as proof of his gratitude to the lower class of people, by whom he had enriched himself, a feast near the garden of the summer-palace . . . announced by hand-bills distributed throughout the city . . . which commenced at two o'clock in the afternoon. A large semicircular table was covered with all kinds of provision, piled in different shapes, and in the greatest profusion. Large slices of bread and caviare, dried sturgeon, carp, and other fish, were ranged to a great height, in the form of pent-houses and pyramids, and garnished with craw-fish, onions, and pickles. In different parts of the grounds were rows of casks full of spirituous liquors, and still larger vessels of wine, beer, and quass. Among the decorations, I observed the representation of an immense whale in pasteboard, covered with cloth and gold or silver brocade, and filled in the inside with bread, dried fish, and other provisions.

All sorts of games and diversions were exhibited for the amusement of the populace. At the extremity of the grounds was a large square of ice well swept for the scaters; near which were two machines like the swinging vehicles at Bartholomew Fair. One of these machines consisted of two cross-beams fixed horizontally to a pole in the center by means of a pivot; from the ends of the beams hung four sledges, in which people seated themselves, and were turned round with great velocity; the other had four wooden horses suspended from the beams, and the riders were whirled round in like manner. . . . Beyond these were two ice-hills. . . . Two poles, above twenty feet in height, were also erected, with colours flying; and at the top of each was placed a piece of money, as a prize for those who could swarm up and seize it. The poles, being rubbed with oil, soon froze in this severe climate; many and tedious were the attempts of the various competitors in this slippery ascent to fame. The scene was lively and gay; for about 40,000 persons of both sexes were assembled on the occasion. . . .

It was preconcerted, that, on firing a rocket, the people were to drink a glass of spirituous liquor, and, on the discharge of a second, to begin the repast. But the impatience of the populace anticipated the necessity of a second signal; and the whole multitude was soon and at once in motion. The whale was the chief object of contention; within the space of a few minutes he was entirely divested of his gaudy trappings, which became the spoils of his successful invaders. . . . They rend him into a thousand pieces, to seize the provision with which his inside was stored. The remaining people . . . were employed in uncovering the pent-houses, and pulling down the pyramids. . . . Others crowded around the casks and hogsheads; and with great wooden ladles lapped incessantly wine, beer, and spirits. The confusion and riot, which soon succeeded, is better conceived than described; and we thought it expedient to retire. . . .

But the consequences of this feast were indeed dreadful. The cold had suddenly increased with such violence, that Fahrenheit's thermometer, which at mid-day

127

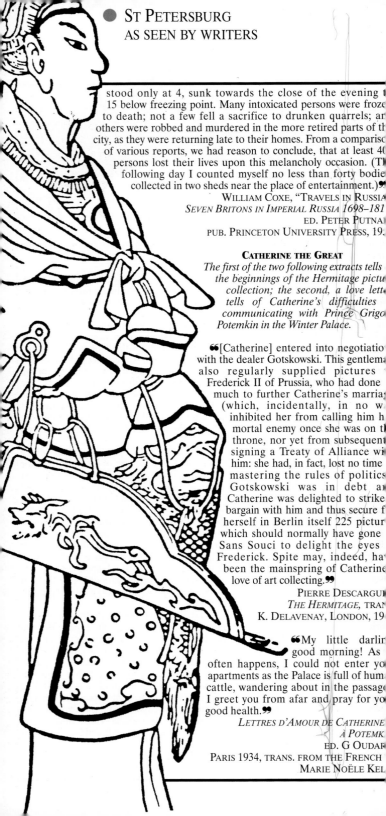

stood only at 4, sunk towards the close of the evening t
15 below freezing point. Many intoxicated persons were froze
to death; not a few fell a sacrifice to drunken quarrels; an
others were robbed and murdered in the more retired parts of th
city, as they were returning late to their homes. From a comparison
of various reports, we had reason to conclude, that at least 40
persons lost their lives upon this melancholy occasion. (Th
following day I counted myself no less than forty bodie
collected in two sheds near the place of entertainment.)**

WILLIAM COXE, "TRAVELS IN RUSSIA"
SEVEN BRITONS IN IMPERIAL RUSSIA 1698–181
ED. PETER PUTNA
PUB. PRINCETON UNIVERSITY PRESS, 19.

CATHERINE THE GREAT
*The first of the two following extracts tells
the beginnings of the Hermitage pictu
collection; the second, a love lett
tells of Catherine's difficulties
communicating with Prince Grigo
Potemkin in the Winter Palace.*

**[Catherine] entered into negotiatio
with the dealer Gotskowski. This gentlem
also regularly supplied pictures
Frederick II of Prussia, who had done
much to further Catherine's marria;
(which, incidentally, in no w
inhibited her from calling him h
mortal enemy once she was on th
throne, nor yet from subsequent
signing a Treaty of Alliance wi
him: she had, in fact, lost no time
mastering the rules of politics
Gotskowski was in debt a
Catherine was delighted to strike
bargain with him and thus secure f
herself in Berlin itself 225 pictur
which should normally have gone
Sans Souci to delight the eyes
Frederick. Spite may, indeed, ha
been the mainspring of Catherine
love of art collecting.**

PIERRE DESCARGUE
THE HERMITAGE, TRAN
K. DELAVENAY, LONDON, 19

**My little darlir
good morning! As
often happens, I could not enter yo
apartments as the Palace is full of hum
cattle, wandering about in the passage
I greet you from afar and pray for yo
good health.**

*LETTRES D'AMOUR DE CATHERINE
À POTEMK*
ED. G OUDAR
PARIS 1934, TRANS. FROM THE FRENCH
MARIE NOËLE KEL

By the Fortress in winter ▲

The Moika Canal ▲

The Sphinx landing stage, University Embankment ▽

silyevsky Island, from the Admiralty Embankment ▲   Palace Embankment and the Hermitage ▼

The frozen Neva and the Peter and Paul Fortress ▼

Palace Bridge ▲   Trinity Bridge (also called Troitsky Bridge) ▼

From the
Peter and Paul Fortress
to the islands of the delta

1. PETER AND PAUL FORTRESS **2.** PETER AND PAUL CATHEDRAL **3.** TRINITY BRIDGE

🕐 **Half a day**

◆ **A-B-C**

FROM THE BASTION TO THE MAUSOLEUM CHAPEL
The Peter and Paul Fortress has never been a residential area. Its only inhabitants were the garrison and the clergy attached to the Cathedral. It was, however, the symbolic center of the Russian Empire because successive sovereigns from Peter the Great onward (including the executed Czarevich Alexei ● *36*) are buried there.

FORTIFICATIONS

With the coming of the age of artillery a Vauban-style fortress with bastions was planned for the defense of the island. It is likely that Peter the Great was inspired in this by what he had seen in the West (1696–8). After the first earthworks had been raised the walls were continued in stone under the supervision of the architect Trezzini. The bastions bore the name of the princes who were given responsibility for each military sector. Thus, from Peter's (Petrovsky) Gate these are known as the CZAR, NARYSHKIN, TRUBETSKOY, ZOTOV, GULUKIN and MENSHIKOV BASTIONS. In about 1740 the initial fortifications were doubled around each gate leading to the mainland by a curtain wall with moats; the latter were filled in during the 19th century. As a result it is necessary to pass through St John's Gate in order to reach Peter's Gate. When she built up the Neva embankment Catherine II added a granite dressing to the fortifications in 1779. Although it stands on the Petrograd Side the Arsenal, or Kronverk, complements the ramparts of the fortress and is an integral part of them. In the event, the Peter and Paul Fortress never had to play the defensive role for which it was designed.

THE GATES

PETER'S GATE. The decoration of this gate, with its imperial eagle and wooden bas-relief, refers to the victories of Peter the Great. On either side statues of the goddesses Bellona and Minerva serve as reminders of Peter's military prowess and political sagacity.

NEVA GATE. Built by Lvov between 1784 and 1787, this gate leads to the Fortress' only deep-water landing stage. It is crowned by a triangular pediment and framed by two groups of twin columns, joined by two blocks of facetted stone. The image of SAINT NICHOLAS guards this gate, which serves as the fortress exit toward Vasilyevsky Island, while SAINT BASIL stands sentry over the gate between the Trubetskoy and Zotov bastions.

"The fortress of St Petersburg was built, like all fortresses, to be a visible symbol of the antagonism between the people and its sovereign. No doubt it defends the city, but it threatens it to a far greater extent; no doubt it was built to repel the Swedes, but in practice it has been a prison for Russians."

Alexandre Dumas,
Voyage en Russie

After the annexation by Russia of the mouth of the Neva during the Northern War the first fortress was built, in May 1703. This structure was close to the sea and naturally defended by the Neva itself. The island of Petersburg on which it stood was small enough to be entirely enclosed, leaving no room for enemy forces to gain a foothold. It was the last upstream island of the delta, and no ship could enter the waterway without passing it.

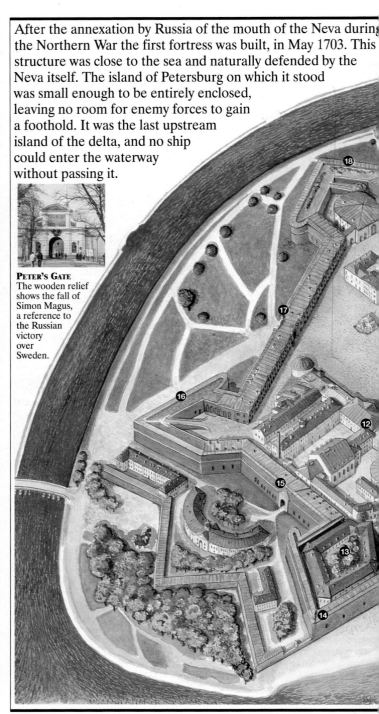

PETER'S GATE
The wooden relief shows the fall of Simon Magus, a reference to the Russian victory over Sweden.

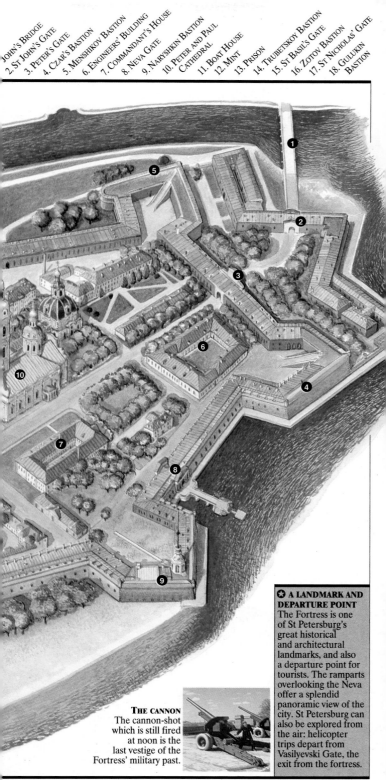

JOHN'S BRIDGE
2. ST JOHN'S GATE
3. PETER'S GATE
4. CZAR'S BASTION
5. MENSHIKOV BASTION
6. ENGINEERS' BUILDING
7. COMMANDANT'S HOUSE
8. NEVA GATE
9. NARYSHKIN BASTION
10. PETER AND PAUL CATHEDRAL
11. BOAT HOUSE
12. MINT
13. PRISON
14. TRUBETSKOY BASTION
15. ST BASIL'S GATE
16. ZOTOV BASTION
17. ST NICHOLAS' GATE
18. GULUKIN BASTION

★ A LANDMARK AND DEPARTURE POINT
The Fortress is one of St Petersburg's great historical and architectural landmarks, and also a departure point for tourists. The ramparts overlooking the Neva offer a splendid panoramic view of the city. St Petersburg can also be explored from the air: helicopter trips depart from Vasilyevski Gate, the exit from the fortress.

THE CANNON
The cannon-shot which is still fired at noon is the last vestige of the Fortress' military past.

PETER AND PAUL CATHEDRAL ★

The first church inside the fortress was built of wood. Its construction began on June 29, 1703, the feast day of Saint Peter and Saint Paul. The construction of the present cathedral (PETROPAVLOVSKY SOBOR; Петропавловский собор) was undertaken in 1712 under the direction of the architect Trezzini, who opted for the Western style of the period. The tower has been struck by lightning and rebuilt several times, and the cathedral was reconstructed following a fire in 1753. Its nave is conventional European Baroque, both in its floor plan and its elevation. There is also a pulpit, which is unusual for a Russian Orthodox cathedral.

ICONOSTASIS ● 56. The architectural framework, which is ill-adapted to the Russian ritual, imposed an original solution for the iconostasis; in effect it occupies the entire breadth of the cathedral, and its royal doorway runs the width of the central nave.

CHIMING CLOCK. After 1724 the cathedral was equipped with a Dutch clock, presented by Peter the Great. Its bells originally sounded a carillon in honor of the Czar. Later, with the change of political regime, it sounded the Soviet anthem. Today every six hours it chimes *God Save the Czar*, a tune by the 18th-century composer Bortniansky and every hour the Orthodox *Alleluya*.

THE GOVERNOR'S MAUSOLEUM. Against the east wall of the
Cathedral is the mausoleum reserved for governors of the
fortress who died during their tenure. Among other duties
the governors had to alert the sovereign to the fact that the
Neva was once again navigable at winter's end, by bringing
him a goblet of water from the river.

THE BOAT HOUSE

THE PAVILION. The Boat House (Botny Dom/Ботный дом),
built by the architect Alexander Wist (1761–5) in the
Baroque style, is crowned by an allegory of navigation
sculpted by David Jensen (1891). Today it is occupied by
a luxury souvenir shop.

ST PETERSBURG HISTORY MUSEUM

ENGINEERS' BUILDING. The whole Fortress precinct houses
the St Petersburg History Museum; the collections in the
Engineers' Building demonstrate certain aspects of daily
life, in particular through a series of highly colored shop
signs painted in a naive style. On the way through to the
Commandant's House stands Mikhail Shemyakin's statue
of Peter I (1990).

THE COMMANDANT'S HOUSE. This building, which dates
from the 1740's, contains an exhibition documenting
the history of the Fortress, from the first human
occupation of the site to the fall of the monarchy.
The naval aspect of its history is especially well
presented.

THE OLD ARSENAL

Between 1705 and 1708 the
Fortress was protected on
the Petrograd Side by
the construction of
the original Kronverk.
Of this auxiliary earthwork
nothing remains today except
ruins, with a stream running at
their foot.

MONUMENT TO THE DECEMBRISTS.
The execution of the Decembrists
● 42 took place at the Arsenal.
The obelisk commemorating the five
victims bears a medallion showing
their profiles.

ARTILLERY MUSEUM. The
Arsenal building is a brick-built
construction with a façade
regulated by pilasters; each
segment includes a carriage
gateway and twinned bays on the
second floor. In 1856 the military
collections assembled since 1776
were installed in the arsenals of the
Kronverk, where they may still be
seen today.

149

THE FIRST MARKET BUILDING
In the early 18th century the island of Petersburg was the site of the city's food market, the first Gostiny Dvor (right), a restaurant, and the port with its customs house where foreign ships (mostly Dutch) unloaded their cargos. Later the customs officers were moved to Vasilyevsky Island ▲ 156.

MATHILDA KSHESINSKAYA (1872–1971)
A pupil of the choreographer Petipa, Kshesinskaya (right) was one of the ballet stars who trained a new generation of dancers in the Paris schools.

MONUMENT TO THE "STEREGUSHCHY"
Built on a stone plinth, this monument on the corner of Kamennoostrovsky Avenue and the Gorky Prospekt commemorates a destroyer captured by the Japanese in 1907 and scuttled by her two surviving crewmen. The sculptor Karl Isenberg chose to represent his theme on a stele of sheet-metal. On the reverse side is an inscription describing the event and listing the names of the dead.

THE PETROGRAD SIDE

PETERSBURG ISLAND. In the early days of the city this island (known today as the Petrograd Side) was important because it was close to the Fortress. All commercial and social life was concentrated around the old Revolution Square, now renamed TROITSKAYA. It suffered decline with the development of the left bank; by the second half of the 19th century wooden houses without gas or running water were in evidence, just as they were on the right bank.

RAPID MODERNIZATION. At the turn of the 20th century land was cheap and the influx of money into St Petersburg gave a powerful incentive to construction. The Petrograd Side was quickly built up, almost uniformly in the Art Nouveau style ● 92. The construction of the TRINITY BRIDGE (1897–1903) (Troitsky Most) gave the district further cachet by linking it to the grander quarters of the far bank. This bridge replaced a floating one ● 91, which had to be dismantled each year when the Neva swept away all the ice from Lake Ladoga.

MUSEUM OF POLITICAL HISTORY. In 1904, the architect A.I. Hogen built a townhouse ● 92 for Mathilda Kshesinskaya, favorite ballerina of Nicholas II. It was commandeered by the Bolsheviks in March 1917, and later became the Museum of the Great October Socialist Revolution. Now the Museum of Political History, it also incorporates a display devoted to the life of Mathilda Kshesinskaya and is the venue for musical evenings.

ALEXANDER PARK

The Gorkovskaya metro station (Горьковская) is surrounded by an immense park, until recently named after Lenin but

ow with its old title of Alexander Park
estored. It occupies the old military training
grounds around the Kronverk ▲ 149 and is
a favorite place for St Petersburgers.

THE ZOOLOGICAL GARDENS. West of the
Kronverk is the zoo, converted from a 19th-
century private menagerie. It has seen better
days; nevertheless, although giraffes and elephants are
urrently absent, the zoo does have a comprehensive
ollection of northern animal species, some of them virtually
nknown to the Western public. Children visiting this zoo will
liscover that minks, sables and martens exist in other forms
han coats and stoles; they will also be interested by rare
nimals from Siberia, such as the long-eared hedgehog and
he Przewalsky horse. In addition, there is a large aviary of
irds of prey, and a number of bears, the emblem of Russia.

CABIN OF PETER THE GREAT ★

WOODEN LODGE ● 83. Facing the Neva is the small cabin
ccupied by Peter the Great (DOMIK PETRA; домик Петра)
n the summer of 1703. The roof is made of wooden slats in
he shape of tiles, while the brick imitation of the exterior is
eminiscent of a Dutch cottage. One of the two rooms was
nade into a chapel under Nicholas I; dismantled in 1930, this
as replaced by an 18th-century style interior. The stone
ouse built around the cabin also
ncloses a boat built by Peter the
reat himself,
long with an
xhibition of
ngravings.

THE MOSQUE
(МЕЧЕТ; мечеть)
Islam is the second
most popular religion
in Russia, with about
20 million adherents.
Although Muslims
were present in
St Petersburg from
the earliest years, the
city had no mosque
until 1910. Designed
by Vasilyev, who took
as his model the Gour
Emir Mausoleum at
Samarkand (15th
century), the mosque
is thoroughly oriental
in style, with an entry
porch and two
minarets covered in
polychrome tiles.

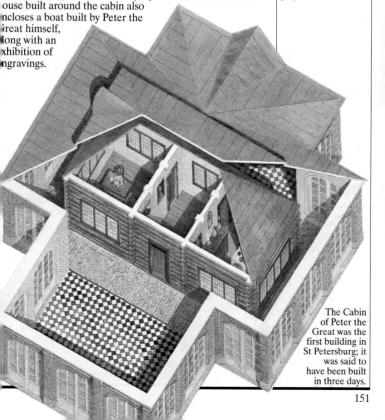

The Cabin
of Peter the
Great was the
first building in
St Petersburg; it
was said to
have been built
in three days.

151

THE "AURORA"

Built in the city's shipyards, this cruiser inherited the name of a famous fighting frigate of the Crimean War. Moored in front of the Nakhimov Naval Academy since 1948, it is one of the most celebrated symbols of the Revolution.

THE CRUISER "AURORA" ★

The cruiser *Aurora* (KREISER AVRORA; крейсер Аврора) of the Baltic Fleet was launched in 1903; it became a cadet training vessel after the war with Japan in 1904. The crew, many of whom had progressive ideas, played a key role at th start of the Revolution ● 46; at a signal given from the Fortress, one of the *Aurora*'s guns opened the people's attac on the Winter Palace. It is open to the public as part of the Naval Museum (Stock Exchange).

LENIN SQUARE

In the middle of Lenin Square (PLOSHCHAD LENINA; пл.Ленина) stand a bronze effigy of the great revolutiona sculpted by Sergei Yevseyev. The statue unveiled in 1926, shows Lenin standing on the turret of an armored vehicle, his right arm thrust out and left thumb grasping his waistcoat. An inscription reads "Long Live the Socialist Revolution throughout the World".

THE POINT (STRELKA)

ne of the finest vantage points on Vasilyevsky Island is the relka, meaning Arrow or Point. Peter I intended this site be the prestigious center of his capital, with a broad square d magnificent government buildings.

NAVAL MUSEUM (TSENTRALNY VOENNO-MORSKOY MUZEY; ентральный Военно-морской музей). The heart of this chitectural ensemble is the old Stock Exchange building 87, rebuilt between 1804 and 1810 by Thomas de Thomon. he Exchange, with its massive granite base, was the place of usiness to which merchants came on their arrival at the port St Petersburg ▲ 192. Since 1940 the building has been located to the Naval Museum.

HISTORY OF THE RUSSIAN FLEET
The collections of the Naval Museum include over 1,700 model ships, from the oldest (Peter I's small vessel) to the most modern, along with designs and maquettes.

157

RARE SPECIES
The St Petersburg Zoological Museum is one of the largest of its kind in the world. It has examples of over forty thousand different animal species, with about fifteen million specimens in reserve.

ROSTRAL COLUMNS ★
● 87. On the square in front of the Exchange are the two rostral columns (the term is derived from the Latin *rostrum*, the bows of a vessel), to which are attached metal ships' prows. These are flanked by colossal statues, allegories of the four great rivers of Russia – the Volga, the Dnieper, the Volkhov and the Neva – sculpted in stone from studies by I. Chamberlain and J. Thibaut. For some time beacons, fueled by hemp oil, burned on the top of the columns, and these functioned as lighthouses at the entrance to the port.

OLD PORT WAREHOUSES. On either side of the Exchange are port warehouses, built between 1826 and 1832 by the architect Giovanni Luchini. The south building is now the ZOOLOGICAL MUSEUM (ZOOLOGICHESKY MUZEY; Зоологический музей), founded in 1896. This was the former site of the palace of Czarina Prascovia Fyodorovna (1664–1723), the wife of Peter I's half-brother, Czar Ivan Alexeyvich (1666–96) and mother of the future Empress Anna Yoannovna ● 36. The north warehouse is now the DOKUCHAYEV MUSEUM OF SOIL SCIENCE (TSENTRALNY MUZEY POCHVOVEDENIYA IM. V. DOKUCHAYEV; центральный музей Почвоведения им. В. Докучаева),

MUSEUM OF LITERATURE
(LITERATURNY MUZEY; Литературный музей). The old Customs House was built between 1829 and 1832 under the supervision of Luchini. Since 1927 this building has served as the Institute of Russian Literature (or Pushkin House) and the Museum of Literature. Both establishments were founded after the 1899 exhibition in honor of Pushkin's centenary ● 114. Their archives include over two thousand manuscripts from the 13th to the 18th centuries, along with a number of texts by Tolstoy and Dostoevsky ▲ 207. The museum houses an extraordinary collection of original oil paintings and watercolors.

opened in 1904. This museum is devoted to the
study and protection of Russia's soils and to
increasing their productivity.

MAKAROV EMBANKMENT

The embankment is named for Stepan Makarov
(1849–1904), the famous Russian Navy Admiral.
The granite facing of the embankment was built
between 1806 and 1809, as were the buildings by the
Customs House pier (note the broad stairway with its
sculpted lions).

LIBRARY OF THE ACADEMY OF SCIENCES (BIBLIOTEKA
AKADEMII NAUK; библиотека Академии наук). The main
façade completes the view from the main Neva waterway
along the Mendeleev "line", named for the chemist
Mendeleev (1834–1907). Founded in 1714, the Library of the
Academy of Sciences (1912–25, architect R. Marfeld) is one
of the oldest scientific establishments in the city. It contains
over twenty million volumes, as well as engravings, drawings,
watercolors, manuscripts, maps and charts.

THE TWELVE COLLEGES (DVENADTSAT KOLLEGI; Двенадцать
Коллегий). Constructed between 1722 and 1742 by Domenico
Trezzini ● 83 and Theodore Schwertfeger, and now attached
to the University of St Petersburg, this complex is made up of
twelve identical buildings in an unbroken line, intended for
the various government bodies: the Senate, the Synod and the
ten "colleges" or ministries. The glazed second floor is now
the corridor of the University and is famed for its length. In
1835 all these buildings were handed over to the University
authorities, by whom they were partially reconstructed.
Visitors are admitted to the museum named after the chemist
Mendeleev, who devised the periodic table of chemical
elements, and lived and worked here from 1866 to 1890.

THE POINT (STRELKA), CENTER OF SCIENTIFIC RESEARCH

Although Vasilyevsky
Island did not in fact
become the hub of the
city as Peter I had
intended, it is,
however, the nerve
center of research and
of the human sciences.
Students, researchers
and museum curators
account for much of
its population, hence
its nickname "Island
of Light". It is also
pleasant to browse
in the bookstores
clustered around the
university, and to stop
at one of the many
cafés were students
can be seen putting
the world to rights.
The monument to
Mikhail Lomosonov
● 53, built in 1986
on University
Embankment, is a
fitting symbol of the
spirit of the island.

A CONCENTRATION OF BUILDINGS

The Twelve Colleges
constitute the west
side of an immense
architectural
ensemble built in the
early 1830's. Apart
from the warehouses,
it includes the
Merchants'
Courtyard of the
New Exchange (now
part of the
University) along
with an annex of the
Museum of the
Academy of Sciences,
currently used by the
St Petersburg
department of the
Nauka science
publishing
organization. In 2003
a monument was
erected as a homage
to Andrei Sakharov,
between the Twelve
Colleges and the
Academy of Sciences
library.

UNIVERSITY EMBANKMENT

At the beginning of the University Embankment
(UNIVERSITETSKAYA NAB.; Университетская наб.) are a
number of buildings which are linked to the history of the
Academy of Sciences.

THE KUNSTKAMMER ★ ▲ 250. The Kunstkammer, Peter the
Great's gallery of curiosities, is an interesting example of early
Russian Baroque. Built between 1718 and 1734 by the
architects G. Mattarnovy, N. Herbel, G. Ciaveri and
M. Zemtsov, the Kunstkammer has wings of two stories with

a tower between. The Kunstkammer was the first Natural
Science Museum in Russia, and it included a library and
an observatory. From 1783 to 1796 the Academy was
directed by E. Dashkova, a friend of Catherine II and
one of the most cultivated women of her time. In 1878 it
became the Museum of Anthropology and Ethnology
(MUZEY ANTROPOLOGII I ETNOGRAFII IM. PETRA
VELIKOVO; музей Антропологии и Этнографии им.
Петра Великого). The museum's displays include items
which illustrate the daily lives and cultures of many
different countries, along with their weapons, clothes
and religious objects.

M. LOMONOSOV MUSEUM (MUZEY M. LOMONOSOVA;
музей М. Ломоносова). In 1949 the M. Lomonosov
Museum ● 53 was installed inside the Kunstkammer, in
memory of the great scientist. Among its attractions are
Lomonosov's scientific instruments and his writings, in
addition to a reconstitution of the Academy of
Sciences' conference hall.

ACADEMY OF SCIENCES (AKADEMIYA NAUK; Академия наук).
Beside the Kunstkammer, also on the embankment at no. 5 is
the main Academy of Sciences building, which was
constructed between 1783 and 1789 by Giacomo Quarenghi
● 86. In 1925 the main staircase in the vestibule was
embellished with a mosaic panel by Lomonosov, which was
entitled *The Battle of Poltava*. In the same year the Academy
became known as the
Academy of
Sciences of the
Soviet Union,
before its
headquarters
were
transferred to
Moscow nine
years later, in
1934.

THE GLOBE
At the Lomonosov
Museum is a
reconstruction of the
huge terrestrial globe
of the Academy of
Sciences. Made in the
1600's for the Duke
of Holstein-Gottorp,
it was presented as a
gift to Peter the Great
in 1713.

**CABINET OF
CURIOSITIES**
The collections of
monstrosities and
curiosities in the Kikin
Palace ▲ 250 were
amassed by Peter I
and transferred to the
Kunstkammer in
1727.

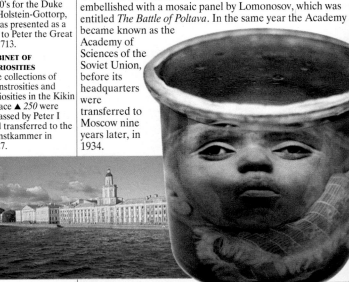

MENSHIKOV PALACE (DVORETS MENSHIKOVA; дворец Меншикова) ★ ● *82*. At no. 15 on the embankment stands the architectural ensemble of the Menshikov Palace. In the early years of the 18th century Prince Menshikov, who was a close friend of Peter the Great, had his private mansion here. The building has two floors and a mansard roof; it was designed by the architects Giovanni Maria Fontana and Gottfried Schädell. It was here that Peter I held lavish assemblies and celebrations of Russian victories, and received foreign embassies. In 1781, two years after Menshikov's death, the palace was the barracks of an elite regiment, the Foot Guards, before it was passed on to the Army's First Cadet Corps. The left wing of the palace was enlarged by the addition of a new building, which was itself enlarged during the 1770s. Works initiated in 1966–81 restored the palace's original aspect, which was remarkable for its famously splendid interiors. A spacious vestibule leads to the formal oak staircase, with wrought-iron banisters struck with the monograms of Peter the Great and Menshikov himself. The stairs go up to the apartments of Prince Menshikov and his sister-in-law Varvara Arseneva (who was responsible for educating his children); the two areas are separated, however, by formal drawing rooms. The ASSEMBLY ROOM, which is over a thousand square feet in size, is the largest room in the palace. The WALNUT ROOM, with its painted ceiling and boiseries of Persian walnut wood, was Menshikov's favorite room; his BEDROOM (below) is covered with no fewer than 27,811 Delft tiles ● *64*. The restoring of the architectural decoration of the palace was completed in 2002, with the installation of the princely crowns and vases. The palace is now an annex of the Hermitage and contains an exhibition on "Russian Culture 1700–30".

ALEXANDER MENSHIKOV (1672–1729)
The son of a baker, Menshikov was a childhood friend of Peter the Great. He wielded immense influence on affairs of state, and distinguished himself in a number of military campaigns (he was promoted to general in 1705). He later directed part of the construction of St Petersburg. Following the death of Peter the Great, Menshikov, who had become a member of the Secret Supreme Council and had married off his daughter to the future Peter II, was sole master of Russia for over two years. But he aroused the hostility of the nobility and his grip on power ended with his arrest in 1727. All his property was confiscated and he was deported with his family to Siberia, where he died two years later.

MENSHIKOV'S OFFICE
On the walls are portraits of Menshikov's four daughters.

PAINTING, SCULPTURE, ARCHITECTURE
The Academy of the "three noble arts" was founded in 1757, at the instigation of Lomonosov.

ACADEMY OF ARTS (AKADEMIYA KHUDOSHESTV; Академия художеств). Further along the embankment, at no. 17, the building of the Academy of Arts may be found, which was constructed between 1764 and 1768 by the architects Alexander Kokorinov and Jean-Baptiste Vallin de la Mothe ● 86. The traditions of this academy are maintained today by the Repin Institute of Painting, Sculpture and Architecture. Also housed within the building is the Arts Academy of Research, and on the first floor a department exhibiting plaster casts of original artworks from all over the world. The department of architecture displays a variety of designs and projects, together with scale models of Smolny ● 84, St Isaac's Cathedral ● 88, the Engineers' Castle, and the Stock Exchange ● 87.

LIEUTENANT SCHMIDT EMBANKMENT

SPHINX QUAY ★
(SPUSK SO SPHINXAMI; Спуск со Сфинксами) This quay was built (1832–4) to a plan by Konstantin Thon. The two sculpted sphinxes on either side of the steps leading down to the river were found at Thebes, the capital of ancient Egypt. Their features are those of the Pharaoh Amenophis III.

LIEUTENANT SCHMIDT BRIDGE. Both the bridge and the embankment are named for Nikolai Schmidt (center), who distinguished himself during the 1905 Revolution ● 44. The Lieutenant Schmidt Bridge (originally named the Nicholas Bridge) was the first permanent bridge across the Neva; it was built between 1847 and 1850 by the engineer S. Kerbedz and the decoration (sea shells and sea horses) is by Bryulov.
THE ACADEMICIANS' HOUSE (DOM AKADEMIKOV; дом Академиков). At no. 1 Lieutenant Schmidt Embankment (NAB. LEYTENANTA SCHMIDT; наб. Лейтенанта-Шмидта) stands the Academicians' House, which was constructed in the 1750's by Savva Chevakinsky. The building was completely reshaped in the early 19th century by the architects A. Bezhanov and Andrei Zakharov ● 87. The classical structure of the house is typical of the period; it has twenty-six plaques affixed to its walls, which commemorate the intellectuals who occupied it.

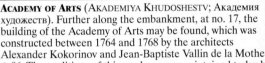

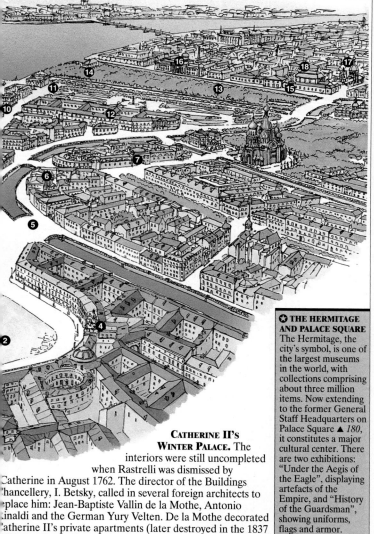

CATHERINE II'S WINTER PALACE. The interiors were still uncompleted when Rastrelli was dismissed by Catherine in August 1762. The director of the Buildings Chancellery, I. Betsky, called in several foreign architects to replace him: Jean-Baptiste Vallin de la Mothe, Antonio Rinaldi and the German Yury Velten. De la Mothe decorated Catherine II's private apartments (later destroyed in the 1837 fire), the Throne Room, the church, the apartments of the ladies of honor on the third floor, and the apartments of Count Grigory Orlov on the mezzanine floor. Velten reorganized the Portrait and the Mirror galleries, and Rinaldi changed the Throne Room into an oval salon. Catherine II had ten grandchildren, and the imperial apartments (including the theater) were altered to meet their needs by Giacomo Quarenghi and Ivan Starov. But the really major changes were to come with new construction work.

✪ THE HERMITAGE AND PALACE SQUARE
The Hermitage, the city's symbol, is one of the largest museums in the world, with collections comprising about three million items. Now extending to the former General Staff Headquarters on Palace Square ▲ *180*, it constitutes a major cultural center. There are two exhibitions: "Under the Aegis of the Eagle", displaying artefacts of the Empire, and "History of the Guardsman", showing uniforms, flags and armor.

167

Built by Bartolomeo Rastrelli (1754–62), Elizabeth I's Winter Palace is laid out around an immense closed courtyard with four projecting pavilions at the corners. The main portions of the building facing the Neva and Palace Square are linked by closed lateral galleries with apartments, service areas and staircases giving on to them. The center of the façade giving onto the Neva is barely evident by comparison with the projecting pavilions on either side of it. Although the Palace Square was built much later, the entrance to the courtyard was always by way of the triple arch on the city side.

The entrance to the New Hermitage was from Khalturin (Millionaires') Street, through a monumental gateway. It was built by the German architect Leo von Klenze between 1839 and 1851 and is supported by ten sculpted figures of Atlas.

DURING THE REVOLUTION Guards occupying the Winter Palace, October 24, 1917.

THE THEATER (E)

Built in the antique style, it has a semi-circular auditorium and décor inspired by the Olympic Theater at Vicenza (Italy).

E WINTER
ACE (A)

jor alterations
re made to the
nter Palace's
rner pavilions in
19th century.
e Ambassadors'
ircase (or Jourdain
ircase) was built in
northeast corner:
sovereign used
s staircase on
uary 6 (Epiphany)
ch year on his way
less the waters of
Neva in memory
Christ's Baptism.

THE SMALL
HERMITAGE (B)

Beginning in 1736,
Vallin de la Mothe
built a hanging
garden here, with a
pavilion at each end.
The north pavilion,
which was called
the Hermitage, was
finished in 1770.
But Catherine II's
growing art collection
eventually required
another building, the
Large Hermitage, to
be built.

THE LARGE
HERMITAGE (C)

Built in two stages,
the Large Hermitage
was the work of Yury
Velten (1771–87).
It occupies a site
between the palace
and the Winter Canal
dug by Peter the
Great between the
Neva and the Moika.
Its name was changed
in the 19th century to
the Old Hermitage.

THE NEW
HERMITAGE (D)

The imperial
collections were
saved from the fire
which devastated the
Winter Palace in
December 1837.
To house and display
them to the public,
it was decided in
1839 that a New
Hermitage should be
built. The museum
was opened by
Nicholas I in 1852.

"COMPOSITION VI"

The work of
Vasily Kandinsky is
played on the third
floor of the south
wing of the Winter
Palace, after the
Fauvist section.
This painting,
Composition VI, is an
example of a work
from the artist's
Abstract period.

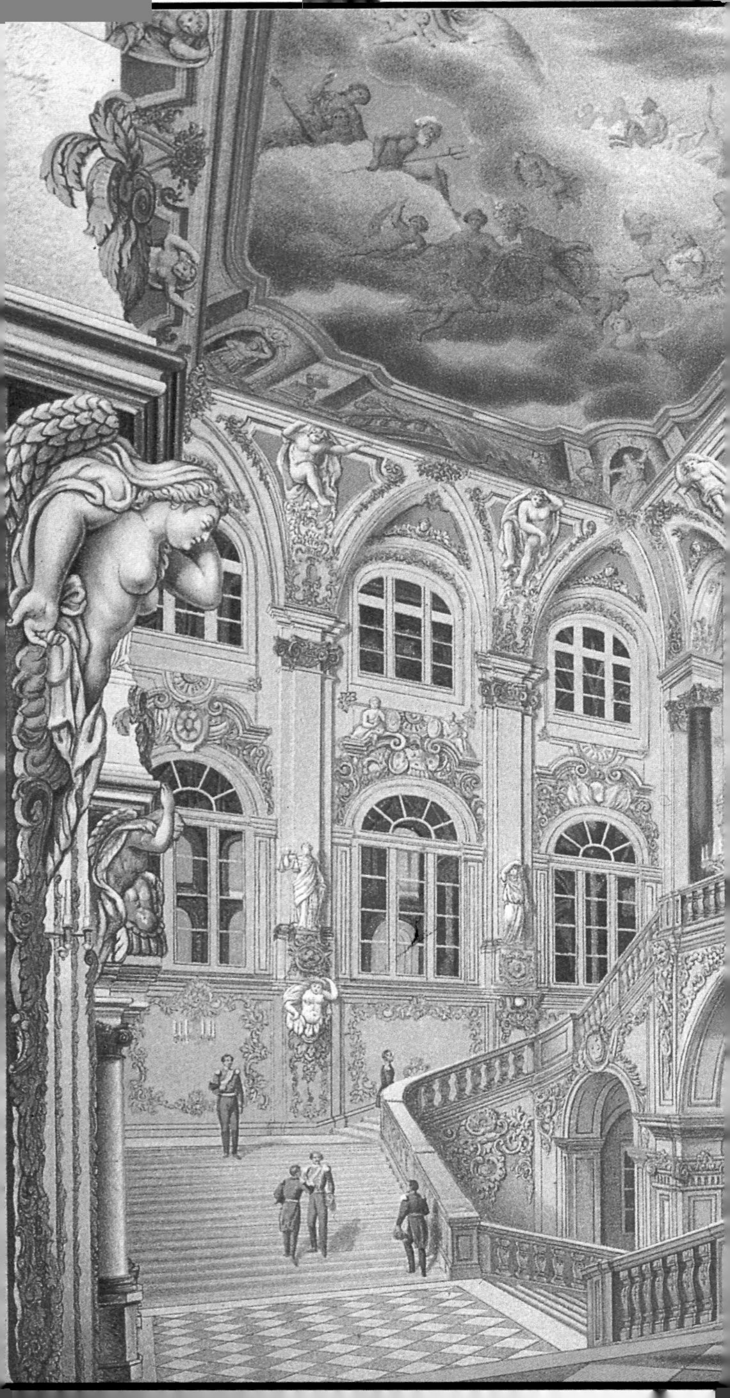

The War of 1812 Gallery (**2**) still bears the stamp of Rossi, its decorator. Here are displayed the portraits of the Russian generals who took part in the war against Napoleon. The Alexander Hall (**1**) contains a medallion with the profile of Alexander I, and moldings of warlike themes symbolizing the Czar's victory in the war of 1812–14. Bryulov decorated this with clusters of Gothic columns, two-headed eagles and classical medallions. The Hall of St George (**3**) is decorated with Carrara marble columns with gilded bronze capitals. The Throne, now installed in the Hall of Peter I, formerly stood below the bas-relief of Saint George and the Dragon. In the Pavilion Hall (**4**) copies of mosaics from Roman spas are set in the floor. This hall also contains reproductions of the Fountain of Tears from the Bakhtchisarai Palace in the Crimea. On the orders of Catherine II Quarenghi painted a reproduction of Raphael's *Loggia* (**5**) at the Vatican along the Winter Canal side of this room (1783–92).

The history of the Hermitage as a museum began with Peter the Great, who himself bought a number of works of art – among them *David and Goliath* by Rembrandt and the *Tauride Venus*. In the reign of Catherine II the imperial collections occupied rooms in the Hermitage of the Winter Palace, which gave its name to the museum. The museum is considered to have been officially born in 1764, when the Berlin dealer Gotzkowski sent the Empress of Russia 225 paintings intended for Frederick II of Prussia, in payment of a debt. Later, on the advice of Diderot and many of the best art connoisseurs of the time, Catherine bought many more works of art (and above all complete collections) in Paris, Dresden and London. Toward the close of her reign the Hermitage collection numbered 3,000 paintings, almost 7,000 drawings as well as some 70,000 engravings, 10,000 carved stones and 38,000 books.

VENETIAN PAINTERS
The museum contains an outstanding collection of Italian paintings from the 13th to the 18th centuries. The Venetian collection at the Old Hermitage is particularly rich and includes works such as *Judith* (left) and *Madonna and Child* by Giorgione (1477–1510). One room is entirely devoted to paintings by Titian (c. 1490–1576), among which are several masterpieces, including *Danaë*, *Mary Magdalen*, *Portrait of a Woman*, *Christ Carrying the Cross* and *Saint Sebastian*.

17TH–18TH CENTURY SPANISH PAINTINGS
The Spanish collection includes impressive works by El Greco (*Saint Peter and Saint Paul*), José de Ribera (*The Vision of St Jerome*), Velasquez (*The Meal*, also known as *The Drinkers*), Zurbaran (*Saint Laurence*), Murillo (*Child with Dog*) and Goya's *Portrait of Antonia Zárate* (right) .

THE GOLDEN COMB OF SOLOKHA
(above)
The collections of antique,
oriental and Scythian jewelry, as well as
gold and silverwork from Western Europe,
are displayed in a special area. This golden
comb is from the collection of Scythian
jewelry, of which the Hermitage has some
outstanding examples.

ITALIAN ART, 13TH–18TH CENTURIES

Among the many
masterpieces in
the section, don't
miss the following:
*The Virgin of the
Annunciation*
(Simone Martini);
*The Vision of Saint
Augustine* (a fresco
by Filippo Lippi);
*Virgin and Child
with Saint Thomas
and Saint Dominic*
(Fra Angelico);
*Saint Dominic and
Saint Jerome*
(Botticelli). The
Italian majolica
room has two
paintings by
Raphael: *Madonna
Conestabile* (above)
and *The Holy
Family*. In the first
glazed gallery are
Veronese's
*Conversion of
Saint Paul* and
Tintoretto's *Birth
of John the Baptist*.
In the large glazed
gallery are 17th-
and 18th-century
paintings, including
works by Tiepolo
and Canaletto.

THE "BENOIS MADONNA"
The great gallery of the Old Hermitage
exhibits two famous piantings by Leonardo
da Vinci : *Benois Madonna*(1478, above)
and the *Litta Madonna* (early 1490-1).
This painting, previously known as the
Madonna of the Flower, is named after
one of its former owners.

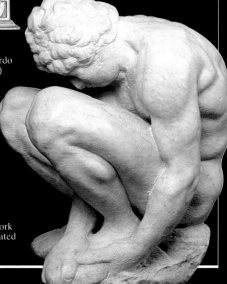

Crouching Youth (right), the only work
by Michelangelo in Russia, was created
for the Medici Tombs in Florence.

DUTCH PAINTING OF THE 15TH AND 16TH CENTURIES

The most remarkable works in this collection are Campin's diptych, *The Trinity* and the *Virgin at the Hearth*, *Saint Luke Painting the Virgin* by Van der Weyden, *The Healing of the Blind Man at Jericho* by Van der Weyden, and *The Adoration of the Magi* by Van der Goes. All 16th-century genres and great masters are represented, except for Vermeer. There are two portraits by Hals, landscapes by Van Goyen and Van Ruisdael, and pictures by Van Ostade, Steen, De Hooch and Ter Borch. In the Rembrandt Room are seventy-five pictures spanning the painter's entire career, from *The Sacrifice of Abraham* (1635) (right) and *The Descent from the Cross* (1634) to *David and Uriah* and *The Return of the Prodigal Son* (mid-1660's).

17TH–19TH CENTURY ENGLISH PAINTING

This section of the museum comes after the room devoted to works by Fragonard and Greuze. Note in particular *Love Untying Venus's Girdle* and *The Infant Hercules Killing the Serpents* (below, by Reynolds); and *The Duchess of Beaufort* (by Gainsborough). Also here is the work of landscape painters contemporary with Constable, including *Boats near the Shore* by Richard Parkes Bonington (1801–28

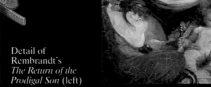

Detail of Rembrandt's *The Return of the Prodigal Son* (left)

"SASKIA AS FLORA"
This painting by Rembrandt dates from the first years of his marriage to Saskia van Uylenborch, shown here as a goddess of Roman mythology.

15TH–19TH CENTURY GERMAN PAINTING

In this section religious painting is displayed alongside Renaissance portraits and 17th-century still lifes. The great masterpieces here include Cranach the Elder's *Venus and Cupid* (below), *Virgin and Child Under an Apple Tree* and *Portrait of a Woman*; as well as *Portrait of a Young Man* by Ambrosius Holbein and *Erasmus of Rotterdam* by Hans Holbein the Younger (1497–1543).

There are also some fine still lifes by Christoph Pudiss (1618–66) and Hendrik van der Borcht the Elder (1583–1660).

Nineteenth-century German paintings are shown on the third floor, in a series of rooms parallel to those housing the Matisse collection. The group of paintings by the Romantic artist Caspar David Friedrich (1774–1840) are not to be missed.

17TH-CENTURY FLEMISH PAINTINGS

Many of the paintings exhibited in this section are works by the major Flemish portraitists of the period. The section includes twenty-six pictures by Van Dyck, including his fine *Portrait of Charles I*, *Self-Portrait* and *St Peter the Apostle*. Of the forty works by Rubens the most notable are *Christ with Crown of Thorns* (above), *The Alliance of Earth and Water*, *Perseus and Andromeda*, *Landscape with Rainbow* and *Portrait of Isabella of Spain's Lady-in-Waiting*. The fame of the collection of Flemish paintings in the Hermitage rests on the museum's holdings of works by these two masters.

"LA MUSIQUE"

The collection of paintings by Matisse (1869–1954) in the Hermitage is one of the largest and most representative in Europe. The thirty-seven paintings exhibited include *La Danse* and *La Musique*.

15TH–18TH CENTURY FRENCH PAINTING

This collection of French painting rivals that of the Louvre itself. The major works here are Le Nain's *The Milkmaid's Family*, Poussin's *Tancredi and Hermine* and *Landscape with Polyphenus*, Watteau's *The Little Savoyard* and *The Awkward Proposal*, and Fragonard's elegantly suggestive *Stolen Kiss* (left).

19TH CENTURY FRENCH ART

This collection is the pride of the Hermitage, particularly because it includes some paintings of international importance. Among the works dating from the first half of the 19th century are *Bonaparte at the Bridge of Arcole* (Gros); *Morpheus and Iris* (Guérin, left); *Portrait of Count Guriev* (Ingres); *Lion Hunt in Morocco* and *Arabs Saddling a Horse* (Delacroix).

BLOODY SUNDAY
Gathered on Palace
Square on January
22, 1905, the
demonstrators asked
to be allowed to
present a petition to
the Czar Nicholas II
(who was not in the
palace).

PALACE SQUARE

AN IMPERIAL ESPLANADE. Even though the entrance to the
courtyard of the Winter Palace ▲ *168* was originally planned
not for the Neva side but for the city side of the building,
Palace Square (DVORTSOVAYA PLOSHCHAD; Дворцовая
площадь) was laid out at a relatively late date. The architect
Bartolomeo Rastrelli ● *84* had proposed a semicircular
colonnade to transform the area into a gigantic courtyard and
provide a counterpoint to the Baroque façade of
the Winter Palace. But Empress
Elizabeth died

The police fired on
the crowd; the
resultant carnage
created an
unbridgeable gulf
between the Czar and
his people and
provided the impetus
for revolution.

before the
completion of the
project and Catherine II
dismissed Rastrelli when she ascended the
throne. All this time the square was no more than a
huge field; but in 1772 the architect Starov resurrected the
idea of a colonnade, which Catherine had rejected, although
the semicircular plan appealed to her. Finally, in 1779 the
Arts Academy launched a competition, which was won by
Yury Velten ▲ *162*. Opposite the palace he built a half-circle
of houses with identical façades. Still, th
ensemble lacked real grandeur, and
Carlo Rossi ● *86* was commissioned in
1819 to lay out a more regular square.
THE GENERAL STAFF HEADQUARTERS.
The main function of the buildings
fronting the square was to provide a
general headquarters for the Army's
main staff. In 1819 it was decided that
Russia's administrative center should
also be moved here, concentrating the
Ministry of Finance and the Foreign
Ministry in the same place. Carlo Rossi
went back to the old semicircular layout as defined by the
existing buildings, and put all of them behind a single façade
the center of which was pierced by a huge triumphal arch, th
ARCH OF THE GENERAL STAFF. The skill with which this was
accomplished is famous in the annals of architecture. The
arch, sited directly on the axis of the main palace entrance,
had to link the square with the curved street coming from th

PALACE SQUARE
The Winter Palace,
Admiralty Gardens,
former headquarters
of the General Staff,
and the Guards'
former headquarters
bound this huge area.

Nevksy Prospekt. Rossi therefore devised a "turning" arch – that is, one doubled with a part forming an arc of a circle which made it possible to pass from the fixed plane to the curve of the street while preserving the illusion of depth. The Arch is decorated Roman-style with military trophies and laurel-crowned worthies. On its top is a team of six bronze horses harnessed to the chariot of Glory. In 1840 the square was rounded off on its east side by the Headquarters of the Guard, designed by Alexander Bryulov.

THE ALEXANDER COLUMN (ALEKSANDROVSKAYA KOLONNA; Александровская колонна). This gigantic column was raised in the middle of the square (1830–4) in honor of Alexander I ● *36*, who prevailed against the

CARLO ROSSI (1775–1849)
Rossi was born in St Petersburg, the son of an Italian ballerina. Beginning his career as the assistant of Brenna, he studied in Italy before returning to Russia to complete his architectural masterpieces, among them the Palace Square.

THE ALEXANDER COLUMN
The 600-ton column, brought from Finland in 1832, was raised onto its base using a system of winches similar to that later used for St Isaac's Church ▲ *195*. Myth has it that the column is perfectly balanced and whoever can lift it will find gold and treasure hidden underneath.

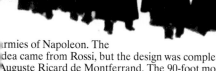

armies of Napoleon. The idea came from Rossi, but the design was completed by Auguste Ricard de Montferrand. The 90-foot monolith of pink Finnish granite is crowned by an angel: the total height of the monument is nearly 150 feet. The pedestal is decorated with allegorical bas-reliefs of the rivers Nieman and Vistula (crossed by the Army in pursuit of Napoleon) on one side, and Wisdom and Abundance, Peace and Justice, Victory and Peace on the other.

PUSHKIN'S HOUSE
The poet's study and his 4,000-book library (above) have been carefully preserved as they were when the Pushkin family lived here. Pushkin died in this house on January 29, 1837 ● *117*.

Arms of the Volkonsky Family.

THE MOIKA EMBANKMENT

CAPELLA ● *72*. The original Capella (no. 20), known as the Glinka Singing Academy in this century, was founded by Peter the Great; the present school was built in 1880 by the architect Leonty Benois at the end of a courtyard. The auditorium is separated from the street by high cast-iron railings which link two identical buildings. The Capella ensemble is a fine example of eclectic late 19th-century décor.

DLT STORE (Dom Leningradskoi Torgovli). This store backs on to the Moika Embankment (NAB. REKI MOIKI; наб. реки Мойки), although its main entrance is at no. 21 Bolshaya Konnushenaya. Built by the architect E.V. Virrich (1908–10), it is important in the history of St Petersburg architecture as one of the first metal-and-glass structures in the city. The huge salerooms were patterned on the Parisian *grands magasins* built at the turn of the century.

PUSHKIN MUSEUM (MUZEY-KVARTIRA PUSHKINA; музей-квартира Пушкина). An earlier house on this site (no. 12, built in the 1730's) belonged to the Volkonsky family. This mansion was replaced in 1770 by another in the classical Russian style, and subsequently altered extensively. Six fluted Corinthian pilasters distinguish the projecting central section, of the height of two floors, with a curved façade reflecting the bend in the river. On the courtyard side are broad arches (now glassed in) which still incorporate elements of the original building. The Pushkin family rented the second floor here in 1836.

IMPERIAL STABLES. The first imperial stables were built in 1720 for Peter the Great, by the architect N.F. Gerbel. The buildings were laid out around a polygonal courtyard. Although entirely reconstructed on the same site by Vasily Stasov between 1816 and 1823, they have retained their original form, specifically the curve imposed by the Moika. The CHURCH is contained in the square central portion of the façade giving on to the square. This somewhat complex ensemble included not only the stables and the riding ring, but also several warehouses, the administrative offices (the master of the stables was an

important figure in the imperial service), the lodgings of the staff and the church.

PALACE EMBANKMENT

THE WINTER CANAL BRIDGE. The Winter Canal meets the Neva by the Old Hermitage. The bridge that spans it is characteristic of those built by Yury Velten in the 1770's as part of the works carried out on the banks of the Neva, its tributaries and the various canals.

THE FORMER / NEW MIKHAIL PALACE. Built by Shtakenshneider (1857–61) for Mikhail Nicolayevich, son of Nicholas I ● *36*, this palace (no. 18) occupies a site bordered on one side by the Palace Embankment (DVORTSOVAYA NAB.; Дворцовая наб.) and on the other by Millionaires' Street. It follows the alignment of the other houses, blending well with the other private mansions of the quarter, although its lower level is notable for its French Renaissance-style panels and pilasters. The rear façade, however, is much more modest, and was reserved for the Grand Duke's domestic servants and staff. The dimensions of the palace are impressive, and it is said that one of the Grand Duke's sons would borrow a bicycle to visit his sister-in-law, whose quarters were located in another part of the palace.

Left to right: The galleried bridge across the Winter Canal, built by Yury Velten to link the Winter Palace with the theater ▲ *168*; the façade of the Hermitage ▲ *168* on the Neva side; and a detail of the façade of the Academicians' House. This former palace at no. 26 Palace Embankment, built by Alexander Rezanov (1867–71), includes many Italian Renaissance and Baroque elements. The red sandstone façade is itself strongly reminiscent of Florentine palaces.

BESIDE THE NEVA
The Palace Embankment owes its name to the residence of the Czars, today's Hermitage Museum ▲ *168*. The consolidation of the river banks with granite was undertaken over fifteen years, beginning in 1763, with the architect Yury Velten playing an important role.

THE MARBLE PALACE

FLOOR PLAN OF THE MARBLE PALACE
This follows the traditional U-design of urban palaces, with a courtyard fronting the main entrance.

A GIFT OF THE EMPRESS. For nearly twelve years Catherine II was the mistress of Count Grigory Orlov (1734–83). During this time she presented him with the Marble Palace (MRAMORNY DVORETS; Мраморный дворец). Orlov, with his brothers Alexei and Fyodor, led the conspiracy against Peter III that placed Catherine II on the Russian throne. The palace was built (1768–85) by the architect Antonio Rinaldi on a site between the Palace Embankment and Millionaires' Street. The main façade has four Corinthian columns at its center. The original entrance was via the Red Canal, which ran along the west side of Marsovo Pole. This canal was filled in during the 19th century, when a service wing was added and a new main entrance was built in the courtyard at the side of the palace.

GRANITE AND MARBLE. The contrast between the rough granite of the first floor and the refined marble of the upper levels, from which its name derives, gives the Marble Palace an original if somewhat severe aspect. Its roof was formerly covered in copper sheeting, while the window frames of the *piano nobile* were of gilded bronze, with polished glass panes. Marble was as much in evidence inside the building as outside. The main FORMAL STAIRCASE and the MARBLE ROOM (left) are still in their original state. From 1937 to 1991 the Marble Palace housed the Lenin Museum. Serving since 1992 as an annex of the Russian Museum ▲ *225*, it now contains an exhibition of works by foreign artists living in Russia, and the Lüdwig Donation.

A RECENT ARRIVAL
In the courtyard of the Marble Palace stands an equestrian statue of Alexander III, which replaced Lenin's armored car in November 1994. The statue, originally erected on Insurrection Square (Pl. Vostaniya) ▲ *244*, was brought from the Russian Museum, its home since 1937.

THE FIELD OF MARS

MARSOVO POLE (MARSOVO POLE; Марсово поле). With the Summer Garden to eastward, the Moika to the south, the Red Canal to the west and the Neva to the north, this broad area was not given its final form until 1817–19, when the architect Vasily Stasov (1769–1848) built the Pavlovsky barracks at the same time as Carlo Rossi was completing the Mikhail Palace. Their joint efforts led to a definitive project for the quarter, and the layout of the various green spaces was dictated by the architecture they designed.

BARRACKS OF THE PAVLOVSKY GUARDS REGIMENT (KAZARMY PAVLOVSKOVO POLKA; казармы Павловского полка). The west side of the square is entirely occupied by this gigantic building. At the center of its long yellow façade are twelve Doric columns, crowned by a monumental pediment

decorated with the usual trophies, weapons and winged victories. There are pavilions on either side in front of the building topped by a triangular pediment, which is echoed by a similar arrangement fronting Millionaires' Street. In the middle of Marsovo Pole, now laid out as a park, stands the Liberty Monument (right), formerly known as the Monument to Revolutionary Fighters. On the Neva side the quadrilateral ends at Suvorov Square; and in the center is a statue of Field Marshal Suvorov ▲ 252.

ADAMINI HOUSE. On the southwest side of Marsovo Pole, the corner house (no. 7) with a semicircular colonnade was built by the architect D. Adamini (1823–7) in the later classical style ● 86. The basement of this building was a meeting-place during World War One and the Revolution for Russian artists like Vsevolod Meyerhold, Alexander Blok, Anna Akhmatova,

Mikhail Kuzmin, Vladimir Mayakovsky and Anatoly Lunacharsky.

SALTYKOV AND BETSKY HOUSES. On the north side, fronting the waters of the Neva, Giacomo Quarenghi built the Saltykov House (1784–8); in 1820 it became the Austrian Embassy. It was celebrated for the salon over which presided the ambassador's wife, the grand-daughter of Marshal Kutuzov.

The *Tauride Venus*.

SUMMER GARDEN (LETNY SAD; Летний сад)

A GARDEN IN THE FRENCH STYLE. In 1704 Peter the Great made a rough sketch of a Western-style garden, with rare plant species brought from Siberia, the Urals, Holland and Kiev. The French model won the Czar's favor after his visit to Versailles in 1717, and as a result the gardens, which extend between the Neva to the north, the Fontanka to the east and the Moika to the south, are regular and symmetrical. The gardens were divided into quadrilaterals which were planted with trees and (in the old days) shrubs and flowers. There were also cunningly devised fountains and sculptures.

STATUES FROM ITALY. Most of the statuary in the Summer Garden was bought in Italy, according to the vogue of the early 18th century. Subjects from Greek mythology include

GATES OF THE SUMMER GARDEN
After consolidating the Neva's banks, Velten worked on the Embankment fronting the gardens and on the Summer Palace. The wrought-iron garden gates that he competed in 1784 were considered to be one of the finest examples of metalwork of the period.

✪ **SUMMER GARDEN**
Praised by poets, the Summer Garden is particularly attractive in summer. From November to April its famous statues, masterpieces of European sculpture, are clothed in wooden cases to protect them from frost.

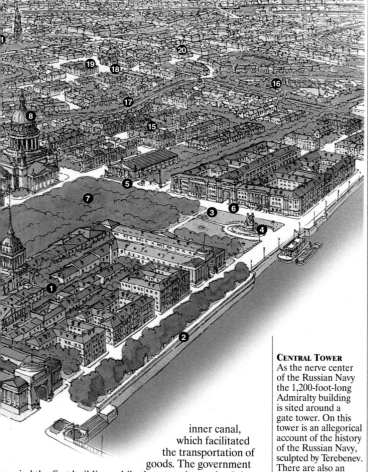

inner canal, which facilitated the transportation of goods. The government

CENTRAL TOWER
As the nerve center of the Russian Navy the 1,200-foot-long Admiralty building is sited around a gate tower. On this tower is an allegorical account of the history of the Russian Navy, sculpted by Terebenev. There are also an Ionic colonnade and various statues.

cupied the first building, while the second contained the rpentry shops, the forges, the cordwainers' shops, the neral workshops and the reserve supplies eded for each body of craftsmen.

EADQUARTERS OF THE GENERAL STAFF. In 1718 e Admiralty became the Headquarters of ter I's General Staff. For a while after this e porches of the pavilions at its ends were onted by a canal on its way to the Neva, which as not filled in until the mid-19th century. In e old days red flags would be hoisted on the ofs of these pavilions to warn the people of pending floods. Later a complex of buildings as erected on the site of the old dockyards tween the Neva and the two wings, effectively ncealing the Admiralty from passers-by on the bankment. It is now a military zone, closed to e public with the exception of the central tower.

191

▲ NAVAL CONSTRUCTIONS

Confronted by the naval power of Sweden Peter
the Great, the "Father of the Russian Navy",
decided to build a fleet worthy of the name.
Originally the port of St Petersburg was set on Birch Island,
where the city center evolved later in the 18th century. In 1733 i
was transferred to the point of Vasilyevsky Island, and a stock
exchange, a customs house, a merchant's court and other port
installations were built. The Admiralty served both as the Navy
Ministry and as a naval dockyard until 1844. At the close of the
19th century its precinct was densely built up and became
known as the Admiralty Embankment.

KRONSTADT
From the 18th
century onward
Kronstadt was
Russia's principal
naval base; but after
the appearance of
steamships in the
1850's merchant
cargoes began to be
unloaded there, for
transportation to
St Petersburg on
lighters. According to
a popular saying of
the period, "The
voyage from London
to Kronstadt is much
shorter than the
voyage from
Kronstadt to the
point of Vasilyevsky
Island." In 1885 the
port was moved to
Gutuyevsky Island.

**THE "GRANDFATHER
OF THE RUSSIAN
FLEET"**
This was the name
given to Peter the
Great's first ship
▲ *149*, in which he
learned to navigate.

THE ADMIRALTY

Toward 1738 the Admiralty was rebuilt. Its initial floor plan remained the same, but stone now replaced the original wood and clay materials. The Tower was raised to a height of over 200 feet. In 1823, after reconstruction works undertaken by the architect Andrei Zakharov, the building assumed its present appearance. Even before the completion of the works in 1829 the Navy Ministry was transferred here from Moscow, and a bureau was set up for the use of Czar Alexander I.

THE GALLEYS

In Russia the word "galley" was applied to any warship with oars. The crews of these vessels were made up of soldiers and sailors in the pay of the Army. The construction and repair of the galleys was carried out at the dockyards of Galley Island, west of the Admiralty.

THE FIRST DOCKYARDS

The construction of the first factory in St Petersburg, the Admiralty's naval dockyard, began on November 5, 1704. Peter I noted in his diary: "This day we laid the foundations of the Admiralty amid great joy and celebration. The building is to be 200 sagens in length and 100 sagens broad [1 sagen = 6½ feet]."

THE EMBLEM OF THE CITY

A spire was added to the Admiralty Tower in 1719, with a golden apple and a weathercock in the form of a caravel.

193

PETER THE GREAT
Peter I surveys the city he founded from horseback, in the pose imagined for him by the French sculptor Etienne Falconet, who won a competition arranged by Catherine II in 1765. The sculpture was not completed until 1778; it represents the Czar ascending a rock and trampling a serpent (symbolizing the Swedes) underfoot. This statue was the inspiration for one of Pushkin's most celebrated poems, "The Bronze Horseman" ● *118*. In 2003, another monument dedicated to Peter I was restored to its original position, on the Admiralty's quay. It is a copy of the statue of the "Tsar Carpenter", inaugurated in 1900, then lost during the Revolution. It recalls the stay of the sovereign in Holland.

✪ A VISTA OF BRIDGES
On summer evenings, when the bridges ● *90* spanning the Great Neva are bathed in the mysterious light created by diffused sun beams ● *28* (known in Russia as "white nights"), enthusiasts for the nightly opening of the bridges gather around the statue of the Bronze Horseman. As orchestras assemble on the English Embankment and Admiralty Embankment, bankside cafés and restaurants begin to fill with customers. It is worth being there when the bridges are opened: Palace Bridge opens at 1.35am and Lieutenant-Schmidt Bridge at 1.40am.

DECEMBRISTS SQUARE

DECEMBRISTS SQUARE (PL. DEKABRISTOV; пл. Декабристов) owes its name to the protagonists of one of the more painful episodes in the history of St Petersburg and Russia ● *42*.

EQUESTRIAN STATUE OF PETER I. Contrary to the fashion of the day, the Czar is represented neither as a Roman emperor nor as a prince of his own time. Instead he wears a long robe, a mantle, soft leather boots and a simple sword at his side – the garb of an ordinary Russian prince. Only the crown of laurels on his head, sculpted by a pupil of Falconet's, Anne-Marie Collot, reminds us of his rank. On either side of the plinth are four words, which translate as: "To Peter I, Catherine II".

THE RIDING SCHOOL (THE MANÈGE). Designed by Quarenghi (1804–7), with sculpted décor by Paolo Triscorni, the Riding School is a low quadrangular building not unlike a Greek temple, with a double colonnade and pediment.

VICTORY COLUMNS. Following the disappearance of the Admiralty dockyards, the canal connecting the site with the New Holland district was covered by a brick arch that became the Horseguards Boulevard. On a granite pedestal here are winged Victory figures in bronze, modeled by Christian Rauch (1845–6) and presented to the Czar by the King of Prussia in commemoration of their joint victory over Napoleon.

SENATE AND SYNOD. By creating new institutions for Russia Peter the Great managed to disarm those of his opponents who were obstructing his reforms. He suppressed the Patriarchate which had hitherto wielded absolute power over the Church, and replaced it by a Synod, with authority to settle all religious questions. Likewise in 1711 he outmaneuvered the Duma of the Boyars by setting up a nine-member Senate to manage affairs of state in his absence. The architects Rossi and Stasov designed twin buildings for these institutions

MONUMENT TO PRZEVALSKY
This statue in the Alexander Garden, sculpted by Schroeder in 1882, celebrates the explorer Przevalsky (1839–88), who went out to discover Asia on behalf of the Imperial Geographical Society. In his account of his travels Przevalsky described the wild camel whose image now graces his statue's plinth, along with the rare Siberian horse species which was named after him ▲ *151*.

829–34), which were connected by an arch spanning alernaya Street. The columns are set forward, with a heavy ntablature decorated with statues of angels. A frieze in as-relief emphasizes the attic, in the center of which is a culpted group featuring allegories of Probity and Justice. In e direction of the Neva, the Senate building is distinguished by a colonnade which curves round to meet the embankment. Today the Senate and Synod buildings contain historical archives; they also incorporate the Palace of Count Laval, whose daughter followed her husband, the Decembrist Trubetskoy, into exile in Siberia.

ALEXANDER GARDEN. The Alexander Garden (ALEKSANDROVSKY SAD; Александровский сад) was planted for the two-hundredth anniversary of the birth of Peter the Great, and covers the fortifications and moats which formerly defended the Admiralty. The statues here are mostly copies of antique originals made in the 18th century, along with busts of famous Russians like Gogol, Lermontov, Glinka and Zhukovsky.

ST ISAAC'S CATHEDRAL

St Isaac's Cathedral had difficult beginnings. Between the first church, built of wood on the present site of the Senate, and the project of Rinaldi, inherited by Renna and rejected by ontferrand, nearly a dozen architects em to have tried to build this cathedral its sodden, unstable site.

THE FIRST ST ISAAC'S CHURCH
Wishing to honor the saint on whose feast day he was born, Peter I dedicated what was later to become St Petersburg's largest place of worship to an obscure Dalmatian monk.

Montferrand left an album of watercolors showing the different stages of the cathedral's construction, from the transportation of the columns to their erection.

A TECHNICAL EXPLOIT. The architect Auguste Ricard de Montferrand, who designed the cathedral as we know it (1818–58), gave it a Byzantine floor plan, somewhat lengthened. He solved the problem of unstable foundations by setting the 300,000-ton building on 11,000 pilings, reconciled the dictates of the disposition of the square and the orientation of the Christian sanctuaries, and added deep porches with double rows of columns to the north and south façades. These monolithic columns, made of Vyborg granite brought by sea from Finland, are over 50 feet high and weigh 114 tons each. Before constructing the main dome Montferrand made a study of similar European buildings; his greatest innovation was his use of cast iron for the rafters.

REALISTIC DÉCOR. To give his monstrous brainchild at least a veneer of lightness, the architect used materials of contrasting colors: for example, the gray granite of the walls offsets the pink columns, while the bronze of the pediments, statues, monumental doors and capitals echoes the gold of the domes. The décor of the interior ● *88* is extremely lavish; the two columns supporting the central door of the iconostasis ● *56* are paneled with lapis lazuli, while all the inside columns are covered in malachite.

ST ISAAC'S CATHEDRAL
The upper parts of the building are classical in style, with a huge dome, four smaller bell towers, and abundant statuary on the roof.

ST ISAAC'S SQUARE ★

Conceived as a whole and remodeled by Montferrand as part of the work on the cathedral, St Isaac's Square (ISAAKIEVSKAYA PL.; Исаакиевская пл.) was no more than a huge building site at the time when Rossi was busy with the Senate and the Synod.

MONUMENT TO NICHOLAS I. This equestrian statue (1859), the work of the sculptor Piotr Klodt, represents the Czar in the uniform of the Horse Guards. The pedestal is decorated with four bronze bas-reliefs of the principal episodes of his reign.

The pedestal is decorated with four bronze bas-reliefs of the principal episodes of his reign. Between the motifs are allegorical statues of Justice, Strength, Faith and Wisdom, which have the features of the Empress and the daughters of the Czar, who together commissioned the monument.

MARIINSKY PALACE (MARIINSKY DVORETS; Мариинский дворец). This palace, built (1839–44) by Shtakenshneider, is the final element of the square. Intended for the Grand Duchess Maria, daughter of Nicholas I, it replaced an older construction of Vallin de la Mothe. It was purchased by the State in 1884 and was used thereafter by the Council of the Czar's Ministers. After the Revolution it became the seat of the Provisional Government of the Russian Republic; today it is the headquarters of the St Petersburg Legislative Assembly.

BOLSHAYA MORSKAYA

This main thoroughfare (once Herzen Street) begins at the Arch of the General Staff ▲ *180* and intersects Nevsky Prospekt ▲ *214* and St Isaac's Square.

ASTORIA HOTEL. The Astoria (neoclassical and Art Nouveau) was designed by the architect Lidwal in 1911. The first and second floors are faced with granite decorated with medallions, garlands and mascarons, while the façades are punctuated with pilasters. In 1917 the Astoria was a focus of resistance to the Revolution, which was invested on November 7 by Red Guards and sailors. In the first years of the Soviet regime it was the headquarters of the Petrosoviet. In 1990 it was merged with the neighboring Angleterre Hotel (where poet Sergei Esenin committed suicide in 1925) and was entirely renovated.

THE BLUE BRIDGE
Despite its diminutive span the Blue Bridge (SINY MOST; Синий мост) across the Moika is the broadest in St Petersburg (nearly 300 feet). It was once made of wood and painted blue – hence the name – while its neighbors were red and green.

LOBONOV-ROSTOVSKY MANSION
This majestic private mansion on the corner of Decembrists Square and the Voznesensky Prospekt occupies a three-cornered site. It was built by the architect of St Isaac's Cathedral, Auguste Ricard de Montferrand (1817–20).

DEMIDOV MANSION
The gateway here is flanked by Atlas figures and caryatids supporting a richly sculpted balcony. At the turn of the 20th century Demidov Mansion was the Italian Embassy; today it is a machine-tool training institute.

GAGARIN HOUSE
The pavilion at no. 45, next door to Demidov Mansion, was built in the 1840's. It is now the Composers' House.

DEMIDOV MANSION. This building (no. 43) bears the name of an industrialist whose family made a fortune from mines in the Urals. Constructed between 1836 and 1840, the Demidov Mansion was inspired by Italian Renaissance architecture and is laid out around an inner courtyard. Formerly it had a hall that was entirely covered in malachite taken from its owner's mines, and this served as the model for the one in the Winter Palace ▲ 172.

NABOKOV'S HOUSE. Vladimir Nabokov (below, with his mother) was born in St Petersburg in 1899 and grew up in no. 47. The scion of a liberal aristocratic family, Nabokov was a privileged child and idolized by his mother; he recalls his happy youth in his memoir *Other Shores*. Following the October Revolution the Nabokovs left Russia for Europe; the writer then emigrated to the United States in 1940, adopting U.S. citizenship. The house contains the Nabokov Museum.

POLOVTSEV MANSION. This lavish townhouse (no. 52), also called the Architects' House, was built (1835–6) by Pel. The Senator A. Polovtsev, who acquired it in 1860, was also the president of the Russian Historical Society. The interior is notable for its neo-Gothic library, a gilded hall and a salon decorated with malachite and bronze. The restaurant at Polovisev Mansion, which was once used exclusively by architects, is now open to all.

CENTRAL POST OFFICE

The first post office, or Postamt, founded by Peter I in 1714, was on Suvorov Square ▲ 186. It was later transferred to larger premises on the present Millionaires' Street; and in 1782 Catherine II moved it to the present site. This was the departure point for the post coaches which criss-crossed the Russian Empire; all the milestones in the nation indicated their exact distance

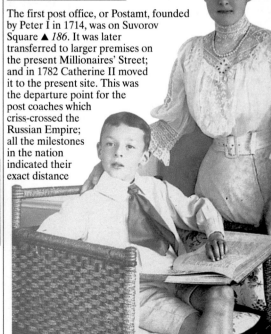

from the Postamt. In 1859, when the Post Office was in need of more space, it expanded to the other side of Postamt Street and a covered gallery in the form of an archway was built to connect the two buildings. Clocks were hung here, showing the time in the major foreign capitals. Today the Postamt still fulfills its original function.

NOVAYA GOLLANDIYA (NEW HOLLAND DISTRICT)

THE FORMER TIMBER STORES. The Novaya Gollandiya district covers an area that was once a Navy storage depot constructed on an artificial island skirted by the Admiralty, Kryukov and Moika canals. Before the depot was built, timber used for shipbuilding was kept at the Admiralty ▲ 190, in close proximity to the yards, where it was seasoned in the Dutch fashion; for this reason the wood store was known as "New Holland". The immense building with its rounded corners is characteristic of the work of the architect Vallin de la Mothe, who was commissioned to construct the market galleries. The bare brick edifice that ultimately resulted is virtually blind on its exterior, with nothing but small-paned bay windows on the corners.

THE ARCH ● 88. A large pool stands at the center of the store area, which can be reached by boat through an archway high enough to admit fairly substantial superstructures. This arch is classical in design, framed by two columns bearing a Doric frieze. The arch itself rests on smaller columns. The austerity of the architectural design is relieved to some extent by the colors of the brick walls and the metopes, which contrast with the gray granite columns and triglyphs. The district of Novaya Gollandiya has been associated with the Russian Navy for as long as it has been in existence; today it remains a military zone, and is not open to the public. In the 19th century it was used as a prison. In more recent times it has been suggested that the Novaya Gollandiya district should be converted into a cultural center, or a tourist area which would incorporate hotels and boutiques. A third project has been proposed that would move the Naval Museum into the precinct, as this institution is at the moment somewhat cramped in its present building at the Stock Exchange ▲ 157.

"My mother's boudoir had an overhanging window, which was convenient for looking outside, since it had a view across Morskaya Street toward Mariya Square . . . from this window, a few years later, at the start of the Revolution, I observed more than one skirmish, and for the first time in my life I saw a dead man.**"**

Vladimir Nabokov

APARTMENT OF ALEXANDER BLOK
The apartment in which the writer spent a few months (no. 57, Decembrists Square) is now a museum displaying mementos of his life, amid the sober surroundings he favored.

From the 18th century onward the Mariinsky was the imperial ballet theater. Among the five theaters maintained by the court (two in Moscow and three in St Petersburg) it was especially favored from the time of Nicholas I. Nothing was too lavish for the ballets of the Imperial Theater, which was endowed with sumptuous décors created by court artists such as Roller and (later) Golovin and Benois. Known as the Kirov under the Soviet regime, the Mariinsky reverted to its original name in 1992.

MARIUS PETIPA (1818–1910)

A world-renowned choreographic genius, Petipa was ballet master at the Mariinsky from 1869 to 1903. He put on more than sixty performances and was one of the architects of academic ballet.

THE KIROV BALLET

From 1935 the Mariinsky Ballet was known as the Kirov Ballet, in honor of Sergei Kirov ● *49*. The repertoire of the Soviet period included Tchaikovsky's *Queen of Spades*, among other productions.

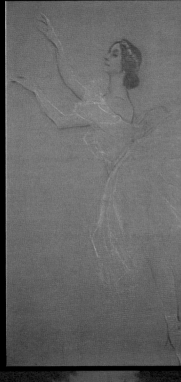

PAVLOVA (1881–1931)
No choreographer
before Petipa had
celebrated the
ballerina with so much
brio. His ballets
brought a whole
constellation of
dancers to the fore,
including Mathilda
Kshesinskaya,
O. Presbrazhenskaya
and Anna Pavlova.

**THE CORPS DE
BALLET**
The genius of Petipa
reached its climax in
his collaboration with
the composers
Tchaikovsky and
Glazunov. With
The Sleeping Beauty
(1890), *Swan Lake*
(1895) and
Raymonda (1898)
Petipa created a style
in which the *corps de
ballet* became an
essential component
of the choreographic
language.

YUSUPOV PALACE

Built by Vallin de la Mothe in the 1760's, the Yusupov Palace (YUSUPOVSKY DVORETS; Юсуповский дворец) was converted at the end of the 19th century for Princess Zinaida Yusupov. Seriously damaged during World War Two, it has since been heavily restored and its magnificent art collection moved to the Hermitage. The interior decoration of the palace testifies to its former brilliance; the formal salon, the MOORISH SALON, and the Buffet Room (where the acoustics are extraordinary) in particular. So as not to overload the slender vaulting of the BALLROOM, which was not strong enough to support crystal or gilded bronze, the chandeliers were fashioned of gilt papier-maché so that they resembled metal. An Italianate THEATER (above) is situated in the North Wing of the building.

THE DEATH OF RASPUTIN. On the first floor of the Moika side of the building a concealed entrance leads to a salon in which exclusive parties were given; it was in this salon that Rasputin ● 37, the hypnotic monk who oscillated between spirituality and debauchery, met his horrible end. In the uneasy atmosphere of the period, Rasputin's mesmeric gift had given him enormous power over the Empress and her entourage. To rid the court of this inconvenient character Prince Felix Yusupov plotted his murder, in which the Grand Duke Dmitry also had a hand. Felix Yusupov died in Paris in 1967.

THE POISONING OF RASPUTIN
In the basement of the Yusupov Palace there is a waxwork which recreates the décor and atmosphere of Rasputin's gruesome murder.

THEATER SQUARE ✪

Theater Square (TEATRALNAYA PL.; Театральная пл.) contains, in close proximity, two of the main institutions of the musical life of St Petersburg.

THE MARIINSKY THEATER. Between 1847 and 1848, A. Kavos, St Petersburg's chief theatrical architect, built a theater that also doubled as a circus. Circus acts with performing horses, acrobatic shows and trapeze acts took place in its central arena.

Badly damaged by fire in 1859, the building was replaced the following year by a conventional theater. Named the Mariinsky Theater in honor of the Empress Maria Alexandrovna, consort of the Emperor Alexander II, the theater began its first season with *A Life for the Czar*, a work by Glinka that signaled the birth of classical Russian opera. It was nationalized in 1917, and from 1935 to 1993 was known as the Kirov Ballet. It has now

✪ NEW LIFE FOR THEATER SQUARE
The area around Theater Square is the focal point of the city's artistic life. Once the place where wealthy princes bought residences for their favorite ballerinas, the area later became an official showcase for Soviet culture. Today it has a new lease of life, thanks to the Mariinsky Theater. This musical theater, which is renowed for its festival "Stars of the Night", has broadened its repertoire by staging innovative productions of such classic works as Tchaikovsky's *The Nutcracker* and Mussorgsky's *Boris Godunov*, with a cast featuring eminent performers from other countries.

reverted to its original name. During
the Soviet era the theater continued to
mount operas and ballets by native
Russian composers such as Prokofiev
and Shostakovich. The theater's current
director is Valery Gergiev, whose primary
objective is to revive the great
masterpieces of Russian opera. The
ballet company, which still enjoys
international renown, continues to tour
the major capitals of the world.

THE CONSERVATOIRE. The site on which
the Conservatoire now stands was
originally occupied by the Great Theater.
Built in the late 1770's, during the reign
of Catherine the Great, it was at the
time the only permanent theater in
St Petersburg. Between 1891 and 1896 it

was completely rebuilt: the new building, designed by the
architect V. Nicol, was to house the Conservatoire that the
pianist Anton Rubinstein had founded in 1862. It was the first
advanced music school in Russia, teaching seven disciplines;
these were musical theory and composition; choir and
orchestra conducting; singing; orchestral instruments; piano
and organ; ballet and opera direction; and traditional
instruments. The Conservatoire has two auditoriums: in the
larger of the two, pupils give public performances; the smaller
one, which has magnificent acoustics, a painted ceiling and
a gallery of portraits of musicians, is used for Russian and
international festivals and competitions.

Statue of Nikolai
Rimsky-Korsakov
▲ 239 in front of the
Conservatoire.

SYNAGOGUE
The Jewish
community of
St Petersburg was
heavily repressed
prior to the reforms
of Alexander II ● 36.
In 1893 the
construction of a
synagogue and
cultural center
confirmed these
reforms; the
synagogue, at no. 2
Lermontov Street, is
built in the Moorish
style.

In an area once overwhelmingly inhabited by sailors, this cathedral was understandably dedicated to their patron, Saint Nicholas. With its blue, white and gold exterior, St Nicholas' Cathedral is similar in many ways to Smolny, which was built by Rastrelli; indeed Chevakinsky, the architect of St Nicholas, was a pupil of the Italian. A remarkable illustration of religious Baroque, this church remained open throughout the Soviet era.

BESIDE THE KRYUKOV CANAL
The cathedral is built to the classic Greek cross plan, with a central cupola and four turrets at each corner, topped by onion domes ● 57. On the exterior the composition is punctuated by columns backed against the walls. The lower church (there is no crypt, because of likely flooding) supports a richly embellished upper one. Services are held on the upper level, where the décor is especially lavish because of the largesse of Catherine II, who presented ten gold-covered icons to commemorate ten naval victories. The equally gold-laden

iconostasis ● 57, of carved wood, was executed between 1755 and 1760. The bell tower is separate from the church proper ● 85, standing at the entrance to the cathedral precinct, where it is reflected in the Kryukov Canal ▲ 210.

1. Main entrance
2. Secondary entrance
3. Lower church
4. Stairs leading to upper church
5. Iconostasis
6. Portal
7. Altars
8. Central cupola
9. Onion-domed corner turret

SENNAYA PLOSHCHAD
In Dostoevsky's time the crowded and filthy Haymarket was known for its low dives, taverns, cabarets, brothels and prostitutes' hotels. The district exercised a deep fascination on Raskolnikov, the hero of *Crime and Punishment*: at the close of the novel, visiting the Haymarket for the last time, ". . . he let himself fall to the ground . . . on his knees in the center of the square, he bent and kissed the muddy stones with ecstasy and delight . . . then he straightened, and prostrated himself a second time."

HAYMARKET SQUARE

From St Nicholas' Cathedral, Sadovaya Street (SADOVAYA UL.; Садовая ул), typical of 19th-century St Petersburg, leads through to Haymarket Square (SENNAYA PL.; Сенная пл.). At the end of the 18th century there was a huge market here where hay, oats and straw were sold, hence the name. The Haymarket area was once one of the worst slums of St Petersburg, but today the old buildings have been replaced by buildings constructed after World War Two. The only original edifice still standing is the Police Station, with its four-columned classical portico.

THE CHURCH OF THE ASSUMPTION IN HAYMARKET SQUARE, now demolished, was built in the mid-18th century to a project by A. Kvasov, in which Rastrelli had a hand. It was the architectural focus of the square. Closed in 1938, the church was knocked down in 1961 to make way for the Sennaya metro station.

DOSTOEVSKY DISTRICT ★

A HERMETIC SPACE. Dostoevsky never had a house of his own in St Petersburg; instead he was constantly on the move,

> "Few places exercise on the human spirit so somber,
> violent, and strange an influence . . ."
>
> Fyodor Dostoevsky

hanging his domicile a score of times in the eight years he lived in the city center. As a rule he chose buildings that faced churches. Whether large and spacious or narrow and closed off, a room for Dostoevsky had a profound underlying meaning. Time and again the image of the oppressive, constricting bedroom appears in his books. This hermetic space, bounded by a corner, a wall, a palisade or an alleyway, is a frequent characteristic of his work; it has the value of a symbol, expressing the inner life of the hero and his state of mind.

CUT OFF FROM THE WORLD. Dreamers, "men of the underworld" with ravaged consciences, the heroes of Dostoevsky always live in "corners"; they flee the reality that surrounds them. The writer himself nearly always lived on street-corner houses, which made him feel even more isolated from the rest of the world than he actually was. He had a clear preference for Vladimir Square ▲ *238* and the Haymarket. It was here that he set his characters, who walked the same streets as he did and saw the same buildings and scenes from their windows as he saw. The lives of both Dostoevsky and his heroes are seamlessly blended with the life of St Petersburg itself. Indeed, this may be one reason why Dostoevsky moved with such regularity: once he had completed a novel, he became impatient to leave the places which his art and his imagination had transformed into fiction.

A CITY REINVENTED
Dostoevsky's St Petersburg has two dimensions, one real, the other imaginary. On the one hand, there is the city which really existed, with real people and locations; and on the other, there is the imagined metropolis, peopled by invented characters, which is such a strong characteristic of his work. Dostoevsky loved his city, where he had grown up and made his literary career. St Petersburg is present in about twenty of his thirty novels, sometimes as a background but more often as a character in its own right.

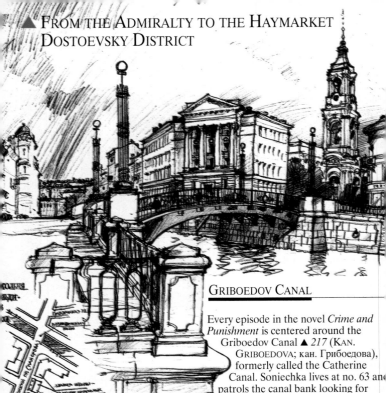

GRIBOEDOV CANAL

Every episode in the novel *Crime and Punishment* is centered around the Griboedov Canal ▲ *217* (КАН. ГРИБОЕДОВА; кан. Грибоедова), formerly called the Catherine Canal. Soniechka lives at no. 63 and patrols the canal bank looking for clients. On the far side of the canal stands the building occupied by the moneylender Alena Ivanovna, the old woman whom Raskolnikov robs and kills with an axe. No. 65 was the old Police Station to which Raskolnikov is summoned, and which Dostoevsky himself visited.

PRZEVALSKY STREET

RASKOLNIKOV'S HOUSE. The corner house here, no. 5, is thought to be the model for Raskolnikov's. In the mid-19th century this three-story building belonged to a man called Joachim. If you turn right after entering the porch you will see in the corner the door which gives onto the staircase described in the novel. Dostoevsky gives an exact account of Raskolnikov's comings and goings, and his hero's fate is decided by a series of coincidences. Thus Raskolnikov, who has carefully thought out everything he needs to do before he commits his crime, finally forgets to bring an axe with which he intends to do the deed.

ASCENSION BRIDGE
❝Raskolnikov went straight to X Bridge, stopped in the middle of it, leaned his elbows on the parapet, and looked down . . . with his head craned over the water, he began mechanically to contemplate the last pink rays of the setting sun … Eventually red circles emerged before his eyes, and the houses, passers-by, quays, coaches and everything else began spinning and dancing around him.❞
Crime and Punishment

TREASURY STREET

Dostoevsky occupied three different houses in Treasury Street (KAZNACHEYSKAYA UL.; Казначейская ул.), close by the Haymarket, known as Petit Bourgeois Street until the turn of the century. The writer, who was already famous, lodged in one of the most wretched slums in St Petersburg; not

**KARL BRYULOV
(NO. 6)**
The painter Karl Bryulov stayed at this address in 1836, where Nikolai Gogol visited him several times to pose for his portrait.

UNNY SIDE (EVEN NUMBERS)
espite their diversity

the façades of the buildings along the sunny side of the

Prospekt give an overall sense of elegance and unity.

**KARL BRYULOV
(NO. 6)**

MALAYA MORSKAYA STREET

MALAYA MORSKAYA STREET
From 1902 to 1992 this street bore the name of one of its most famous residents, Nikolai Gogol, who lived in

an apartment at no. 17 between 1833 an 1836. He wrote *Taras Bulba* here.

213

No. 14 has a poignant reminder of the siege of Leningrad: a plaque reads, "Comrades! In the event of artillery fire, this side of the street is the most dangerous."

BOLSHAYA MORSKAYA STREET
Before reverting to its original name Bolshaya Morskaya Street was rebaptized Herzen Street, after the writer (right) who lived at no. 14. Bolshaya Morskaya Street cuts directly across Nevsky Prospekt. The even street numbers end at the Arch of the General Staff. At nos. 3–5 the former Azovsko-Donskoy bank (1908–9) provides another example of the luxurious tastes of the old financiers. This building has now been converted into a telephone exchange.

"WOLFF AND BÉRANGER" (NO. 18)
Pushkin met his second, Danzas, at this pastry-shop on January 27, 1837, before his final duel ● 116. The literary café here opened in 1985.

No. 14

BOLSHAYA MORSKAYA STREET

CHICHERIN PALACE (NO. 15)

POLICE BRIDGE
The rearrangement of the banks of the Moika took place earlier than that of the other canals. Nevertheless it was only in the years 1798–1810 that these were completely reconstructed in granite. The Police Bridge, which spans the Moika, owes its name to its proximity to the Chicherin Palace (no. 15) and the central police building.

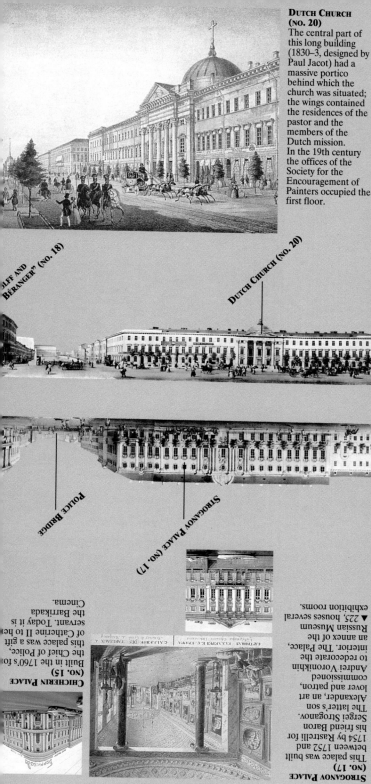

DUTCH CHURCH (NO. 20)

The central part of this long building (1830–3, designed by Paul Jacot) had a massive portico behind which the church was situated; the wings contained the residences of the pastor and the members of the Dutch mission.
In the 19th century the offices of the Society for the Encouragement of Painters occupied the first floor.

"OLFF AND BÉRANGER" (NO. 18)

DUTCH CHURCH (NO. 20)

POLICE BRIDGE

STROGÁNOV PALACE (NO. 17)

CHICHÉRIN PALACE (NO. 15)

Built in the 1760's for the Chief of Police, this palace was a gift of Catherine II to her servant. Today it is the Barrikáda Cinema.

EKATEPNHA ΓΑΛΛΕΡΕЯ Ε.С. ГРАФА.   Lithographie R. Geisel de Muenchen   GALLERIE DES TABLEAUX. A.

STROGÁNOV PALACE (NO. 17)

This palace was built between 1752 and 1754 by Rastrelli for his friend Baron Sergei Stroganov. The latter's son Alexander, an art lover and patron, commissioned Andrei Voronikhin to redecorate the interior. The Palace, an annex of the Russian Museum ▲ 225, houses several exhibition rooms.

"DOMINIQUE" (NO. 24)
Before the Revolution
no. 24 was the famous
restaurant *Dominique*
where the young

Dostoevsky habitua[lly]
dined in the 184[0s]
Later the interior w[as]
sketched by [the]
painter Rep[in]

**SMYRDIN PUBLISHING
HOUSE (NO. 22)**
Formerly the
bookseller
A. Smyrdin, the

publisher of Pushkin
and Gogol, occupied
the right wing of the
Lutheran church
building.

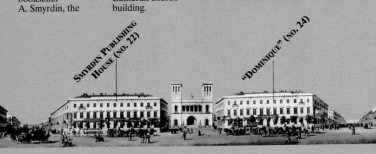

SMYRDIN PUBLISHING HOUSE (NO. 22)

"DOMINIQUE" (NO. 24)

MERTEN'S STORE (NO. 21)

CATHEDRAL OF OUR LADY OF KAZAN

**MERTEN'S STORE
(NO. 21)**
The enormous glazed
arcades formerly
housed the Merten's
fur store, designed by
the architect
Lialevich in 1912.

GRIBOEDOV CANAL

This waterway was cut between 1764 and 1790 to avoid flooding. Hilarion Kutuzov, the father of Marshal Kutuzov, originally proposed this idea to Elizabeth I.

SINGER BUILDING (NO. 28)

The Singer Sewing Machine Company decided to build a ten-story building on this site and, despite the opposition of the municipality, constructed it in 1907 with a glass globe on its dome.

SINGER BUILDING (NO. 28)

GRIBOEDOV CANAL

The tomb of Marshal Kutuzov (1745–1813) is preserved in the cathedral.

ninety-six columns, forms one of St Petersburg's most majestic squares.

KAZAN SQUARE

The church of Kazan, with its semicircular colonnade of

CHURCH OF OUR LADY OF KAZAN

Designed by Voronikhin and built between 1801 and 1811, this church reflects both Russian and Western styles. While it respects the Orthodox canon of an altar facing east, its lateral colonnade (like that of St Peter's in Rome) is very striking. It was reinstated as a functioning church in 1999.

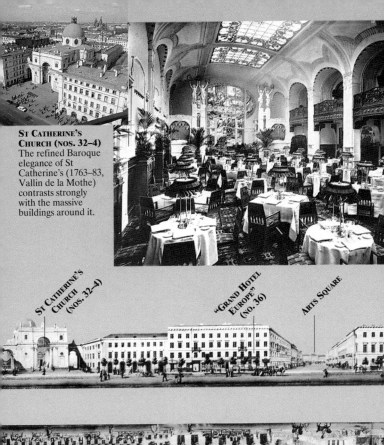

ST CATHERINE'S CHURCH (NOS. 32–4) The refined Baroque elegance of St Catherine's (1763–83, Vallin de la Mothe) contrasts strongly with the massive buildings around it.

ST CATHERINE'S CHURCH (NOS. 32–4)

"GRAND HOTEL EUROPE" (NO. 36)

ARTS SQUARE

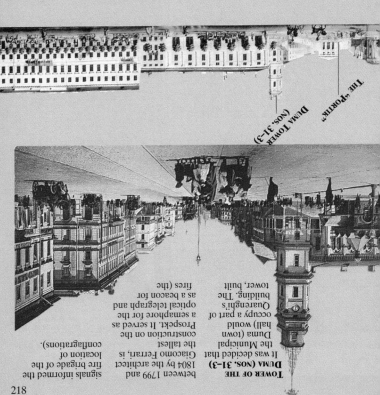

DUMA TOWER (NOS. 31–3)

THE "PORTIK"

TOWER OF THE DUMA (NOS. 31–3) It was decided that the Municipal Duma (town hall) would occupy a part of Quarenghi's building. The tower, built between 1799 and 1804 by the architect Giacomo Ferrari, is the tallest construction on the Prospekt. It served as a semaphore for the optical telegraph and as a beacon for fires (the signals informed the fire brigade of the location of conflagrations).

GRAND HOTEL EUROPE (NO. 36)

Beyond the Grand Hotel Europe, now restored by European investors to its pre-Revolutionary glory, cross Mikhailovskaya Street, to reach the Arts Square.

ARMENIAN CHURCH

This wonderful little church was built by Yury Velten in 1780 and restored between 1835 and 1837 by the architect A. Melnikov.

MEETING PLACE OF THE DECEMBRISTS (NO. 42)

The Decembrist Gavril Batenkov (1793–1863) lived at no. 42, where he entertained other conspirators such as Kondraty, Ryleyev, Trubetskoy and Bestuzhev (left).

ARMENIAN CHURCH

NO. 42

GOSTINY DVOR (NO. 35)

GOSTINY DVOR (NO. 35)

After a series of fires and lootings, the tradespeople of Nevsky Prospekt decided to finance the construction of a stone galleried market by Vallin de la Mothe. Behind these façades, which have a total length of more than half a mile, is the largest store in the city. Maintenance work on the gallery in 1965 brought to light over 300 lbs of gold hidden by merchants.

The "Port... This neoclassi... portico, the work... (1802–6), w... the architect Rus... restored in 19... Today it is a s... office for theater a... exhibition ticke...

THE "PASSAGE" (NO. 48)

This 180-yard gallery, built in 1846, was commissioned by Count Essen-Stenbock from the architect R. Zheliazevich as a site for shops, a concert hall and a *salon de thé*. The façade, which the tradesmen thought modest, was altered 1902 by the engineer Kozlov.

THE "PASSAGE" (NO. 48)

SADOVAYA STREET

SCHROEDER PIANO WORKS (NO.

ALTMAN– SHCHEDRIN LIBRARY (NO. 37)

A MAJOR RESERVE In addition to a large stock of French books (among them the 7,000 books of Voltaire's library) are a number of other treasures, notably rare 11th- and 12th-century manuscripts such as the *Ostromir Gospels* (1056), documents and autographs of Peter the Great and Mozart ▲ 231.

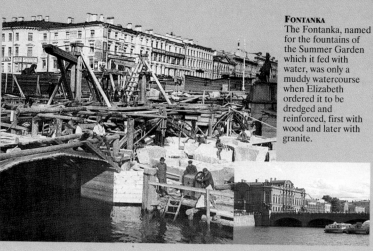

FONTANKA

The Fontanka, named for the fountains of the Summer Garden which it fed with water, was only a muddy watercourse when Elizabeth ordered it to be dredged and reinforced, first with wood and later with granite.

ANICHKOV BRIDGE

ANICHKOV PALACE (NO. 39)

"A PERPETUAL STREAM OF CARRIAGES GOES BY AT FULL SPEED, AND CROSSING THE PROSPEKT IS NO LESS PERILOUS AN UNDERTAKING THAN CUTTING OVER THE BOULEVARD FROM RUE DROUOT AND RUE DE RICHELIEU IN PARIS."

THÉOPHILE GAUTIER

THE HEIRS OF THE PIONEERS

After 1817 the Anichkov Palace became the residence of the heirs to the Russian throne. Alexander III liked it so much that he remained there after his coronation, filling the house with his art collections, which were later to be exhibited at the Russian Museum ▲ 225. In 1935 the Anichkov buildings became the Palace of the Pioneers, where the red-scarfed pioneers came to spend their free time.

223

1. ARTS SQUARE 2. STATUE OF PUSHKIN 3. BRODSKY MUSEUM 4. MUSSORGSKY THEATER 5. BENOIS PAVILION 6. MIKHAIL PALACE 7. ETHNOGRAPHIC MUSEUM 8. SHOSTAKOVICH PHILHARMONIA 9. CHURCH OF THE RESURRECTION 10. MIKHAILOVSKY GARDEN 11. ENGINEERS' CASTLE 12. STATUE OF PETER THE GREAT / 13. RUSSIAN MUSEUM (ENTRANCE)

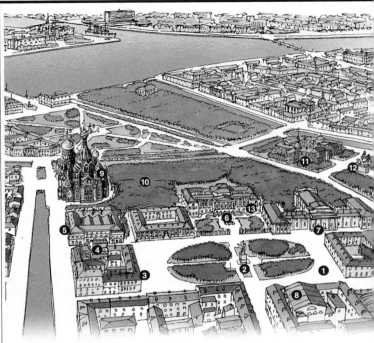

☑ **Half a day**

◆ **A-E**

STATUE OF PUSHKIN
Sculpted in 1957 by
Mikhail Anikushin,
the statue is the first
thing you see when
you arrive from the
Mikhail Street side.

T he former Mikhail Square thoroughly deserved its new
name of Arts Square (PL. ISKUSSTV; площадь Искусств)
since institutions of music, literature, painting and sculpture
are all concentrated here behind Carlo Rossi's façades, on a
site which was no more than a swamp at
the beginning of the 19th century. In the
center of the square is a statue of the
poet Pushkin ● *114*, whose imperious
gesture seems to invite you to begin
your visit on the left hand side of the
square.

BRODSKY MUSEUM

The painter Isaac Brodsky (1883–1939),
after whom Mikhail Street was named
during the Soviet era, lived between
1924 and 1939 at no. 3, which was a building constructed in
the early 19th century according to plans by Rossi. Those who
admire socialist realism will look for Brodsky's edifying
canvases, such as *Lenin's Speech at
the Putilov Factory Workers' Meeting*
(1929) and *Lenin at Smolny* (1930
▲ *248*. Others, however, may
prefer his comprehensive
collection of 19th- and 20th-
century paintings, which includes
works by Repin, Surikov and
Serov.

LITTLE THEATER OF OPERA AND BALLET

THE FORMER MIKHAILOVSKY THEATER

● 68. At no. 1 Arts Square is the old Mikhailovsky Theater (now called the Little Theater of Opera and Ballet, Maly Theater or Mussorgsky Theater), built by the architect Alexander Bryulov, partly to plans by Rossi, between 1831 and 1833. "Certain productions have their premieres in St Petersburg almost at the same time as in Paris. We may be forgiven a certain pride at seeing, some six or seven hundred leagues from Paris, at a latitude of sixty degrees, that our language is sufficiently widely spoken to maintain full houses in an exclusively French theater." Thus Théophile Gautier described the "French Theater of St Petersburg", as it was sometimes known at that time; it is now a mecca for ballets and musical productions.

RUSSIAN MUSEUM ★

MIKHAIL PALACE (RUSSKY MUZEY/MIKHAILOVSKY DVORETS; Михайловский дворец). The central building of the Russian Museum, with its Corinthian façade, was built between 1819 and 1825 for the Grand Duke Mikhail, brother of Alexander I, by Carlo Rossi. This architect, who laid out Mikhail Square in its entirety, also arranged the interior details of the palace. All that survives of this today is the vestibule and main staircase, along with the White Room (where visitors can see sculptures by Mikhail Kozlovsky, bas-reliefs by Stepan Pimenov and murals by Vighi).

FIRST RUSSIAN MUSEUM. In 1898 Nicholas II transformed the Palace into the Russian Museum of Alexander III, bringing in some of the paintings and art objects earlier assembled by his father at the Anichkov Palace ▲ 223. Works from private collections, from the Hermitage ▲ 168 and from the Fine Arts Academy ▲ 162 were added to these, leading to the construction of a west wing in the direction of the Griboedov Canal, by Leonty Benois, between 1914 and 1916. The nationalization of private property in 1917 also greatly enriched the museum.

✪ ARTS SQUARE
With three museums, two theaters and the Shostakovich Philharmonia building, Arts Square is an artistic hub. A café on the square, the Stray Dog (Brodiarchaya Sobaka), was popular in the 1910's with artists and writers like Vladimir Mayakovsky and Anna Akhamatova. Nearby, beside the Mikhailovsky Garden, is the art market, a picturesque place between four bridges.

Created by an *ukaze* of the Emperor Alexander III, the Russian Museum opened its doors on March 7, 1898 in Carlo Rossi's Mikhail Palace. Today it is one of the largest museums in the world, with reserves of over 380,000 paintings and *objets d'art*. The purpose of the museum is to exhibit Russian works of art that range in date from the 10th century to our own time; among them is an extraordinary collection of some six thousand icons.

"THE SWAN PRINCESS" (1900)
Superb and disquieting, *The Swan Princess* by Mikhail Vrubel (1856–1911) illustrate Pushkin's story *The Czar Saltan*

"EVGRAV DAVYDOV" (1809)
Since the creation of the Academy of Arts of St Petersburg the teaching reflected mainly French art. The Russia of the early 19th century did not escape the vogue for Romanticism, fueled by the patriotic war of 1812, as this portrait of Evgrav Davydov by Orest Kiprensky (1782–1836) shows.

"THE DINNER" (1902)
The collections of the museum reflect the artistic and cultural blossoming of Russia on the eve of the Revolution. One of the movements of the period, the World of Art, adopted an esthetic that was simultaneously predominant in Berlin, Vienna and Paris. Leon Bakst (1868–1924) went to the French capital; a lover of 18th-century painting and the poetry of the French Symbolists, he knew how to pay homage to them without compromising any of the essentially Russian character of his art.

"The Zaporozhian Cossacks Write a Letter to the Turkish Sultan", Ilya Repin (1891)
National traditions, historical episodes, legends and tales supplied many favorite themes of the 19th century.

"The Promenade" (1917)
Marc Chagall, who was initially influenced by the World of Art movement, later looked for a means of escape into the world of fantasy.

"Anna Yoannovna" (1741)
Artists whose destinies were closely linked to that of Russia were also represented: left, the Empress Anna Yoannovna and her servant, by Rastrelli.

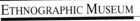

Details of the façade of the Church of the Resurrection, representing the arms of all the regions of Russia

ETHNOGRAPHIC MUSEUM

The Mikhail Palace is flanked, on its left, by a wing built (1900–11) by Vasily Svinin to house the ethnographic section of the Ethnographic Museum (MUZEY ETNOGRAFII; Государственный музей Этнографии). Founded in 1901, it was not opened to the public until 1923; it became a separate museum in its own right in 1934. The richness of its collection makes it far and away Russia's most important ethnographic museum. All the peoples of the former Soviet Union are represented: for example, Moldavians and Bielorussians, Azeris and Turkmens, Evenks and Nenets.

MARBLE HALL. The great entry hall of the museum is sumptuous: Svinin had its walls covered with delicate pink Carelian marble, while the sculptor Kharlamov executed a 300-foot frieze representing all the peoples of the former Russian Empire.

SHOSTAKOVICH PHILHARMONIA

The building constructed by Paul Jacot in 1839 for the Assembly of the Nobility was the scene of major concerts organized by the St Petersburg Philharmonic Society; here, in the Great Hall, Tchaikovsky, Berlioz and Wagner came to conduct their own works, and Isadora Duncan danced. After the Revolution the Great Hall and auditorium became the property of the Philharmonic Society (founded in 1921); a year after the death of Shostakovich (left) in 1976 it was renamed after him. The Philharmonia building projects into the ITALIANSKAYA with two further theaters, the MUSICAL COMEDY THEATER (no. 13) and the KOMISSARZHEVSKAYA THEATER (no. 19). The latter opened in October 1942, hence its nickname the "Blockade Theater".

THE "LENINGRADSKAYA". On the evening of August 9, 1942, the date that had been fixed by Hitler for the fall of Leningrad, the Philharmonia gave the city's first performance of Shostakovich's *Leningrad Symphony*, or *7th Symphony*, which was broadcast from the Great Hall by all the nation's radio stations. Some of the members of the orchestra were still in uniform, having been recalled from the front for the occasion. Others wore the traditional white tie and tails.

CHURCH OF THE RESURRECTION ★

THE NEO-RUSSIAN STYLE ● 89. The twisted onion domes, proliferating mosaics and asymmetry of the Church of the Resurrection (KHRAM VOSKRESENIY KHRISTOVA; храм Воскресения Христова) come as a surprise in this city known for its Baroque curves and classical rigor. The mosaics have just been restored and are magnificent.

Alfred Parland, who built the church (1883–1907), won the competition set up by Alexander III, which stipulated that it had to be in the "purely Russian style of the 17th century".

ENGINEERS' CASTLE ★

A walk through the MIKHAILOVSKY GARDEN will take you past the rear façade of the Mikhail Palace to the Engineers' Castle (INZHENERNY ZAMOK; Инженерный замок), which since 1991 has served as an annex of the Russian Museum ▲ 225.

STATUE OF PETER THE GREAT. Bartolomeo Carlo Rastrelli, the father of the architect, began this equestrian statue of Peter I while the Czar was still alive, and ultimately used his death-mask as a model. In 1800 Paul I placed the statue in front of the Castle's main entrance, with the inscription: "To the great-grandfather, the great-grandson."

MIKHAILOVSKY CASTLE. Paul I decided to build a secure fortress on the site of Empress Elizabeth's Summer Palace. The castle was inaugurated on November 8, 1800, St Mikhail's Day in the Orthodox calendar. The name Mikhailovsky, contrary to that of Arts Square or the Russian Museum, has nothing to do with the Grand Duke Mikhail; instead it refers to the Archangel Mikhail, who, according to Paul I, appeared and commanded him to build a chapel bearing his name on his site. This inspiration, which obliged the architect Brennan to design each of his four façades completely differently, did not mitigate the castle's frowning, military aspect.

SCHOOL OF ENGINEERING. Alexander I abandoned the castle, with its sinister associations. It later became the barracks of a squadron of the Imperial Guard, the headquarters of an institute for the blind, and the Chancellery of the Ministry of Instruction and Religious Affairs. In 1822 the Military Engineering School moved here, and it assumed the name of Engineers' Castle. Fyodor Dostoevsky ▲ 207 was a student at the school in 1838, occupying a corner room on the third floor overlooking the Fontanka, where he liked to read and work.

229

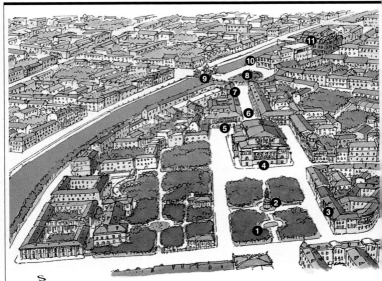

⏱ **Three hours**

◆ **A–E**

"If God did not exist, it would be necessary to invent him." One of the famous Voltaire manuscripts in the Public Library.

OSTROVSKY SQUARE (PL. OSTROVSKOVO; площадь Островского) is bordered on one side by Rossi's Saltykov-Shchedrin Library ▲ *221*, and on the other by the pavilions of the Anichkov Palace ▲ *223* and its gardens. This square, even more than Arts Square, is an example of the architectural ensemble of balanced proportions and restrained ornamentation for which Carlo Rossi was famous ▲ *181*. It formerly bore the name of the wife of Nicholas I, Alexandra; in 1923 this was changed in honor of the celebrated Russian dramatist Alexander Ostrovsky, whose most famous works were *Poverty No Vice* (1854), *The Storm* (1860) and *Snegurochka* (1873), which had been performed at the Alexandrinsky Theater.

CATHERINE II SQUARE

STATUE OF THE EMPRESS. This massive monument (over 40 feet tall) standing in the center of the square was sculpted in 1873 by Matvei Chizhov and Alexander Opekuchin, after a project by Mikhail Mikeshin. Catherine the Great is shown in her state robes, while around the plinth cluster sundry personalities of the period: the officers Suvorov ▲ *252*, Rumantsev, Orlov ▲ *184* and Chichagov, the statesmen Potemkin ▲ *251*, Bezborodko and Betskoy, the poet Derzhavin and Princess Dashkova, President of the Academy of Sciences.

ALEXANDRINSKY THEATER ★

Known as the Pushkin Theater during the Soviet era, the Alexandrinsky Theater (ALEXANDRINSKY THEATR; Александринский

earp) was built in 1832, to a project by Carlo Rossi in
the Russian classical style ● *86*. It was named in honor
of the Empress Alexandra Fyodorovna. The troupe at
this theater, one of the oldest in Russia, was founded
in 1756 during the reign of Elizabeth I ● *36*. In 1836 it
staged the first production of Nikolai Gogol's
The Government Inspector.

RUSSIAN DRAMA. The history and development of theatrical
genres in Russia (classicism, Romanticism, Realism) are
linked to the evolution of this theater, which became the
de facto national dramatic academy. The repertoire during
the second half of the 18th century included the works of
Russian authors such as Alexander Sumarokov, Iakov

Kniazhnin, Vasily Kapnist and Ivan Krylov, as
well as Western European masters, such as
the French playwrights Corneille, Racine,
Molière and Beaumarchais. At the dawn of
the 20th century the Imperial Alexandrinsky
Theater turned to the new drama of Anton
Chekhov, whose *Seagull* flopped badly
in 1896. After the 1917 Revolution
the theater actively promoted new
Soviet-style plays, and today it remains
one of the most popular with the
St Petersburg public. Its repertoire
is a blend of Russian and Western
classics, along with contemporary
plays. The leading actors of the
decades between 1950 and 1980 used
the title of "Artists of the People of
the USSR".

**ORIENTAL
MANUSCRIPTS**
The Saltykov-
Shchedrin
Library has,
among its
oriental treasures,
this manuscript of
the Hindu poem, the
Bhagavad-Gita.

THEATER MUSEUM ★

This museum, founded in 1918, was established on
the premises of the former Management of the Imperial
Theaters of Russia. Its collections were assembled from
the imperial archives and from the private collections of
people connected with the
theater; today the Theater
Museum includes many items, all
of which are on display, which
document 250 years of Russian
music and theater.

Another special jewel of the Theater Museum is its collection of ballet shoes, which gives an idea of the technical evolution of the ballerina's art.

COLLECTIONS. The museum also displays the personal archives of Marius Petipa, Maria Savina and Fyodor Shalyapin (including the jeweled robe that he wore as Boris Godunov), along with the autographed musical scores of Nikolai Rimsky-Korsakov, letters of Piotr Tchaikovsky and projects for costumes and décors of many different periods throughout the history of Russian theatrical production. The museum's collection of costumes is one of the world's largest, and includes, among others, those of SLEEPING BEAUTY (1890).

FOR MUSIC LOVERS. In the evenings people crowd into the museum's small concert hall. The piano on which Tchaikovsky once played bursts into sound; recordings of former stars are played; contemporary artists perform, and videos of the greatest ballets and operas are screened.

5. ACTORS' HOUSE 6. "NEVSKY PALACE" 7. SAMOJLOV MUSEUM 8. MUSEUM OF THE ARCTIC AND ANTARCTIC 9. MARATA STREET 10. DOSTOEVSKY MUSEUM 11. VLADIMIR CHURCH 12. VLADIMIR SQUARE 13. FOUNTAINS HOUSE 14. HOUSE OF LETTERS 15. FONTANKA 16. BELOSELSKY-BELOZERSKY PALACE

NEVSKY PROSPEKT

AKHMATOVA MUSEUM. (MUZEY ANNY AKHMATOVOI; музей Анны Ахматовой). The poet Anna Akhmatova lived from 1924 to 1952 in the apartment on the third floor of the south wing, overlooking the courtyard. During the 1920's this place was frequented by poets, painters and writers, among them Mayakovsky, Tatlin, Lebeder and Tyrssa. Akhmatova's rooms were made into a museum in 1989; one of them has been redecorated to look as it would have appeared between 1938 and 1941. Here Akhmatova's husband and later her son were arrested. In the other room a display of her poetry explains how she won so important a place in the history of Russian society, culture and literature between 1910 and 1960. There is also a portrait of the poet by Modigliani, executed during a visit to Paris in 1911.

HOUSE OF LETTERS

The house that was situated at the intersection of Nevsky Prospekt and the Fontanka Embankment (nos. 40–60) was entirely destroyed during the siege of World War Two ● *50* but subsequently rebuilt. The critic Vissarion Bielinsky lived here from 1842, in what was known during the 19th century as the "House of Letters". Bielinsky was an influential journalist, and had a powerful effect on the younger generation of writers. He gathered around him a circle of Russia's intellectual avant-garde which included the writers Nekrasov, Turgenev, Grigorovich and Dostoevsky. Today the house is used by the regional tax office.

VISSARION BIELINSKY (1811–48)
Bielinsky's ideas about the condition of the people and the role of Russian writers are expressed in his letter to Gogol, which was clandestinely circulated among the intelligentsia. Dostoevsky spent four years in a labor camp and six years in exile in Siberia, partly because he had read this letter.

237

BELOSELSKY-BELOZERSKY PALACE

The house of Prince Shakhovskoy was bought in the mid-18th century by Myatlev, the head of the Assignat bank. It was subsequently altered by the classical architect Thomas de Thomon and became the palace of Prince Beloselsky-Belozersky. The new owners were wealthy and famous, members of a family that dated back to Vladimir Monomachus, the Kievan Grand Duke. Their double-barreled name originated in 1798, when Paul I gave Beloselsky the right to use the name of Belozersky, in recognition of his ancestors' services to Russia. The palace was rebuilt between 1846 and 1848 by the architect Shtakenshneider. From 1898 to 1917 it belonged to the imperial family; one of its last owners was the son of Alexander II, Prince Sergei Alexandrovich.

MUNICIPAL CULTURE CENTER AND MUSEUM
After the Revolution the Beloselsky Palace was occupied by the Communist Party's regional committee. Today it is the Municipal Culture Center. The Hall of Mirrors and the Oak Room are used for plays and concerts, while other rooms provide exhibition areas. The palace also houses the Museum of the Development of Russian Democracy, which is named after Anatoli Sobtchak, the first mayor of the city following the Soviet period.

VLADIMIR SQUARE
Vladimir Prospekt leads to the square of the same name, whose buildings form a circle around the Vladimir Church (dedicated to the Virgin and Saint John of Damascus).

VLADIMIR PROSPEKT

LITTLE (MALY) DRAMATIC THEATER ● *69*. At no. 18, on the corner of Rubinstein and Count streets, is the Little Dramatic Theater (MALY DRAMATICHESKY TEATR; Малый драматичесий театр). Since its creation in 1944, it has gained worldwide fame under the direction of Lev Dodin.
LENSOVIET THEATER (LENSOVETA TEATR; Леисовета театр). This single-story building (no. 12) has a striking façade with an eight-column portico, Ionic pilasters and masks. It was built in the 1820s by the architect Mikhailov as a wealthy mansion for the Korsakov family. After the Revolution it was occupied by a number of different theatrical institutions. Today it is once again known by its original name, the Lensoviet Theater, and is under the direction of Vladimir Paze.

VLADIMIR SQUARE (VLADIMIRSKAYA PL.; Владимирская пл).

The first church in the center of this square was built in 1747 and replaced in 1761 by a stone building. Its anonymous architect may have been Trezzini, who worked under Rastrelli. In 1783 a two-story bell tower was erected alongside the chirch by Quarenghi; in 1848 the architect Ruska added two further stories. Closed since 1932, the Vladimir Church has been reopened by the Russian Orthodox authorities.

RIMSKY-KORSAKOV MUSEUM

The famous composer Rimsky-Korsakov lived for the last teen years of his life at no. 28 Zagorodny Prospekt. In 1971 his apartment was transformed into a museum (MUZEY-KVARTIRA RIMSKOVO-KORSAKOVA; музей-квартира Римского-Корсакова). The vestibule, study, salon and dining room here recreate the atmosphere of what was one of the centers of St Petersburg culture, where Rimsky-Korsakov held his musical enings, the "Korsakov Wednesdays". Glazunov, Lyadov, Rachmaninov, Taneyev and Shalyapin all attended these events. Today an entire room is devoted to musical life in St Petersburg in the late 19th and early 20th centuries, and every Wednesday meetings of singers and musicians are once more held in the concert room. In this apartment Rimsky-Korsakov wrote over forty romances, as well as his *Principles of Orchestration*, *Chronicle of My Musical Life* and the operas *Sadko*, *Czar Saltan*, *The Czar's Bethrothed* and *Kashchey the Immortal*.

"LOUSE EXCHANGE"
The intersection of Nevsky Prospekt, Vladimir Prospekt and Liteiny Prospekt used to be known as the "Louse Exchange"; porters and craftsmen looking for work used to gather here, along with itinerant barbers who sat their clients on stools to cut their hair.

RIMSKY-KORSAKOV (1844–1908) ● 72
The composer's name is closely linked with the Conservatoire, where he taught the composition class.

DOSTOEVSKY MUSEUM ★

This museum (MUZEY-KVARTIRA F.M. DOSTOYEVSKOVO; музей-квартира Ф. М. Достоевского) was opened in 1971, ninety years after the death of Dostoevsky ▲ 206. The apartment had to be reconstituted, but its atmosphere remains faithful to the personality of the master and to the spirit of his time.

A WRITER'S PRIVACY. Dostoevsky lived in this apartment on two occasions (for a few months in 1846, and during the last years of his life) with his wife Anna Grigorievna and their two children, Lyuba and Fedya. Here he wrote his celebrated *Discourse on Pushkin*, as well as *The Brothers Karamazov*. Dostoevsky liked his study (above) because it was spacious and isolated from the rest of the apartment. The place was austere and ascetic. Above the sofa on which he slept is a reproduction of Raphael's *Virgin of Saint Sixtus*, a painting he especially loved. Beyond the windows are the domes of the Vladimir Church, of which he was a parishioner. The streets and the passers-by in this district still compose the same ". . . inexhaustible, magnificent almanac, which one can leaf through in one's spare moments, when one is bored, after a meal . . .".

MARATA STREET

MUSEUM OF THE ARCTIC AND ANTARCTIC (MUZEY ARKTIKI I ANTARKTIKI; музей Арктики и Антарктики). The former St Nicholas Church is the only building of the United Schismatics (a branch of the Old Believers ● 56) which remains intact at St Petersburg; it was closed in 1932 to make way, in 1937, for the Museum of the Arctic and Antarctic, which houses, among other exhibits, stuffed polar wildlife and items from expeditions. Today there is a project to return the church to the Old Believers and move the museum elsewhere.

NEVSKY PROSPEKT

On the section of Nevsky Prospekt between Liteiny and Vladimir prospekts and Marata Street is a series of apartment blocks dating from the second half of the 19th century and early 20th century. At no. 60 lived the satirical writer Mikhail Saltykov-Shchedrin ▲ 221; in 1815 Vladimir Zhukovsky, the translator of English, French and German poetry, lived at no. 82.

RADISHCHEV (1749–1802)
This celebrated writer, the first thoroughgoing Russian dissident, lived at no. 14 Marata Street from 1775 to 1790. He was arrested, imprisoned at the Peter and Paul Fortress, and sent to Siberia on the orders of Catherine II for his revolutionary *Journey from Petersburg to Moscow*. Freed in 1796 by Paul I, he was amnestied in 1801 by Alexander I, but killed himself in 1802.

ACTORS' HOUSE. This building (no. 86), with its white-columned portico, is known in St Petersburg as the Actors' House. It unites several theatrical associations, such as the Union of Theater Workers, the Russian Theater Society and the Stanislavsky Palace of the Arts. Built in the 18th century as a private mansion, then reconstructed between 1820 and 1830 by the architects Ovsianikov and Fossati, it belonged in the 19th century to the Yusupov family, who organized concerts and exhibitions there. Today the Actors' House still mounts soirées, seminars, conferences, and exhibitions of theater décor as well as international festivals and competitions.

"NEVSKY PALACE". No. 57, opposite the Actors' House, was built in 1861 by the architect Langé and belonged to the craft school of Czarevich Nicholas ● *36*. It was formerly the Renommée Hotel, which rented furnished rooms, before it became the Hermès and finally the Baltic Hotel at the end of World War Two. It was restored in 1993, and is today a luxury establishment.

SAMOILOV MUSEUM. In the same block as the Nevsky Palace, on the Groom Street side, is the Samoilov family museum which was opened 1994. From 1869 onward a number of famous actors, composers, painters and writers frequented this house.

PUSHKIN STREET

On a square halfway down Pushkin Street (PUSHKINSKAYA UL.; Пушкинская ул.) is a statue of the writer, which was the first to be erected to him in St Petersburg. It is the work of the sculptor Opekushin, who was also responsible for the Moscow statue of Pushkin (1880), this monument was unveiled in 1884.

NO. 10 PUSHKIN STREET. Today a number of artists inhabit this derelict house. As representatives of alternative culture in St Petersburg they organize exhibitions, entertainments and concerts in the courtyards of the building and in the street outside. The creative drive behind this unusual center is currently a popular phenomenon in St Petersburg.

VASILY SAMOILOV MUSEUM
This establishment pays homage to Vasily Samoilov, an actor at the Alexandrinsky Theater, where he played more than fifty different roles. His personal effects are displayed in the main rooms, along with 19th- and 20th-century theatrical mementos and the interior of one of the imperial boxes. Costumes made in the workshops of the imperial theaters are also exhibited, on Yves Saint-Laurent dummies, from the *200 Years of the Ballets Russes* exhibition at the Paris Opera.

MUSEUM OF THE ARCTIC AND ANTARCTIC
This museum contains several sections (The Nature of the Arctic, History of Polar Scientific Expeditions, Economy and Art of the Nordic Peoples). One of its major curiosities is a 1930 three-seater amphibious plane, which hangs above the entrance.

The first Russian production company was founded in 1907. St Petersburg at that time appears (with the help of Czarist censors) as a 19th-century city, a sumptuous décor perfect for adaptations such as *The Queen of Spades* (1916) by Iakov Protazanov, the greatest director of the early Russian cinema.

Max Linder, immensely popular in Russia, came to St Petersburg in 1913. The public flocked to see his movie, which ended with a ballooning scene. Then the theater lights came on, and Linder himself appeared on the end of a rope, as if he had come in through the roof.

St Petersburg's first movie theater was established on the Nevsky Prospekt, on the initiative of the Lumière brother. Although Moscow was the cinematic capital for Russia under the Czars, St Petersburg was an inspiration to a number of directors and developed a distinct cinema tradition of its own. Today directors no longer seem threatened by censors, but the new economic situation of the Russian cinema is making movie production extraordinarily difficult.

АКВАРІУМЪ

4-го Мая 1896 года

Внимаше! Откр

Съ 4 Мая и ежед. первый разъ въ Росс
Живая фотографія Синемотографъ-
Мізрь последнія чудеса науки.
Завтра, въ Воскресенье, 5 Мая, выходъ
вая ФОТОГРАФІЯ последнія чудеса на

Certain Soviet directors rapidly established their "Leningrad" credentials, notably Kozintsev and Trauberg. Ermler (with Johanson) was mainly concerned to film a city transformed by socialism (*Ruins of Empire*, 1929).

This was held on May 4, 1896 at the Aquarium Theater, and was organized by the Lumière brothers.

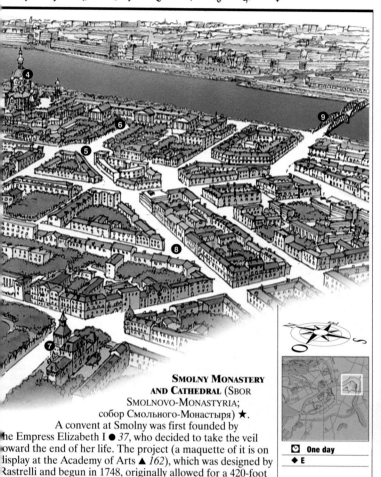

SMOLNY MONASTERY AND CATHEDRAL (SBOR SMOLNOVO-MONASTYRIA; собор Смольного-Монастыря) ★.

A convent at Smolny was first founded by the Empress Elizabeth I ● 37, who decided to take the veil toward the end of her life. The project (a maquette of it is on display at the Academy of Arts ▲ 162), which was designed by Rastrelli and begun in 1748, originally allowed for a 420-foot bell tower. Catherine II, once she was on the throne, sacked the Italian architect in 1764 and founded a school for young ladies in the convent.

🕓 **One day**

◆ **E**

A LAVISH CATHEDRAL ● 85
The cathedral as completed by Vasily Stasov in 1835 preserves the style of Rastrelli, in which the ornamental exuberance of Baroque includes purely Russian elements such as the five onion domes.

247

▲ Lenin and the Revolution

For taking part in an illegal political meeting the seventeen-year-old student Vladimir Ilyich Ulyanov was arrested, banned from the University and exiled to a distant village in Kazan. Thus began Lenin's life as a dedicated revolutionary. By 1916 he was living in Zurich and had despaired of any revolution in his lifetime; the spontaneous rising of the Russian masses in October 1917 came as a total surprise to him.

A CLANDESTINE EXISTENCE
Lenin lived clandestinely in St Petersburg during the 1905–7 Revolution ● 44 and in the same city (by then named Petrograd) under the Kerensky regime from July 5 to October 25, 1917. Left, Lenin disguised as a worker, under the name of K. Ivanov.

APRIL 1917
Lenin outlined his program at the Tauride Palace in April 1917. He declared the "Tasks of the Proletariat" to be of the utmost urgency; and to the astonishment of his listeners he proposed an immediate end to the war, the overthrow of the government, and the handing over of all political power to the soviets.

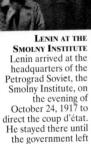

LENIN AT THE SMOLNY INSTITUTE
Lenin arrived at the headquarters of the Petrograd Soviet, the Smolny Institute, on the evening of October 24, 1917 to direct the coup d'état. He stayed there until the government left for Moscow on March 11, 1918. He ran the Council of People's Commissars within the Palace, wrote, and received delegations and journalists; among the latter was J. Reed, author of a celebrated account of the October Revolution, *Ten Days that Shook the World*.

POWER TO THE BOLSHEVIKS

On October 25, 1917, at 10.40pm, even as the attack on the Winter Palace ● *44* was under way, the Second Pan-Russian Congress of Soviets opened at Smolny. The Mensheviks and right-wing Socialist Revolutionaries disapproved of Lenin's coup d'état. They proposed to open talks with the Provisional Government, with a view to setting up a democracy. After a short, violent debate they walked out in a body, abandoning the field to the Bolsheviks.

BACK IN PETROGRAD

In July 1920 Lenin took part in the Second Congress of the Komintern at the Tauride Palace. The same month he sent a message to Stalin, then fighting at Kharkov:

"The situation in the Komintern is excellent. Zinoviev, Bukharin and I believe that we should immediately encourage the Revolution in Italy. In my view, we should first Sovietize Hungary and perhaps the Czech state and Romania. This requires mature consideration. Let us know your conclusion."

LENIN'S TRAGEDY

On May 25, 1922 Lenin fell ill, with a paralyzed right arm and leg and acute aphasia. He returned to work in October, but by December was once more confined to his bed. His health declined progressively thereafter, and he was cut off from the levers of power within the Kremlin.

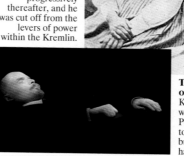

THE DEIFICATION OF LENIN

Krupskaya, Lenin's wife, entreated the Politburo in vain not to embalm his body but to bury it as he had wished.

NIKOLAI KARAMZIN (1766–1826)
The great historian and writer Nikolai Karamzin spent the final years of his life at the Tauride Palace.

THE FIRST KUNSTKAMMER
After Kikin's death his palace was used for the Kunstkammer, Peter the Great's assemblage of curiosities. Here was displayed a collection bought from the Dutch anatomist Frederik Ruysch (1717), a specialist in embalming. In 1727 the Kunstkammer was transferred to Vasilyevsky Island ▲ *160*.

SMOLNY INSTITUTE (SMOLNY INSTITUT; Смольный институт) ★. This long neoclassical building, built by Quarenghi in 1806–8, was a school for young ladies until August 1917, at which time the Soviet of Workers' and Soldiers' Deputies of Petrograd ● *46* was installed there. On October 24, 1917, in the evening, Lenin arrived to seize control of the insurrection. The long corridors of the Institute swarmed with Red Guards, soldiers, sailors and factory delegates seeking weapons, tracts or newspapers. On October 25, while the fighting was still going on, the Second Pan-Russian Congress of Soviets opened, at 10.40pm in the Lecture Hall. At 3.10am the delegates greeted the news of the fall of the Winter Palace with wild cheering. That evening they ratified the decrees proposed by Lenin on peace and land ownership, as well as on the formation of the Council of People's Commissars. The Council, headed by Lenin, operated from Smolny until it was moved to Moscow in March 1918. Since 1991 the Institute has housed the offices of the Mayor of St Petersburg, but the historic Lecture Hall, Lenin's study and the bedroom he occupied with his wife, Nadezhda Krupskaya, now form part of the SMOLNY MEMORIAL MUSEUM. There is also a permanent exhibition about the Institute as it was at the time of Catherine II.

KIKIN PALACE

At the Stavropol intersection stands one of the oldest buildings in St Petersburg, the palace of the Boyar Alexander Kikin. Kikin was an opponent of Peter the Great's policies who supported the Czarevich Alexei in his doomed attempt to overthrow the Emperor ● *39*. After fleeing to Austria on the advice of Kikin the Czarevich returned to Russia in January 1718 and was condemned to death a few months later. Most of the people he denounced as his accomplices, among them Kikin, were executed. Nowadays the Kikin Palace building houses a music school.

"Stand up straight and speak French!" was the admonishment given to the six- to eighteen-year-old pupils at the Smolny Institute. Here the young ladies were taught such subjects as religion, languages, arithmetic, drawing, dancing, sewing and good manners.

TAURIDE PALACE

Nearby, on the left-hand side of Shpalernaya Street, runs the 760-foot yellow façade of the Tauride Palace (TAVRICHESKY DVORETS; Таврический дворец), which has a stark Doric pediment crowned by a green dome. Constructed between 1783 and 1789, this was one of the first classical buildings in Russia ● 86.

POTEMKIN'S REWARD. Catherine II was much given to showering palaces on her favorite, Prince Potemkin. After presenting him with the Anichkov Palace ▲ 222 she had the Tauride Palace built for him, modeled on the Pantheon in Rome. Scarcely was it finished than she offered to buy it back for 460,000 roubles; Potemkin, a notorious spendthrift, was always heavily in debt and needed the money. In February 1791, on his return from Iasi, the former capital of Moldavia, where he had negotiated an advantageous peace with the Turks, Catherine gave the palace to Potemkin a second time. He used it to throw parties of legendary extravagance.

OTHER OCCUPANTS. After Prince Potemkin's death the Tauride in 1792 was decreed an imperial palace. When the Empress died Paul I revenged himself on his mother and her favorite by stripping the place bare and converting it into a

POTEMKIN, PRINCE OF THE TAURIDE
The Greeks called the Crimea the Tauride; they believed that its barbarian inhabitants were in the habit of burning foreigners on sight (Euripides states this categorically in his *Iphigenia*). When the Crimea was annexed to Russia in 1783 it reverted to its original name; and Potemkin, who led the campaign against the Ottomans, was named Prince of the Tauride by Catherine II. His palace, built at this time, was given the same name.

A MAJESTIC FAÇADE
The stylistic restraint shown by the architect Starov in his design for the palace provoked the enthusiasm of poet Gavril Derzhavin: "Its exterior is distinguished neither for its sculptures, nor its gilding ... old-fashioned, elegant good taste is the true source of its dignity and majesty."

barracks. The Column Room was converted into a stable, and its furnishings and works of art were moved to the Mikhail Castle ▲ 229. Alexander I had the palace restored by Luigi Rusca (1802–4).

FROM THE DUMA TO THE SOVIETS. After the February Revolution ● 46 the left wing of the palace was occupied by the Soviet of the Workers and Soldiers of Petrograd, while the right wing was used by the Committee of the Duma, which formed the Provisional Government. The Tauride Palace was later used as the Leningrad Higher Party School before becoming the seat of the Assembly of the CIS.

TAURIDE GARDENS. (TAURICHESKI SAD; Таврический сад). Although probably not as luxuriant today as in Potemkin's time these gardens are still a pleasant place to walk. In winter its avenues are used by cross-country skiers.

WATER MUSEUM
Situated opposite the Tauride Palace is an old water tower, dating from the 19th century. Since 2003, it has housed a water museum.

SUVOROV MUSEUM

The popularity of Field Marshal Alexander Suvorov made possible a nationwide subscription toward the Suvorov Military History Museum (Voenna-Istorichesky Muzey Suvorova/военно-исторический музей А. В. Суворова). In 1904 the architects Guerman Grimm and Alexander Gogen completed this building, with its enormous panels of mosaic illustrating the principal events in Suvorov's life. Inside, a selection of the general's possessions is on display, together with maps, weapons and various other items that have survived from his campaigns.

TOWARD THE MONASTERY

SUVOROV AVENUE (SUVOROVSKY PROSPEKT; Суворовский проспект). This broad thoroughfare, which leads to the Smolny District, used to be known as Elephant Avenue. In the early 18th century the Persian shahs were in the habit of sending elephants as gifts to the Russian emperors (indeed, in 1741 Nadir Shah gave a total of fourteen elephants). One of the special stables constructed for these somewhat cumbersome offerings stood by the side of today's Suvorov Avenue; it was by this route that the elephants would travel on their way to drink from the waters of the river Neva.

NEVSKY PROSPEKT. The section of the Nevsky Prospekt ▲ 212 which leads to the Alexander Nevsky Monastery was built shortly after the foundation of the monastery; the idea behind its construction was to give the monks access to the road to Novgorod, where the metropolitan resided. Close by what has now become Insurrection Square ▲ 244 the monks' route joined with the road linking the dockyards of the Admiralty to this same Novgorod road. It was during the reign of Anna Ivanovna – in fact on April 20, 1738 – that it was finally decreed that "the great thoroughfare from the Admiralty to the Nevsky Monastery should be called the Nevsky Prospekt".

ALEXANDER SUVOROV (1729–1800)
Alexander Suvorov was born in Moscow. His father was a general who had fought with Peter the Great. During the Russo-Turkish War (1787–91) Catherine II conferred on him the rank of Field Marshal after he crushed the Polish uprising (1794).

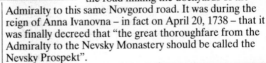

ALEXANDER NEVSKY
Prince Alexander Novgorod was given this sobriquet after he won the 1240 battle by the Neva.

GREAT PALACE ★

As we see it now the Great Palace (BOLSHOY DVORETS; Большой дворец) still has the exterior planned by the Empress Elizabeth I ● 37. After 1745 she had the initial building altered by the architect Bartolomeo Rastrelli ● 84, who, after enlarging Peter I's original palace, added to it a couple of single-floor galleries, each ending with a pavilion (a church on the east side and an armorial pavilion of the west side). He also surrounded the Upper Park with a long railing punctuated by broad pillars, later designing a formal enfilade in the purest Baroque style.

FORMAL STAIRCASE. The stairway to the second floor is typical of the Russian Baroque period. Its décor, designed by Rastrelli in about 1750, combines richly carved and gilded elements in wood (mostly limewood) with numerous trompe-l'oeil features.

CHESME HALL. Contiguous with the ballroom is a large space dedicated to the naval victory of Chesme (1770); this was altered by Yury Velten ● 86 to house major commemorative paintings by Hackert (1737–1807).

THRONE ROOM. In the Throne Room, alongside portraits of Russian sovereigns, is a canvas by the Danish painter Vigilius Erichsen of Catherine II on her horse Brilliant. There are also four pictures of the Battle of Chesme by Joseph Wright of Derby. The Audience Chamber, with its décor by Rastrelli, offers an interesting collection of Russian marquetry gaming tables which date from the latter part of the 18th century.

WHITE DINING ROOM ★. The table set in the White Dining Room, whose neoclassical décor was redesigned by Velten toward 1775, displays a complete set of Wedgwood china delivered from England in 1768.

BAROQUE STAIRCASE
The grand staircase was entirely restored in 1985.

CHINESE ROOMS. On either side of the Portrait Hall are extravagant Chinese Rooms decorated by Vallin de la Mothe with walls set with lacquer screens and exotic marquetry floors.

LAVISH STUCCO
The walls of the White Dining Room are decorated with white stucco bas-reliefs.

FOUNTAINS AT PETERHOF

The wide variety of fountains at Peterhof is the principal feature of the park. Elsewhere (notably at Versailles) all the surviving fountains are classical in design; not so at Peterhof, where their extravagance and sheer playfulness give us a vivid idea of the atmosphere that must have reigned in a park of this kind during the early 18th century. The Great Cascade, with its Samson Fountain, is the most impressive of all.

FESTIVALS AT PETERHOF ✪
The Baroque masterpiece of Peterhof is now a site for several festivals, the most popular of which are those marking the opening and closing of the fountains (in May and October respectively). Cultural events held between these two festivals include the music festival (June) and the festival of the city of Peterhof (July).

GREAT CASCADE
On the slope between the upper and lower terraces, the Great Cascade is a major feature of Peterhof. The statue of *Samson and the Lion* symbolizes the Russian victory over the Swedes at Poltava (1709).

MARLY CASCADE
▲ *260*. Also called the "Golden Mountain", the Marly Cascade is made of white marble and plaques of gilded copper, which cover its successive levels.

CHECKERBOARD CASCADE
The water spouts from the jaws of fierce dragons above giant sloping checkerboards.

THE SUN
The perpetually spinning sun and its silvery rays.

ROMAN FOUNTAINS
Erected in 1739 at the foot of the Checkerboard Cascade, these statues are reminiscent of those by the fountains of St Peter's in Rome. They were reconstituted in 1792; gilded bronze masks spout water from their plinths.

PORTRAIT HALL. In 1764 the Portrait Hall in the central part of the Palace was decorated by the architect Vallin de la Mothe ● 86 with a rare ensemble of 368 portraits of women painted by Count Pietro Rotari.

PARTRIDGE ROOM. The adjoining Partridge Room takes its name from its partridge-design hangings. These hangings were woven in Lyons, France, after cartoons by Philippe de la Salle.

DIVAN ROOM. This room has walls covered with Chinese silk, and contains an enormous sofa framed by a balustrade in the Turkish manner.

CROWN ROOM. The Crown Room is also covered in 17th-century Chinese silk. During the 18th century the imperial crown was kept in this room when the Court was residing at Peterhof.

OAK STUDY
This room, with its carved oak boiseries after drawings by Nicolas Pineau (1684–1754), contains assorted personal possessions of Peter I.

LOWER PARK

LOWER PARK (NIZHNY PARK; Нижний парк) was originally planted with lime trees, oaks, elms and maples from Holland, Germany, Estonia and the regions of Moscow and Novgorod. The geometrical parterres are crowded with the sculptures and fountains that were at that time deemed to be the essential features of any princely park. At the ends of the domain's various prospects there are pavilions designed for the pleasures of the Russian sovereigns and their courtiers.

HERMITAGE PAVILION (PAVILION ERMITAZH; павильон Эрмитаж). In the main room of the Hermitage Pavilion, used for dining, there is a mechanism that lifts the central section of the table, loaded with the dishes ordered by guests, from the first floor straight to the second floor.

MARLY PALACE (DVORETS MARLY; дворец Марли). Marly Palace, a favorite of Peter the Great, is furnished according to his own simple taste.

MONPLAISIR ★ (MONPLEZIR; Монплезир). In 1714, work began on the construction of a small palace the far end of the Lower Park. It was named Monplaisir after the French palace on which it was based. Monplaisir's paintings gallery, which has a ceiling decorated to a design by Philippe Pillement (1684–1730), contains a collection of Dutch and Flemish pictures of battle scenes. In 2001, some of the

A SEA VIEW
Monplaisir, on the seafront, was a favorite with Peter the Great, who liked to spend several months a year there. William Coxe, visiting the palace in 1784, wrote: "We can form an idea of the austere simplicity in which this sovereign was accustomed to live . . .".

BENOIS MUSEUM
East of the Palace are former court buildings which now contain a museum dedicated to the Benois family ● *104*.

MONPLAISIR
In 1723 the Marquis de Campredon gave this report to Louis XV: "One enters the house by way of a remarkably well-kept garden. It is square in shape, with double banks of greenery on either side, contiguous to the rooms, in which one can walk unseen . . . lulled by the sound of the great fountain in the garden."

palace's attractive buildings, including the imperial baths and the Chinese garden around them, were opened to the public.
CATHERINE WING (EKATERININSKY KORPUS; Екатерининский корпус). In the Catherine Wing, added to Monplaisir in the 1740's, a remarkable china service , made at the imperial St Petersburg works between 1809 and 1817, is on display. It is known as the Guriev Service, after the director of the factory. The gilded chandeliers in the Yellow Salon, of pasteboard and carved wood, are remarkable for their quality.

ALEXANDRIA PARK

IMPERIAL STABLES (TSARSKIE KONIUSHNI; Царские конюшни). Beyond the Benois Museum stand the extensive imperial stables (which are now a rest home and closed to the public). They are the work of the architect Nikolai Benois (1856–1928) and their extraordinary neo-Gothic style bears witness to the

Nicholas I's study.

Czar Nicholas I's pronounced taste for this style.
GOTHIC CHAPEL (KAPELLA; капелла). By continuing toward the east through the gates of the Alexandria Park you will reach the imperial family's private oratory, a Gothic chapel built (1831–3) to a design by the Berlin architect Karl Schinkel (1781–1841).
COTTAGE (KOTTEDZH; Коттедж)★. You can reach this small pavilion (right) either by walking through Alexandria Park or by car. The cottage was constructed by the architect Adam Menelaws between 1826 and 1829, and it has now been carefully restored to display collections of objects and furniture, along with Russian porcelain and crystal in the dining room. The original stairway leads to the study of Nicholas I, from which he communicated with his fleet by semaphore. The Czarina's study has a stained-glass screen and a remarkable frieze around the bay window. Another interesting feature is the intricate star-burst ceiling of the Grand Drawing Room next door to the Czarina's study.
NEO-GOTHIC STATION. To the north of Alexandria Park stands the picturesque neo-Gothic railway station, which was built by Nikolai Benois.

"[The Cottage] is a small house built in the new Gothic style currently fashionable in England."
Astolphe de Custine

▲ PALACES ON THE OUTSKIRTS
ORANIENBAUM

COURTYARD/GARDEN
Like Peterhof, the Great Palace is fronted by a huge courtyard/garden surrounded by open land. Two levels of terraces and steps link it to a lower garden area.

About 25 miles from St Petersburg, not far from Peterhof ▲ *256*, is the Oranienbaum estate, which occupies a comparable sloping site and dates from exactly the same period. It was originally given in 1710 by Peter the Great to his companion-in-arms and political advisor Prince Alexander Menshikov ▲ *161* as a summer residence, but it soon reverted to the Crown and was regularly embellished in the 18th century. Until the 1990s, foreign tourists were excluded from Oranienbaum, which stands directly opposite the Kronstadt Naval Base ▲ *192*. Nevertheless, it is one of the very few residences around St Petersburg that did not suffer heavily during World War Two, and has more or less remained in its original state.

CHINESE STUDY
The fine marquetry floors and boiseries of the Chinese Study illustrate large exotic scenes. All are by Russian master cabinet-makers.

GREAT PALACE

Giovanni Maria Fontana began the building works in 1710. The Great Palace (BOLSHOY DVORETS; Большой дворец) takes full advantage of its elevated position, with a central section and two single-story galleries curving round on either side to domed pavilions (a chapel to the west and a Japanese pavilion to the east). Long occupied by government bodies, the Great Palace, also known as the Menchikov Palace, is now once again open to visitors.

CHINESE PALACE ★

Detail of the Glass Study in the Chinese Palace.

The stucco walls and ceilings of the Chinese Palace (KITAISKY DVORETS; Китайский дворец), built by Rinaldi ● *8c* in 1762, provide the background for frescos and oil paintings by Italian artists. The interior style is is Rococo, while outside it is a less flamboyant Baroque.
GLASS STUDY. On the floor, once of glass, are two extraordinary "smalt" marquetry tables.
CHINESE KITCHEN. In the Chinese Kitchen and the Cavalry House, both nearby, are objects from the Far East and 17th- and 18th-century paintings.

PETER III'S PALACE

Near the Great Palace is the Palace of Peter III (DVORETS
ETRA III; дворец Петра III), to which Oranienbaum devolved
in 1743. Peter III, nephew of Empress Elizabeth I ● *36* and a
monarch of rabid military bent, built a fortress here called
Peterstadt, where he had Russian troops parade about in
German uniforms. Nothing remains of it but this small, two-
story palace, constructed by Antonio Rinaldi ● *86* and
decorated in Chinese style with silk hangings, lacquer
paintings and dress cabinets. The Picture Hall houses Italian
and Flemish paintings.

"SLIDING HILL" ★

Heading toward the sea, you come to "Sliding Hill"
(PAVILION KATALNOY GORKY; павильон Катальной горки;
currently closed for repairs), also designed by Rinaldi
(1762–74). Built on a helical plan, until the early 19th century
it had an extension in the form of a 1,500-foot wooden
colonnade, in the middle of which was a *montagne russe* ▲ *185*
for the diversion of the court (a model of this is displayed on
the first floor). From the second-floor windows you can see
the island of Kronstadt, and notably the dome of its huge
Byzantine-style cathedral (1902–13).

ROUND ROOM. The central salon, or Round Room, still has its
original *scagliola* floor, made of powdered marble mixed to
imitate colored marble marquetry.

263

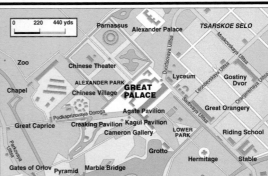

A lthough history tends to associate its name with Catherine the Great the palace of Tsarskoe Selo (TSARSKOÏE SELO; Царское Село) was built at the beginning of the 18th century. In 1710 Peter the Great gave his second wife, Catherine, a small property 15 miles south of St Petersburg. When Elizabeth, Catherine's daughter, came to the throne in 1741 she found the house too small; and in 1743 she commissioned Mikhail Zemtsov to enlarge it. This he did by adding two wings, linked to the main building by single-story galleries leading to pavilions. The finished

ensemble, however, lacked unity, and in 1752 Bartolomeo Rastrelli ● *84* was asked to entirely redesign it. The building we see today is the result of his work, is a surprising 900 feet in breadth.

CATHERINE PALACE ★

FAÇADE. The columns, with composite capitals, are themselves supported by massive Atlas figures; they punctuate most of the bays in the façade of the Catherine Palace (BOLSHOY EKATERININSKY DVORETS; Большой Екатерининский дворец), which incorporates no fewer than five projecting and pedimented buildings. The series of diverse rooms within, restored in the 1960's, gives an idea of the development of the Russian interior through three very different epochs.

STATE STAIRCASE.
This was installed
between 1860 and
1864 by Hippolyte
Monighetti
(1819–78) in the
center of the
palace. On the
upper landing are
folding chairs with
the monogram of
Elizabeth I, made
in the workshops of
Tula ● 60.

Catherine Palace.

GREAT HALL. Decorated
in a generous Baroque
style, with a painted
ceiling representing
"The Triumph of
Russia", this immense
room is the focal
point of the
palace as it was
redesigned by
Rastrelli in the
late 18th century.

State Staircase.

**KNIGHTS'
BANQUETING
HALL.** In this
hall the table is
set with china that
was made to order
for Catherine II by the
Gardner works in Moscow.
The banqueting hall was
formerly heated by a pair
of enormous Dutch faience
stoves.

Great Hall (detail below).

PICTURE GALLERY.
There are 117 works

altogether, by painters such as Luca Giordano, David Teniers
and Jean-Marc Nattier, which hang here side by side in the
decorative spirit of the 18th century.

AMBER ROOM. This famous rococo room – presented to Peter
the Great by the King of Prussia in 1716 and then lost at the
end of World War Two – has been reopened to visitors since
2003. Twenty-four years of work have been necessary to
restore its exquisite panels, decorated in mosaics and amber.

FIRST APARTMENT. The rooms of the first apartment,
converted by the Scottish architect Charles Cameron ● 86
for the heir to the throne Czarevich Paul Petrovich ● 37,
are decorated in the neoclassical style, Catherine II's
favorite. In the GREEN DINING ROOM ★ (details on the
left and right of these pages) the accent is deliberately
innovative; on the ceiling, which is bare of ornamentation,
are ample white stucco figures in relief, alternating with tall
matching antique tripods. The BEDROOM is even more
surprising, with its multiple colonnettes delineating the
alcove and punctuating the walls.

265

CAMERON GALLERY
Catherine II wrote to Baron Grimm in Paris: "If you could only see what a magnificent gallery and what marvelous hanging gardens I shall soon have . . ."

OLD GARDEN

All too often the visit to Tsarskoe Selo is confined to the Catherine Palace, but the park and its many pavilions hold much of interest. Below the eastern façade of the Palace extends the Old Garden (STARY SAD; Старый сад); here are the Upper and Lower Baths, built by the architect Ilya Neelov in the late 1770's.

HERMITAGE

Down from the Old Garden stands the Hermitage (ERMITAZH; павильон Эрмитаж), built by Rastrelli where receptions were held in the summer; nearby is the Hermitage Kitchen, in a remarkably composite style.

AGATE PAVILION ★

In the vicinity of the Palace the Old Garden is delineated by two of the most interesting buildings of Tsarskoe Selo: the Agate Pavilion (AGATOVY PAVILION; Агатовый павильон) and the Cameron Gallery, both built after 1780.
COLD BATHS. The first floor of the Agate Pavilion was occupied by the Tsarina's cold baths. On the second floor the AGATE BEDROOMS open on to a hanging garden, which in turn gives access to the elegant CAMERON GALLERY. There are also a large salon and two studies with walls richly covered in semi-precious agate from the Urals, after which the pavilion is named. (These rooms are currently closed to visitors.)

CATHERINE PARK

The lower reaches of Catherine Park (EKATERININSKY PARK; Екатерининский парк) are taken up by a lake; nearby is a series of follies.

GROTTO, OR MORNING SALON. Originally decorated with thousands of seashells, the grotto was built in the reign of Elizabeth I by Rastrelli. Catherine II liked to come here from time to time, early in the morning, after her marathon work sessions.

AROUND THE LAKE. The Turkish-inspired "Admiralty" and the Chesme Column (CHESMENSKAYA KOLONA; Чесменская колонна) in the middle of the lake are succeeded by the Turkish baths built by Monighetti toward 1850. The Pyramid, where Catherine II's dogs are buried, is close to the Palladian bridge. Other monumental features include the Orlov Gate and the impressive ruined Tower designed by Yury Velten ● 86.

UPPER GARDEN. North of Catherine Park are the Evening Hall, the Concert Hall and the Creaking Pavilion. The Great Caprice, an elaborate arch standing at the end of the avenue that separates Catherine Park from Alexander Park, has a pagoda-like roof supported on Ruskeala marble columns.

ALEXANDER PARK

ALEXANDER PARK (ALEKANDROVSKY PARK; Александровский парк) is named for the Grand Duke Alexander Pavlovich, the future Alexander I and favorite grandson of Catherine II.

CHINESE VILLAGE. This echoes the pavilions described, with its painted roofs, its theater and its various quaint bridges, such as the cross-shaped one with four lamps.

ALEXANDER PALACE (ALEKSANDROVSKY DVORETS; Александровский дворец). This classical building, built by Quarenghi in 1792 for the future Emperor, was also the favorite residence of the last members of the imperial family.

KAGUL OBELISK
This monument stands opposite the side wing of Catherine Palace.

THE ARCH
On the way to Catherine Palace you pass beneath an arch; this communicates with the Lyceum, a building converted into a school in the 19th century. The poet Pushkin was educated here.

АЛЕКСАНДРУ СЕРГЕЕВИЧУ
ПУШКИНУ.

▲ PALACES ON THE OUTSKIRTS PAVLOVSK

Pavlovsk is the most elegant of the summer palaces around St Petersburg, in its decoration and the quality and quantity of the objects it contains. Although PAVLOVSK (Павловск) is no more than four miles from Tsarskoe Selo, visitors from abroad seldom take the trouble to go there. None the less, there is a striking contrast between the majestic aspect of the latter and the more homely character of the former. The histories of the two palaces would have been very similar had it not been for an adventure unique in the annals of the 18th century. In order to get away from the court, and above all to visit the capitals of Western Europe and acquire works of art for their residence, Paul Petrovich and the Grand Duchess Maria Fyodorovna set out on a tour lasting over a year. They left St Petersburg on September 19, 1781 and embarked on a 428-day journey that would take them the length and breadth of Europe, with the objective of embellishing the palace of Pavlovsk.

GREAT PALACE ★

STATE APARTMENTS. The central block of the building is classical in structure. On the second floor are the apartments of Paul and Maria Fyodorovna, set around a central salon known as the Greek Hall. On the Grand Duke's side this leads on to a room called the Hall of War and on the Grand Duchess's side the Hall of Peace. The décor, begun by Charles Cameron ● 86, was mostly completed by Vincenzo Brenna (1740–1819), an Italian artist whom Paul and Maria Fyodorovna met in Poland on their travels.

GALLERIES. After Paul I's accession in 1796 Brenna was commissioned to enlarge the palace, now an imperial residence. He heightened the two single-story side galleries

Paul Petrovich and Maria Fyodorovna.

PAVLOVSK
The original wooden houses on the site, known as Krik and Krak, were succeeded by two small palaces, also in wood, called Marienthal ("Maria's Valley") and Paulslust ("Paul's Joy").
No doubt these were still considered inadequate, so the decision was made to build yet again. The result was what we know as Pavlovsk Palace (Pavlovsky Dvorets; Павловский дворец), much larger and in brick; it was designed by Charles Cameron ● 86, one of Catherine II's favorite architects.

A LAVISH GIFT
Originally a hunting estate, the domain of Pavlovsk was given by Catherine II to her son Paul, when the Grand Duchess produced a male heir for the dynasty, Alexander, on December 12, 1777.

built by Cameron. He then added two ample pavilions to house the new Throne Room and chapel; and finally he included two other service wings, on the same quarter-circle plan.

HALL OF WAR. The carved and gilded wooden *torchères* of the Hall of War (opposite page, top left) are additional tangible proof of the special talent of Russian artisans for woodwork, such as the chairs in the Greek Hall and the marquetry floors of the Grand Duchess's apartment.

BOUDOIR. The Boudoir is decorated with porphyry columns and painted pilasters brought from Italy by the royal couple (left page, center).

☑ **Half a day**

VESTIBULE
The Vestibule (where the tour begins) was decorated by Voronikhin with twelve allegorical sculptures in the Egyptian style, very fashionable at the time. On the upper landing can still be seen the elaborate stucco décor designed by Brenna.

Vase from the toilet service of Maria Fyodorovna.

GRAND DUCHESS'S STATE APARTMENTS. In the apartments of Maria Fyodorovna (center) is a magnificent series of Gobelins and Savonnerie tapestries, along with a sixty-four piece toilet service in Sèvres porcelain kept in a glass cabinet opposite the bed, which was given to Paul I and the Grand Duchess by Louis XVI and Marie-Antoinette during their visit to France.

PICTURE GALLERY. In the picture gallery Russian furniture and vases relate harmoniously with European paintings and French objects in gilded bronze purchased on the orders of Paul I, who originally wanted them for his St Petersburg residence, the Mikhailovsky Castle ▲ *229*.

THE ROSE
Maria Fyodorovna dedicated a pavilion to her favorite flower, the rose, a motif which covers the chairs and everyday objects.

❝. . . 1,500,000 roubles are invested in perpetuity for the upkeep of Pavlovsk . . I give to my son the Grand Duke Mikhail the castle of Pavlovsk . . . the Grand Duke Mikhail will gain possession of Pavlovsk on condition that the castle, the gardens, parks, orangeries, hospital and invalids' home . . . that, in a word, all the dependencies of that beautiful place, are maintained . . . ❞
Maria Fyodorovna

THRONE ROOM ★. In the Throne Room, or State Dining Room (above left), are magnificent displays of porcelain ● *64* from the various palace collections, both French (Sèvres) and Russian (St Petersburg). The dominant feature of this room is its enormous ceiling fresco by the set designer Pietro di Gottardo Gonzaga.

FAMILY ROOM. The Family Room on the first floor is especially touching, with personal mementos of the palace's founders, drawings of Maria Fyodorovna and a charming family portrait.

CORNER SALON. With its 1815 décor by the architect Carlo Rossi ● *86*, the Corner Salon shows the evolution of taste during the reign of Alexander I.

BALLROOM. In the gay pink and blue ballroom are four major canvases by the French artist Hubert Robert, of which Paul I was particularly fond.

MUSEUM OF INTERIORS. On the third floor the Museum of Interiors exhibits a collection of Russian furniture and objects from the late 18th and 19th centuries.

enjoy in peace the lovely colors of St Petersburg's numerous parks and gardens, as well as cruise down the Neva before it becomes solid ice.

■ DEC–JAN

There are barely five hours of sunlight a day in December. With luck you may see the Neva frozen over and may be able to walk on the icy solid Gulf of Finland. The Russians hold four end-of-year celebrations: on Dec. 25 and 31 and on Jan. 6 and 13 (Roman Catholic and Orthodox Christmasses and New Year's Days, respectively). Various public events take place (see p. 284), and major hotels and restaurants also organize end-of-year parties.

■ "WHITE DAYS"

Since 2000, the city has had a winter celebration of its culture, named after the white covering that lies on the ground between November and March. There are programs of ballet, concerts and art exhibitions, and hotels offer attractive rates at this time (except Christmas and New Year). Browse www. whitedays.com for more information.

TRAVEL

→ BY AIR

From the UK, Aeroflot and British Airways operate direct flights to St Petersburg. In the USA, Continental offer direct flights to St Petersburg from Los Angeles. Other major airlines offer connecting flights. International flights arrive in St Petersburg at Pulkovo 2, while domestic flights arrive at Pulkovo 1 (see also p. 276), both about 10 miles south of the city. Check with the following airlines for details of fares and conditions:

■ FROM THE UK

Aeroflot
Tel. 020 7355 2233
www.aeroflot.co.uk
Austrian airlines
Tel. 0845 601 0948
www.aua.com
British Airways
Tel. 0870 850 9 850
www.ba.com
Finnair
Tel. 0870 241 4411
www.finnair.com
Lufthansa
Tel. 0870 8377 747
www.lufthansa.co.uk

■ FROM THE US

Aeroflot
Tel. 1 888 340 6400
www.aeroflot.com
British Airways
Tel. 1 800 AIRWAYS
www.ba.com
Continental
Tel. 1 800 231 0856
www.continental.com
Delta
Tel. 1 800 241 4141
www.delta.com
Lufthansa
Tel. 1 800 399 5838
www.lufthansa.com/us

→ BY TRAIN AND SEA FROM THE UK

■ BY TRAIN

Eurostar from London Waterloo to Brussels, then another train to Berlin. From Berlin the 'Moskva Express' travels direct to St Petersburg (journey time about 36 hours). Trains leave daily (except Sat.) June–Sep.; Tue., Thu. and Sun. only Oct.–May. A Belarus transit visa is required, as well as your Russian visa.
Information
Eurostar (London)
Tel. 0870 160 6600
www.eurostar.com
For train information throughout Europe:
www.seat61.com

■ BY SEA

There are sea links between London, Göteborg, Oslo and Helsinki, and numerous cruises in the Baltic Sea that include St Petersburg on their route. Contact the Russian National Tourist Office or Intourist Travel Ltd (see p. 274) or a specialized tour operator.

HEALTH

→ FIRST-AID KIT

Take your usual medicines with you, such as antibiotics and anti-diarrhea tablets, but make sure all packages are intact in order to avoid trouble at customs when entering the country. If you are undergoing a course of treatment, keep a prescription with you bearing the generic names of the drugs you need.

→ VACCINATIONS

None required from European or American visitors, however DT polio, typhoid, and hepatitis A inoculations are recommended. Any visitor intending to stay in the Russian Federation for more than three months must produce a certificate confirming that they are not HIV-positive. This certificate must mention their passport number and be signed by a doctor. It remains valid for three months. More about health p. 279.

VOLTAGE

220 Volts. Plugs are similar to the straight pins of continental European plugs, but slightly thinner. Adapters and power converters are recommended for all American appliances.

PHOTOGRAPHY AND VIDEO

Film, tapes, batteries available from specialized stores, but make sure you take enough equipment with you. In most national museums you can take photographs without a flash for a nominal fee. Never take pictures in theaters or circuses.

RUSSIA ON THE NET

General information: cultural and travel information on St Petersburg:
www.travel.spb.ru
http://petersburgcity.com
Travelers' Yellow Pages online:
www.infoservices.com/stpete
Travel information on the Russian Federation:
www.geographia.com/russia
www.russian-tours.spb.ru

TEMPERATURE AND RAINFALL					
	JAN.	FEB.	MARCH	APRIL	MAY	JUNE
T. maxi °F	9	10	18	32	43	52
T. mini °F	19	23	32	46	59	68
R. (inches)	1½	1¼	1	1½	1½	2
	JULY	AUG.	SEP.	OCT.	NOV.	DEC.
T. maxi °F	55	55	48	39	28	18
T. mini °F	70	68	59	48	36	27
R. (inches)	2¾	3	2¼	2	1¾	1½

When in St Petersburg you do not need to dial the city code 812 before the seven-digit phone number.

ACCOMMODATION

The number of foreign visitors to St Petersburg has been growing steadily in recent years, and unfortunately the Russian hotel infrastructure has not been able to keep up with the demand. It is still undergoing major transformation, and prices vary greatly according to the season (they actually double during the "white nights" period from mid-May to mid-July). Hotels with fewer than three stars are practically non-existent in the city center.

■ **HOTELS**
Average price for a double room, excluding breakfast:
★★★
US$55–140 (add $13 per day if half-board)
★★★★
US$150–470 (add $25 if half-board)
★★★★★ from US$380 (add up to $110 if half-board)

■ **YOUTH HOSTELS**
US$19–44 per night per person.
www.ryh.ru

■ **STAYING WITH A RUSSIAN FAMILY**
US$38–63 per room
www.homestay.ru
To reserve contact a tour operator (see under Useful addresses p. 283.)

■ **APARTMENTS**
US$38–190 per night for the apartment (may vary according to the size of the apartment and to the distance from the city center).

■ **RENTAL AGENCIES**
Becar
Bolshoy Sampsonievsky Prospekt 61, Business-Center Becar

Tel. 812 324 31 31
Open 9am–10pm, Sat.–Sun. 10am–8pm
http://en.becar.ru/
Itaka
Bolshoy Prospekt VO 36
Tel. 812 325 21 12 or 812 327 98 02
www.petersburg-estate.com
Open Mon.–Fri. 10am–7pm

ARRIVALS AND DEPARTURES

→ **BY AIR**
http://eng.pulkovo.ru

■ **PULKOVO 2 INTERNATIONAL AIRPORT**
Located 10 miles south of the city center, on Startovaya Ulitsa.
International flights
Tel. 812 704 34 44
Tourist Information Bureau
Arrival hall, or Nevsky Prospekt 41
Tel. 812 311 28 43

■ **PULKOVO 1 AIRPORT**
Located 10½ miles south of the city center, on Pulkovsky Road.
Domestic flights (C.E.I.)
Tel. 812 704 38 22

■ **AIRPORT LINKS FROM PULKOVO 1**
Express bus no. 39 to Moskovskaya Metro station (15–20 mins); tickets sold on the bus (under US$1). Change at Moskovskaya for Nevsky Prospekt station (or other destinations), duration: 15–20 minutes.

■ **AIRPORT LINKS FROM PULKOVO 2**
Express bus no. 13 or shared taxi (*marshrutnoye taksy*) to Moskovskaya station. Tickets from the bus driver (under US$1).
Taxis
Taxi rank outside the

terminal; fares go from US$20–50, according to the length of the journey. Many private cab drivers will offer you their services inside the airport arrival hall; agree on the fare before starting your journey. (See City Transportation, p. 282).

■ **AIRLINES**
Aeroflot
– Nevsky Prospekt 7/9
Tel. 812 314 69 59
– Pulkovo Airport
Tel. 812 104 34 44
British Airways
– Sweden House, Malaya Konyushennaya Ulitsa 1/3A, Office B23
Tel. 812 329 25 65
– Pulkovo Airport
Tel. 812 346 81 46
Finnair
– Kazanskaya Ulitsa 44
Tel. 812 326 18 70
– Pulkovo Airport
Tel. 812 324 32 49
Lufthansa
– Nevsky Prospekt 32 (2nd floor)
Tel. 812 320 10 00
– Pulkovo Airport
Tel. 812 324 32 44
Pulkovo Airlines
Pervaya Krasno armeyskaya Ulitsa 5
Tel. 812 303 92 68 or 812 303 92 67
Central Ticketing Office
Nevsky Prospekt 7/9
Tel. 812 571 80 93
Open 8am–8pm, Sat.–Sun. 8am–6pm.

→ **BY BOAT**
Passenger maritime port (*Morskoy Passajirsky Port*)
Morskoy Slavy Pl. 1
Tel. 812 355 13 10 or 812 322 60 52
Also known as Gavan (harbor), it is located at the end of Great Prospekt (Bolshoy Prospekt) on Vasilyevsky Island, on the Gulf of Finland. It is the port of call of all Northern European cruises. The only

regular crossing now operating is between Stockholm and St Petersburg.

→ **BY TRAIN**
(See Regional Transportation p. 283.)

BRIDGES

St Petersburg's 300 or so bridges form an intergal part of its architectural heritage. Between them they link the 42 islands that make up the city. Between April and November – when the rivers are not frozen – the swing bridges (20 in total) stay raised for part of the night in order to let commercial vessels through. You are advised to be aware of the bridge opening and closing times to avoid being stranded on the wrong island. The opening times of the bridges listed below must be verified by calling 063 between 8am and 10pm.

■ **SWING BRIDGE LIFTING TIMES**
Alexandra Nevskogo
1.30–5.05am
Birzhevoy
2.10–4.50am
Bolsheokhtinsky
2–5am
Bolshoy Krestovsky
2.05–3.55am and 4.40–5.20am
Bolshoy Petrovsky
1.25–2am and 5–5.45am
Dvortsovy
1.50–2.55am and 3.15–4.50am
Elagin I
by special order
Elagin II
by special order
Elagin III
by special order
Grenadersky
2.45–3.45am and 4.20–4.50am
Kamennoostrovsky
2.15–3am and 4.05–4.55am
Kantemirovsky
2.45–3.45 am and

STAYING IN ST PETERSBURG FROM A TO Z ◆

Cars, children, cost of living, emergencies

4.20–4.50am
Lazarevsky
1.55–2.35am and
4.45–5.20am
Leitenanta Schmidta
1.40-4.55am
Liteiny
1.50–4.40am
Sampsonievsky
2.10–2.45am and
3.20–4.25am
Trotsky
1.50–4.50am
Tuchkov
2.10–3.05am and
3.35–4.45am
Ushakovsky
2.15–2.55am and
3.55–4.30am
Volodarsky
2–3.45am and
4.15–5.45am

CARS

→ DRIVING
■ **DRIVING LICENSE**
You are advised
to carry an
international
driving license.

■ **HIGHWAY CODE**
Roundabouts:
cars entering the
roundabout have
right of way over
those already
engaged.

■ **SPEED LIMITS**
In built-up areas:
37 miles/hr (60km/hr)
On the road:
56 miles/hr (90km/hr)

■ **ALCOHOL LEVELS
IN THE BLOOD**
Zero tolerance.

■ **GASOLINE**
After Jan 1, 2003,
the price of gasoline
in Russia rose from
20% to 30%.

■ **TRAFFIC JAMS**
Traffic and
congestion are
severe, especially
in the city center in
the rush hours,
between 8am–10am
and 5pm–8pm.

■ **PARKING**
Parking in the city
center is unmarked
and free of charge.
There are some
attended parking lots,
charged by the hour,
near the major hotels
and tourist sites.

■ **RESCUE SERVICE**
Tel. 320 90 00

→ CAR RENTAL
Not necessary if
you're planning to
stay in the city.

■ **CONDITIONS**
You must be over
21 and have held a
driving license for
at least a year.

■ **PAYMENT**
By credit card
(Amex, Visa, DC,
Mc/Ec, JCB, Hertz
Charge Card).

■ **CAR RENTAL
AGENCIES**
Prices average
US$115–150 per
day. Make sure you
have full insurance.
Astoria-service
Borovaya Ulitsa
11/13
Tel. 812 112 15 83
Avis
Konnogvardesysky
Bul. 4
Tel. 812 312 63 12
Rex
Kievskaya Ulitsa 3,
Office 206
Tel. 812 320 6662
www.rexlux.spb.ru/
Executive car
2 linia 35
Tel. 812 213 11 21

Hertz
– Pulkovo airport
terminals 1 and 2,
11am–11pm
– Malaya Morskaya
Ulitsa 23
Tel. 812 324 32 42
www.hertz.spb.ru

CHILDREN

If your children are
accompanying you,
take them to:
■ **ST PETERBURGSKY
TSIRK** (Circus)
Reki Fontanky nab. 3
Tel. 812 314 84 78
www.circus.spb.ru
Ticket office
11am–7pm

■ **CENTRAL LEISURE
PARK (ELAGIN ISLAND):**
giant wheel,
rowing boats...

■ **VICTORY PARK
"PRIMORSKY"**
(Krestovsky Island):
tennis courts,
rollerskating rink,
dolphins, ponies.

■ **ZOO** and other
attractions in
Alexandrovsky Park.

■ **ZOOLOGICAL
MUSEUM**
One of the largest
natural history
museums in
the world.

EMERGENCIES

■ **AMBULANCES**
Tel. 03
■ **FIRE BRIGADE**
Tel. 01
■ **POLICE (MILITSIA)**
Tel. 02 or 164 97 87
for foreign visitors
■ **GAS LEAK**
Tel. 04
■ **SOS ON THE ROAD**
Tel. 812 320 90 00
■ **ALL-NIGHT
DRUGSTORE**
9pm–8pm
Tel. 812 311 20 77
■ **LOSS OR THEFT**
Go to the police
station nearest to the
place of loss or theft
in order to make a
declaration and
obtain an official
police report (Tel. 02)
which you will need

TRINITY BRIDGE

◆ STAYING IN ST PETERSBURG FROM A TO Z

Finding your way, food and drink

to submit to your consulate for lost documents, or to your insurance company.
Loss of luggage: Luggage retrieval service Pulkovo 2 Airport, open 24 hours Tel. 812 324 37 87

FINDING YOUR WAY

Nothing could be simpler than finding your way around the center of St Petersburg, where the main tourist attractions (the Admiralty, Peter and Paul Fortress, St Isaac's Cathedral) and the canals provide you with clear landmarks. Out of the center, it is a little more difficult to find your bearings and you need to pay more attention.

→ **TOPOGRAPHY**
In the heart of St Petersburg (the oldest part of the city), the streets are laid out in a radial system, the main arteries fanning out from a central point while the canals curve around them. Later, more outlying areas were constructed mainly to an orthogonal design, dividing the whole area into a network of streets running at right angles to each other and forming "microdistricts" bound by the main arteries radiating out from the center.

→ **SIGNPOSTS**
Although the city has readopted many of the pre-revolutionary street names, the streets still tend to be known by both their Soviet and post-

NEVSKY PROSPEKT

Soviet names. Newly installed signs are now often sponsored by commercial companies; don't be surprised to find the trademark of a distinctly Western company displayed under the name of the street.

→ **STREET NUMBERING**
In theory, all streets are numbered starting from the Neva. In practice, in the majority of cases, the direction of street numbering varies from area to area. Guidelines are as follows:

■ in the mainland area of the city (south of the Neva): from north to south and from west to east;

■ on Vasilyevsky Island: from south to north and from east to west;

■ on Petersburg Island (also known as Petrograd Side): from south to north and from west to east.

FOOD AND DRINK

→ **BISTROS**
You will find several cheap bistro and fast-food chains.

→ **BRASSERIES AND BREWERIES**
There are a great number of brasseries in the city, and several brands of beer are produced in St Petersburg (Baltika, Nevskoye, Stepan Razin).

→ **CAFÉS**
The number of cafés in the city center is growing rapidly, and many now offer a fine selection of coffees, teas and cakes.

→ **RESTAURANTS**
There is a wide range of cuisine available in St Petersburg: the most common are Russian and Georgian, then Korean, Chinese and Latin-American.

→ **RUSSIAN CUISINE**
"Russian cuisine," writes travel journalist Jo Durden Smith, "is a mixture of elements of various origins: its starters (*zakusky*) come from a German and Scandinavian tradition imported by Peter the Great. Its noodles, ravioli (*pelmeny*) and tea derive from the Mongols; its buckwheat *kasha* from central Asia; its shish kebab (*shashlyk*) from the Caucasus; its *borshch* from central Europe – with the whole mix made more sophisticated and varied by imported 19th-century French chefs. Ice-cold vodka is traditionally drunk with *zakuski* (and often throughout the meal). Local beers are now excellent (try, for instance, Baltika no. 7). Georgian red wines are rather sweet to the Western palate, but you could try *kinsmarauli*, Stalin's favorite wine, as well as a dry white called *tsinandali*. Of Russian champagnes, the best is brut (the dryest); it's an agreeable alternative to its distant French cousin which, like all imported wines in Russia, is very expensive. French wines, for all this, are part of the old Russian tradition. Both Ivan the Terrible and Peter the Great had a fondness for Burgundy; and the Hotel Grand Europe, before the Revolution, is said to have had the finest champagne cellar in the world."

→ **GLOSSARY**
Bitky: meatballs.
Borshch: beetroot soup, potatoes, cabbage and meat.
Goluptsy: small meat-stuffed cabbage.
Kulibiak: salmon or meat pie.

Upp. case	Low. case	Phon.
А	а	a
Б	б	b
В	в	v
Г	г	g
Д	д	d
Е	е	ié
Ё	ё	io
Ж	ж	j
З	з	z
И	и	i
-	й	ï
К	к	k
Л	л	l
М	м	m
Н	н	n
О	о	o
П	п	p
Р	р	r
С	с	s
Т	т	t
У	у	ou
Ф	ф	f
Х	х	kh
Ц	ц	ts
Ч	ч	tch
Ш	ш	ch
Щ	щ	chtch
-	ъ	-
-	ы	y
-	ь	-
Э	э	è
Ю	ю	iou
Я	я	ia

Okhroshka:
cold soup.
Pelmeny:
a type of ravioli.
Pirozhky: small
meat or cabbage
pies.
Po-Pojarsky: poultry
meat in flat pies).
Shashlyk:
meat kebab.
Shchy:
cabbage soup.
Ukha: fish soup.
Zakusky: varied
hors d'œuvres.

HEALTH

→ PREVENTION
Avoid drinking
tap water and bathing
in lakes or pools
(risk of leptospirosis,
or Weil's disease).
Be aware of the
expiry dates on food
packages (especially
frozen food) and
avoid "homemade"
vodka and other
spirits sold at kiosks
and street stalls.

→ MEDICAL CENTERS
The local *poliklinika*
will handle many
most routine
treatments, but
doctors and nurses
may not speak
English. Many tourist
hotels have their
own doctors (inquire
at the front desk).
■ **POLIKLINIKA #2**
Moskovsky
Prospekt 22
Tel. 812 292 62 72

■ **GASTELLO HOSPITAL**
Gastello Ulitsa 20
Tel. 812 291 79 60

■ **MEDICAL CENTERS
FOR FOREIGN VISITORS**
**American Medical
Center**
Serpukhovskaya
Ulitsa 10
Tel. 812 326 17 30
www.amcenters.com
Metro Teknolo-
gitchesky Institut
Open 24 hours daily
(office Mon.–Fri.
9am–6pm).
Private practice.
Euromed Clinique
Suvorovsky
Prospekt 60
Tel. 812 327 03 01
www.euromed.ru/en/
Private practice.

LANGUAGE

English is the foreign
language most widely
spoken by the
population, especially
by young people and
staff in tourist
locations. Russian
is the official
language, so if you
want to be able to
find your way around

easily you will need
to become familiar
with the Cyrillic
alphabet and its
English phonetic
transcription
(see table, left).

MAIL

→ POST OFFICES
There are many post
offices throughout the
city. They can also be
found in major hotels.
Usually open 9am–
8pm, closed one
day a week.

■ **CENTRAL POST
OFFICE**
(Glavpotchtamt)
Potchtamtskaya 9
(in the St Isaac's
Cathedral district)
Tel. 312 83 02
and 312 80 39

■ **EXPRESS SERVICE**
DHL
Tel. 812 326 64 00
UPS
Tel. 812 327 85 40

■ **STAMPS**
US$0.66 for Europe.
US$1 for the US.
Sold at post offices.

MARKETS

→ FOOD, FRUIT AND
VEGETABLES
Food markets are
open daily. The
products are
generally fresher and
cheaper than in
stores.
■ **KUZNECHNY MARKET**
Kuznechny Per. 3,
Tel. 812 312 41 61
Mon.–Sat. 8am–8pm,
Sun. 8am–6pm
The largest market in
the city center.

→ ART AND
ANTIQUES
St Petersburg is
known as the
"antiques capital".
There is a market
on Konnyushennaya
Square, near the
Church of the
Resurrection of
Christ. There are also
many sale-or-return
stores, see Shopping
p. 296.

→ FLEA MARKETS
The place to find
anything from military
belt buckles to
antique china sets.
They are on the
outskirts of the city:
– Udelnaya Metro
station, next to the
railway tracks.
– Avtovo Metro
station
– Marshala Kazakova
Ulitsa 40 (Yunona
Market, mostly for
micro-electronics).

MONEY

→ EXCHANGE
Rubles cannot
be converted on
the open market.
Exchange can
only take place in
Russia at bureaux
de change, hotel
receptions, in
banks and in the
larger stores.
Warning:
*Do not take the risk
of changing money
on the black market,
and beware of the
numerous conmen
operating in the city*
.

■ **BANKS**
Usually open
Mon.–Fri. 9.30am–
1pm and 2–4pm.
Alfa-Bank
Kanala Griboyedova
Nab 6/2
**Association of the
commercial banks
of St Petersburg**
Sadovaya Ulitsa 21
Tel. 315 65 09
Baltysky Bank
Sadovaya Ulitsa 34
and Nevsky Prospekt
85 (in the Moscow
railway station
building).
Menatep
Nevsky Prospekt 1
Promstroy bank
Nevsky Prospekt 140
Dumskaya Ulitsa 7
Sberbank
Nevsky Prospekt 153,
82 and 101, Liteyny
Prospekt 7,
Sadovaya Ulitsa 35

■ **FOREIGN-CAPITAL
BANKS**
BNP-Dresdner Bank
Isaakyevskaya Pl. 11

◆ STAYING IN ST PETERSBURG FROM A TO Z

Newspapers, nightlife, opening times, public holidays, religion

When in St Petersburg you do not need to dial the city code 812 before the seven-digit phone number.

■ **BUREAUX DE CHANGE**
Open daily 10am–8pm

→ **AUTO-TELLERS**
They are located in the city center, major hotels and banks. The maximum amount you can take out is set by your bank. Commission is 3%–4%.

→ **FORMS OF PAYMENT**
■ **CASH**
Although payment is often made in rubles, the US dollar, known as *kapusta* (cabbage), is the preferred local currency; it is a good idea to bring dollars with you in small denominations to use for tips – clean US$1, US$5, US$10 bills issued after 1990. As well as US dollars, euros are accepted for unofficial transactions such as the purchase of souvenirs.

■ **CREDIT CARDS**
Accepted in most restaurants, hotels, stores.
Warning:
Check all bills and receipts, and only use credit cards in reputable establishments. Beware of fraud.

■ **TRAVELER'S CHECKS**
They are not recommended as they are accepted only by banks and the commission is 5% to 7%, and sometimes more.

→ **COST OF LIVING**
Prices are volatile and inflation is rife. The tariffs applied to foreign visitors in tourist areas are those of Western Europe. Admission fees to sites and museums are higher than those charged to Russians in order

to finance the restoration of the national heritage, while allowing local people access to their own culture.
Cup of coffee: US$1.90
Pint of beer: From US$1.25
Bottle of wine: From US$12
Lunch: From US$4
Dinner in a restaurant: From US$19 per person
Museum admission fee: From US$6–12
Theater ticket: From US$30
Single room in a hotel: From US$60

NEWSPAPERS

→ **LOCAL NEWSPAPERS**
■ **IN ENGLISH**
The St Petersburg Times, a weekly publication for foreign residents, gives information on cultural events and is distributed free to hotels, restaurants and cafés.
www.times.spb.ru

■ **IN RUSSIAN**
Cultural magazines
Na Nevskom, Krasny journal, Sobaka.ru (very trendy).
Dailies
Vecherny Peterburg, Smena, Sankt-Peterburgskiye Vedomosty.

→ **ENGLISH-LANGUAGE NEWSPAPERS**
Sold in hotels and at newsagents in the city center.

■ **IN ENGLISH AND RUSSIAN**
Pulse St Petersburg is a weekly publication that gives information on life in the city.

■ **IN ENGLISH**
Neva News and

Estate News (real estate in the Russian Federation and Eastern Europe) are both published monthly.

NIGHTLIFE

→ **ART AND MUSIC**
From permanent exhibitions to special events, there is always something to see or do in St Petersburg. Arts and music have always flourished here in the city that was known as the "Rock capital" during the Soviet era. Nightclubs, theaters, opera halls and cultural venues offer a wide range of concerts and shows all year round. (See Leisure p. 293, Celebrations, festivals and events p. 284).

→ **"WHITE NIGHTS"**
The widest range of events occurs in the summer, during the period of the "white nights", when nightlife becomes more intense and the city center is full of local people out on the streets until dawn (Vasilyevsky, Petrograd Side and Nevsky districts).

■ **INFORMATION**
From the Tourist Information Bureau, the Cultural Program Institute, or the local press.

■ **RESERVATIONS**
Ask at your hotel or at the venue itself.

OPENING TIMES

Vary greatly, but the standard opening times (with most places closing for lunch between 1–3pm) are:

■ **BANKS**
Mon.–Fri. 9.30am–1pm and 2–4pm

■ **BUREAUX DE CHANGE**
Daily 10am–8pm

■ **DEPARTMENT STORES**
8am–9pm (some stay open 24 hours)

■ **FOOD STORES**
8am–8pm or 9am–9pm

■ **OTHER STORES**
10am–7pm

■ **RESTAURANTS**
Times may vary, but restaurants usually serve until 10pm or 10.30pm. Russians tend to have lunch around 2pm and dinner between 9pm and 10pm.

■ **MUSEUMS**
See Places to Visit p. 300 for addresses and opening times.

PUBLIC HOLIDAYS

■ **JANUARY 1**
New Year's Day
■ **JANUARY 7**
Orthodox Christmas
■ **FEBRUARY 23**
Defenders of the Nation's Day
■ **MARCH 8**
International Woman's Day
■ **MAY 1 AND 2**
Labor Day
■ **MAY 9**
Victory Day (1945)
■ **JUNE 12**
Russian Independence Day
■ **NOVEMBER 7**
Reconciliation Day

RELIGION

■ **JEWISH**
Synagogue Lermontovsky Prospekt 104; Metro Baltiskaya

■ **MUSLIM**
Mosque, Kronversky Prospekt 7; Metro Gorkovskaya

■ **ORTHODOX**
– St Nicholas', Nikolskaya Pl. 1/3; Metro Ploshchad

Mira
- The Holy Trinity,
Nevsky Monastery
Metro Ploshchad
A. Nevsky

PROTESTANT
Lutheran Church,
Saltikov-Shedrine 8
Metro
Chernyshevskaya

■ **ROMAN CATHOLIC**
Our-Lady-of-Lourdes
Kovenski Prospekt 7
Metro Ploshchad
Vosstanya

SHOPPING

Make sure you are
given receipts and
that you keep them,
as you may be
required to produce
them by the Russian
customs when
leaving the country.

→ **WHAT TO BUY**
■ **GOLD AND SILVER**
objects, jewelry, and
clocks and watches.

■ **FURS** (*shapkas*),
scarves and shawls,
natural fabrics wool.
silk, etc. from
Central Asia.

■ **WOODEN OBJECTS**
Russian dolls
(*matryoshkas*),
lacquered boxes,
sculpted pictures...

■ **ST PETERSBURG
PORCELAIN**
from the Lomonosov
factory (originally the
famous imperial
works).

■ **RECORDS**, cassettes
and CDs (classical or
folk music).

■ **RARE BOOKS**
in European
languages
(especially French)
in the numerous
second-hand
bookstores or stalls.

■ **ANTIQUES**,
paintings, etc.
Warning:
Russian law
stipulates that you
can't export

HELICOPTER TRIP ABOVE THE NEVA

BOAT CRUISE

VASILYEVSKY ISLAND

AVTOVO METRO STATION

antiquities that date
from before 1945,
especially icons.
Any antiques or
works of art taken out
of the country must
be authorized by the
Ministry of Culture
and have a certificate
of export. Otherwise,
customs officials
have the right to
seize goods and
demand that you
pay a fine.

■ **VODKA AND CAVIAR**
A maximum of 7oz

(200g) of caviar per
person is allowed
through customs.
Warning:
Buying vodka or
caviar from street
vendors may seem
like a smart move
because of the lower
price, but
you will have no
guarantee of
freshness or quality.

→ **MAIN SHOPPING
STREETS**
■ **NEVSKY PROSPEKT**
and its commercial

galleries, Gostiny
Dvor and Passage.

■ **KAMENNO-
OSTROVSKY** and
BOLSHOY PROSPEKT
in the Petersburg
Island district.

TELEPHONE

→ **INTERNATIONAL
CALLS**
■ **TO THE UK**
Dial 8 (wait for a long
tone) then dial 10
(international access
code) then 44 for the
UK, the area code
(without the initial 0)
and number.

■ **TO THE US/CANADA**
Dial 8 (wait for a long
tone) then dial 10
(international access
code), 1 for the US,
the area code and
local number.

■ **INTERNATIONAL
OPERATOR**
Dial 077 (072 or 073
from your hotel).

→ **NATIONAL CALLS**
■ **CALLS WITHIN
ST PETERSBURG**
When phoning within
the city, you do not
need to dial the area
code 812.

■ **CALLS TO OTHER
RUSSIAN CITIES**
Dial 8 and wait for a
long tone then dial
the city code and
number.
Information for calls
outside the city:
070.
National city codes:
Moscow: 095
Novgorod: 8162
Ekaterinburg: 3432

→ **PUBLIC
TELEPHONES**
There are many
public phone booths
in the streets, in
museums and hotels.
You are advised to
buy an International
Phone card (sold at
Metro stations and
newsagents) as it will
be much cheaper
than using the normal
city network.

Tipping, tours and excursions, transportation around the city

→ CALL CENTER
(*Tsentralniye Mejdugorodniye Telefonniye Punkt*) Bolshaya Morskaya Ulitsa 28 (next to Palace Square, by Nevsky Prospekt)
Tel. 069
Open 24 hours
Business center (located inside the Call Center) for Internet and fax
Open 9am–9pm.

TIPPING

In restaurants and cafés, bills include a 10–15% service charge, but it is customary to leave a tip by rounding up the amount billed. In taxis, tipping is not usual, unless you wish to show special appreciation.

TOURS AND EXCURSIONS

Guided tours are usually in Russian. If you require a tour in English or have any specific request (expect to pay a lot

more), contact the Tourist Information Bureau or a tour operator (see Useful addresses p. 283).

→ BOAT TOURS
Trips run between April and November.
■ **CRUISES DOWN THE NEVA**
Departures from in front of the Hermitage; in front of the Admiralty (opposite the bronze cavalier); at the Peter and Paul Fortress by the gateway to the Neva; and also near the *Aurora*.

■ **CANAL TRIPS BY WATER-TAXI**
Departures from the quay on the Moyka Canal every night during the 'white nights'; from the Griboedov Canal (water-taxi trips through the Kolomna); and on the Fontanka Embankment, near the Zelieni, Kazansky and Anitchkov bridges.

NEVSKY PROSPEKT

■ **TRIPS TO PETERHOF**
Hydrofoil trips to Peterhof embark opposite the main entrance of the Hermitage.
Duration: 30 mins.
Tel. 812 325 51 20

■ **EXCURSIONS TO KRONSTADT**
Hydrofoil trips to Kronstadt embark opposite 34, Makarova Naberejnaya.
Duration: 35 mins.
Tel. 812 328 22 23

■ **LASTOCHKA OMNIBUS-BOAT**
Cruise in style in 19th-century interiors. Reserve ahead (Kronversky Bridge, near the Peter and Paul Fortress)
Tel. 812 327 25 07

→ COACH TOURS
Operators offer many itineraries and thematic tours. Information, reservations and departures from one of the following three stations in the city center: Palace Square, Kazan Square or near the Ruska Portik (next to Gostiny Dvor).

→ TRAMWAY TOURS
You can visit St Petersburg in one of the streetcars that have served the city faithfully for over a century.
■ **RESERVATIONS**
St Petersburg Tramway Museum Sredny Prospekt 77
Tel. 812 321 5405/06

→ HELICOPTER TOURS
■ **BALTIC AIRLINES (BALTYSKYE AVIALINY)**
Nevsky Prospekt 7/9 Office no. 12
Tel. 812 571 00 84
A15-minute flight in a MI-8. Departures from the strip situated between the Peter and Paul Fortress and

Kronverk; April–Nov., Sat.–Sun. and public hols. Price: around US$40.

TRANSPORTATION AROUND THE CITY

→ BUS, TRAMS AND METRO
St Peterburg has over 290 bus, trolleybus and tramway routes, 4 Metro lines and 57 stations, each reflecting the spirit of the time when it was built (do not miss Ploshchad and Vostanya at Avtovo).
■ **MAP OF THE METRO**
(See Map G p.336) Maps are displayed at the entrance of every Metro station (these are in Russian only). Bilingual city and transportation maps are available from some kiosks in the city center, hotels, bookstores and the Tourist Information Bureau.

■ **TICKETS**
You must buy Metro tickets at station ticket offices, and bus and tramway tickets when boarding. Fares: around US$0.15 at time of going to press but inflation goes up quickly. Various special passes are also available.

■ **OPERATING TIMES**
Buses and tramways run between 6am and midnight. The Metro operates between 5.45am and 0.15am, roughly every 1–5 minutes.

→ PRIVATE SHUTTLES
The numerous *marshrutnoye* taxis, indicated by an "express" sign, are just as convenient to get to the surrounding area: shuttles for Petrodvorets

МУЗЕЙ ЧЕТЫРЕХ СОБОРОВ

государственный музей-памятник

ИСААКИЕВСКИЙ СОБОР

the state memorial museum "St. Isaac's Cathedral"

www.cathedral.ru e-mail: isaac@cathedral.ru

Контроль

Утвержден приказом Минкультуры РФ 17.12.08 №257 ОКУД 079300i

MUSEUM

- Входной билет в музей Исаакиевский собор -

1023748438004

Дата посещения: 05.08.2013

Тест ID: Общ

                    250.00р.

Режим работы: с 11:00 до 19:00 (летом с 10:00 до 19:00).
Выходной день – среда. Вход посетителей прекращается за 1 час до закрытия.
СПб ГБУК ГМП "Исаакиевский собор". ИНН 7812025107. Юридический адрес: 191186 Санкт-Петербург, Невский пр., 29-31, лит. А.

Исаакиевский собор	Храм «Спас на крови»	Сампсониевский собор	Смольный собор
Исаакиевская площадь, 4	наб. кан. Грибоедова, 26	Б. Сампсониевский пр., 41	пл. Растрелли, 1
тел. +7(812) 315-97-32	тел. +7(812) 315-16-36	тел. +7(812) 294-57-51	тел. +7(812) 577-14-21

ООО «ИнфоТех», Санкт-Петербург, Московский пр., 103/3, тел. (812)3279506, ИНН 7810099978. Заказ № 1318, тираж 500000 шт., 2013 г.
TID/MID/AID:
004 79   URN/AUTH:
                    05.08.2013 12:25:17 CHEQUE: 004-2122701 AO №ДЕК: 553898

Hotels
- ⊡ < US$125
- ⊡ US$125–315
- ⊡ > US$315

When in St Petersburg you do not need to dial the city code 812 before the seven-digit phone number.

Mercury
Tavricheskaya Ulitsa 39 ◆ **E** E2
Tel. 812 325 64 44
Metro Chernychevskaya
This building adorned with pediments was turned into a comfortable little hotel in the 1980s. It was originally designed to receive official visitors but it now also welcomes tourists – although there are only 16 rooms, so booking is essential. The subway station is 5 minutes away, but the Tauride Gardens are close by.
16 rooms
⊡

Moskva Hotel
Pl. Aleksandra Nevskovo 2 ◆ **E** E5
Tel. 812 274 30 01
or 812 274 00 52
Metro Ploshchad Aleksandra or Nevskovo
This hotel at the end of the Nevsky Prospekt, in front of the Alexander Nevsky Monastery, has the advantage of a subway station on its doorstep. Its gigantic, Soviet-style façade conceals comfortable rooms, although these are often reserved for groups. Its restaurants and bars have a reputation for providing good value for money.
777 rooms
⊡

Neptun Best Western
Obvodnogo Kanala Nab. 93a ◆ **E** B6
Tel. 812 324 46 10
www.bestwestern.com
Metro Pushkinskaya
Part of the new Neptun business center. Although near the city center this hotel is not very conveniently located: the nearest metro station is 10–15 minutes' walk away.

However, with a tennis court, gym, bowling alley, billiard room, squash court, full-size swimming pool and golf simulator, it has much to please those who like their hotel to offer more than just a bed.
69 rooms
⊡ ⊠⊠

Neva
Ulitsa Tchaikovskogo 17 ◆ **E** C2
Tel. 812 278 05 04
Metro Chernychevskaya
This modest hotel is tucked behind a façade decorated with telamons, just 10 minutes from the Summer Garden on foot. The rooms are simple but their price is appealing.
133 rooms
⊡ C

Novotel St Petersburg Centre
Nevsky Prospekt 102 ◆ **E** E5
Tel. 335 11 88
Metro Mayakovskaya
The most recent of the big hotels in the town center opened its doors in 2005. It has 233 rooms arranged over nine floors. The sober design style gets better on higher floors, where there is a good view. All modern comforts are offered (sauna, fitness studio) and the hotel is equipped with state-of-the-art communications technology.
⊡ C Ⅲ P

Oktiabrskaya
Ligovsky Prospekt 10 ◆ **E** D3
Tel. 277 63 30
Metro Ploshchad Vosstanya
The Oktiabrskaya Hotel stands on the Nevsky Prospekt, midway between the Admiralty and the Alexander Nevsky Monastery. True, it is very central, but its

proximity to Moscow Station means noisy crowds and traffic, and this will be, for many, a disadvantage. The historic 19th-century building, in pure Soviet style, is somewhat charmless but the rooms are being renovated.
Over 500 rooms
⊡ C

Piaty Ugol
Zagorodny Pr. 13 ◆ **E** B5
Tel. 812 380 81 81
Metro Vladimirskaya, Dostoevskaya
This small family-run establishment is located in the Dostoevsky district. Internet access in the rooms, some of which have views of of Our Lady of Vladimir.
27 rooms
⊡ C ⊠ P

🔲 Pushka Inn
Reky Priajky Nab. 14 ◆ **A** C3
Tel. 312 09 13
Metro Nevsky Prospekt
This small hotel is installed in a narrow building on the banks of the Moika, next to the Pushkin Museum. It offers simple but comfortable rooms; those with a view of the river are the most attractive (and also the most expensive). Breakfast is served in the first-floor Pushka Inn restaurant, which is taken over by local customers later in the day.
27 rooms
⊡ ⊡ C Ⅲ ⊠

Radisson SAS Royal
Nevsky Prospekt 49 ◆ **E** C4
Tel. 812 322 50 00
www.radissonsas.com
Metro Mayakovskaya
This hotel near Moscow Station (beyond the Fontanka) is set in an elegant 19th-century building that was originally commissioned by a

wealthy businessman (the hotel's restaurant bears his name). It boasts a highly popular bar that is extended in the summer by a terrace that spills on to the Prospekt. The bedrooms, which are spacious and very comfortable, attract both tourists and business people.
164 rooms
⊡

Renaissance St Petersburg Baltic Hotel
Potchtamskaya Ul. 4 ◆ **A** A5
Tel. 812 380 40 00
Metro Nevsky Prospekt, Sadovaya
This member of the Marriott chain opened in 2004, a stone's throw from the futuristic post office building. The hotel's 19th-century façade gives way to an interior design of the utmost modernity. The rooms are furnished with refinement, and those on the upper floor offer a dizzying view of Saint Isaac's Cathedral.
102 rooms
⊡ C ⊠ P

KOLOMNA DISTRICT

Hotel Sovetskaya
Lermontovsky Pr. 43 ◆ **D** E5
Tel. 740 26 40
Metro Baltiskaya
In keeping with the Soviet penchant for doing things on a massive scale, this 18-story hotel was built in the 1970s with no less than one thousand rooms! Those on the Fontanka wing have been refurbished and are comfortable and attractive. The view of the city and its monuments from the top floor is breathtaking.
Over 1000 rooms
⊡ ⊠

◆HOTELS

Matisov Domik
Reky Priajky
Nab. 3/1 ◆ **D** D3
Tel. 812 495 04 62
Metro Sennaya
Ploshchad
This hotel on Matisov Island, far from the city center, is much appreciated for its tranquility and family atmosphere. The tastefully furnished rooms are set in a small house built around a courtyard bedecked with flowers. A small museum inside the hotel displays Russian antiques.
46 rooms
⬚⬚ **C**

MALAYA OKHTA
Deson-Ladoga
◆ OUTSIDE MAP AREA
Shaumyana
Prospekt 26
Tel. 812 528 53 93
www.deson.lek.ru
Metro
Novocherkasskaya
Don't judge this hotel by its plain concrete façade. The interior is a totally different and thoroughly modern story. The rooms are light, large and comfortable, with pastel décor, and the bathrooms are well equipped. The hotel is slightly east of the city center, but close to the metro station and a five-minute bus ride away from the Alexander Nevsky Monastery.
96 rooms
⬚⬚

MOSKOVSKY
Hotel German Club
◆ OUTSIDE MAP AREA
Ulitsa Gastello 20
Tel. 812 448 51 94
www.germanclub.
narod.ru
Metro Moskovskaya
The hotel's website summarizes the place as "Russian hospitality meets German order". The German Club is rather out of the city center but in a lively and interesting district.

It occupies the third and fourth floors of a tall building typical of the monumental Muscovite architectural style of the Stalin era. The rooms are plain, spotlessly clean and light, with a lot of pine woodwork and high ceilings. All in all, it's a cozy place to stay and worth the extra journey.
16 rooms
⬚⬚

PRIBALTIYSKAYA HOTEL

Pulkovskaya
◆ OUTSIDE MAP AREA
Pobedy Ploshchad 1
Tel. 812 140 39 00
Fax 812 140 39 48
www.pulkovskaya.ru
Metro Moskovskaya
Though it's located at the end of Moskovsky Prospekt, away from the city center, it's still quite handy for getting in and out of town. The Pulkovskaya is on a direct metro line to the heart of the city; Nevsky Prospekt station is no more than a 20-minute ride away. The hotel is also just 10–15 minutes away from Pulkovo airport by taxi. Built in the 1970s, this is again a charmless establishment, but the rooms are adequate, well equipped and inexpensive. The hotel's lobby is impressive and facilities include two restaurants, two saunas, a tennis court and a health club.
840 rooms
⬚⬚

NEAR PETROGRAD
LDM
Ulitsa Profesora
Popova 47 ◆ **C** B3
Tel. 812 234 32 78
www.ldm.ru
Metro
Petrogradskaya
This (very ugly) hotel stands next to the LDM (Leningradsky Dvorets Molodioy – Leningrad Youth Center). Built in 1975, it contains leisure and sports centers,

conference rooms and concert halls where music festivals are held. The picturesque view over the Malaya Nevka and the islands compensates for the fact that the nearest metro station is a good 15 minutes' walk away.
201 rooms
⬚⬚

VASILYEVSKY ISLAND
Hotel Shelfort
3 Linia 26 ◆ **D** E1
Tel. 812 328 05 55
Metro
Vasileostrovskaya
This small hotel opened in 2001 on Vasilyevsky Island, behind the University quay, in a residential area with an abundance of consulates. There are only six rooms (spread over two floors); two of them have preserved their tiled fireplaces. Breakfast is served in a cozy lounge.
6 rooms
⬚⬚

Pribaltiyskaya
Korablestroitley
Ulitsa 14 ◆ **B** A6
Tel. 812 356 30 01
www.pribaltiyskaya.ru
Metro Primorskaya
This typical Soviet-era concrete structure is the biggest hotel in the city, and it was considered the best when built in 1980. The Pribaltiyskaya is well maintained inside, but it is distant from the historic center and rates are steep. Half the rooms, though, have striking sea views since it stands right on the edge of the gulf, high on a promontory. The restaurants serve Russian and Western European food, and in one, Neva, there is live music every evening. Hotel facilities include sauna, pool, gym, massage, beauty salon, bowling and billiard hall, and a nightclub.
1200 rooms
⬚⬚

NEAR VYBORG
Saint Petersburg
Pirogovskaya
Nab. 5/2 ◆ **C** E5
Tel. 812 380 19 19
www.hotel-spb.ru
Metro Ploshchad
Lenina
One of the standard-bearers of Soviet architecture, on the banks of the Neva (just opposite the Aurora cruiser), a 10-minute walk from the subway station. Despite refurbishments, the décor is still imbued with the spirit of the Brezhnev era. The only rooms that offer any real comfort are those on the top floors, with large bay windows overlooking the river, but they are also the most expensive. The hotel relies on group bookings.
410 rooms
⬚⬚

Restaurants
- ◼ < US$30
- ◼ US$30–50
- ◼ US$50–70
- ⊞ > US$70

Prices in restaurants are sometimes given as 'y.e.': eg 25 y. e. y. e. is a conventional monetary unit equivalent to US$1.

AROUND NEVSKY PROSPEKT

1913 God (Year 1913)
Voznesensky
Prospekt 13/2 ◆ **A** A6
Tel. 812 315 51 48
Metro Nevsky
Prospekt
Open noon–1am
With a classic interior, a relaxed, comfortable atmosphere and high-quality service, this place offers Western European cuisine and a range of very rich and varied Russian dishes.
◼ ◼

Admiralteistvo (Admiralty)
Nevsky Palace Hotel
Nevsky
Prospekt 57 ◆ **E** C4
Tel. 812 380 20 01
Open Tue–Sat.
6am–10.30pm
Metro Mayakovskaya
Big, bustling hotel-restaurant where the maritime theme extends to the décor and menu. It is strongest on fish but the reliable menu covers Russian and Soviet classics including caviar, stolichny salad (meat, hard-boiled eggs, gherkins, peas, potato and onion, with mayonnaise), borsch and solyanka (a sharp soup of vegetables and meat or fish). The Georgian fillet of lamb with garlic and coriander sauce is particularly good. Background Russian folk and "urban romance" music.
◼ ◼ ♫

Caviar Bar
Grand Hotel Europe
Mikhailovskaya Ulitsa 1/7 ◆ **C** F5
Tel. 812 329 60 00
Open 6am–11pm
Metro Gostiny Dvor
The Caviar Bar's posh, expensive menu is of course strong on caviar dishes but also includes other favorites of wealthy Russians such as crab, sturgeon, pirozhky (pastry parcels stuffed with meat or cabbage) cooked in champagne. Regular customers here recommend the trout marinated in vodka. Tea is served in samovars, as Russian and gypsy music plays in the background.
⊞ ◼

Dvorianskoye Gnezdo (the Nobles' Nest)
Dekabristov
Pl. 21 ◆ **A** A5
Tel. 812 312 32 05
Metro Gostiny Dvor
Open noon– midnight
A restaurant situated in the tea house at the bottom of the Yusupov Palace garden. The atmosphere is both cozy and imperial at the same time; the excellent menu, original and imaginative, includes dishes taken from the cookbooks of the Yusupov princes. Classical music is performed in the small rotunda. There's a wide selection of high-quality wines.
⊞ ◼ ♫ ♫

Europa
Grand Hotel Europe
Mikhailovskaya
Ulitsa 1/7 ◆ **A** D5
Tel. 812 329 60 00
Metro Gostiny Dvor
Open Mon.–Sat.
7am–11pm; brunch
Sun noon–4pm
Russian and Western European cuisine, excellent choice of wines and cigars. Recommended for the lavish Sunday brunch, to be taken

RESTAURANT OF THE HOTEL EUROPA

lazily with plenty of semi-sweet Russian champagne. But even then, dress at the smart end of casual to feel at ease in this soaring grand, glass-ceilinged Art Deco dining room, where you can expect to see everyone who is anyone in St Petersburg (tie required in the evening).
⊞ ◼

Hermitage
Dvortsovaya pl. 8
◆ **E** A2
Tel. 314 47 72
Metro Nevsky
Prospekt
Open daily 12
noon–11pm
A striking location on the square by the Palace, within the grounds of the old army headquarters (now an annex of the Hermitage Museum). This restaurant was opened for the celebrations marking the city's 300th anniversary, when its vast halls were used for a constant stream of official banquets. They now lie empty, although they have preserved their ornate décor. The menu combines Russian specialties and international dishes. Extensive wine list.
⊞

Kalinka-Malinka
Italianskaya ul. 5
◆ **E** B3
Tel. 314 26 81
Metro Nevsky
Prospekt
Open daily
noon–11pm
The décor, complete with log walls, seeks to recreate the atmosphere of a dacha, while the waiters and musicians all wear appropriate costumes. The menu features classic Russian dishes. This restaurant is very popular at night with the audiences pouring out of the theaters on the nearby Arts Square.
◼ ♫

Kamelot
Bolshaya
Koniuchennaya Ul. 14
◆ **A** C4
Tel. 812 325 99 06
Metro Nevsky
Prospekt
Open noon– midnight
As the restaurant's name suggests, the décor here is inspired by Arthurian legend. Beneath the Gothic vaulting are tables spread with cloths illustrating the adventures of the Knights of the Round Table. Excellent European cuisine, with unusual and

◆ RESTAURANTS

Restaurants
- ▣ < US$30
- ▣ US$30–50
- ▣ US$50–70
- ⊞ > US$70

generous dishes.
▣ ▣

Karavan
Voznesensky Pr. 46
◆ **A** A6
Tel. 812 310 56 78
Metro Sadovaya
Open noon–2am
*Traditional Caucasian
and Central Asian
cuisine served in an
oriental atmosphere.
Dishes include
Georgian shashlyk
(skewered meat),
Azerbaijani Iulia-
kebab (minced meat)
and plov uzbek
(pilau rice).*
▣

Kolkhida
Nevsky
Prospekt 176 ◆ **E** E5
Tel. 812 274 25 14
Metro Ploshchad
Alexandra or
Nevskovo
Open from noon until
the last customer
leaves
*The Kolkhida offers a
traditional Georgian
atmosphere, with staff
dressed in national
costumes. There's
a wide selection
of high-quality
Georgian wines.*
▣

Landscrona
Nevsky Palace Hotel
Nevsky Prospekt 57
◆ **E** C4
Tel. 812 380 20 01
Metro Mayakovskaya
Open 6.30pm–
midnight
*A particularly well-
regarded gourmet
restaurant serving a
wide range of
Mediterranean dishes
with an Italian touch
but also offering
some more unusual
dishes, such as
oysters with caviar
cooked in
champagne. The
game (shot by a
professional hunter
who is a member of
the hotel's staff)
is particularly
recommended. The
restaurant, on
the eighth floor, offers
fine views over the*

rooftops of
St Petersburg.
Live vocal music.
⊞ ▣ ♫

La Strada
Bolshaya
Koniuchennaya 27
◆ **A** C4
Tel. 812 312 47 00
Metro Nevsky
Prospekt
Open noon–11pm
A glass-walled gallery

VALHALL RESTAURANT ON NEVSKY PROSPEKT

VALHALL RESTAURANT

*in a picturesque
courtyard set out in
the style of an Italian
street. The specialty
here is pizza cooked
in front of customers.
This is also a good
place for families:
there is a special
children's menu, and
a children's room with
toys and supervision
by a nanny.*
▣ ▣

Masha i Medvyed
Malaya Sadovaya
Ulitsa 1 ◆ **A** D6
Tel. 812 310 46 31
Metro Gostiny Dvor
Open 11am–11pm
*Plain, simple
basement restaurant
with plain, simple
cooking. Its chief
boast is pike caviar
with onion. Also
serves pirozhky
(pastry parcels
stuffed with meat or
cabbage) prepared*

with beer, onion soup
and kasha (grilled
millet) with
mushrooms.
▣ ▣

Matrosskaya
Tichina (Seaman's
Silence)
Ulitsa Marata 54/34
◆ **E** C4-5
Tel. 812 764 44 13
Metro Ligovsky
Prospekt

Open noon– midnight
*Exceptionally good
fish dishes prepared
by a highly regarded
French chef. The
atmosphere here
evokes the sea: the
sound of waves
whispers in the
background,
waitresses are
dressed as sailors,
and there is a large
aquarium from which
you may select your
fish.*
▣

Nicolaï
Bolshaya Morskaya
Ulitsa 52 ◆ **A** B 5
Tel. 571 14 02
Metro Nevsky
Prospekt
Open daily noon–
11pm
*This restaurant is set
in a private hotel
donated to the
Architects' Union and
rechristened the*

House of the
Architects, but it is
nevertheless open to
all. The building has
lost none of its charm
and its wood trim
provides a delightful
setting for sampling
traditional Russian
food such as beef
stroganoff and
shashlyks (kebabs).
▣

Onegin
Sadovaya Ulitsa 11
◆ **A** B3
Tel. 812 571 83 84
www.oneginspb.com
Open Sun.–Thur.
5pm–2am, Fri.–Sat.
5pm–5am
Metro Gostiny Dvor,
Nevsky Prospekt
*Fashionable
restaurant-club
serving Russian
and European
cuisine.*
⊞

Russian Empire
Nevsky
Prospekt 17 ◆ **A** C5
Tel. 571 24 09
Metro Nevsky
Prospekt
*This restaurant is
located in the elegant
rooms of the
Stroganoff Palace.
The décor revels in
the splendors of a
bygone era (inlaid
tables, fine porcelain
crockery and silver
cutlery) but these do
not come cheap…*
⊞

Senat-bar
Galernaya Ulitsa 1
◆ **D** E2
Tel. 812 314 92 53
Open noon–2am
Metro Nevsky
Prospekt
*A restaurant in the
cellars of the Senate
where the imperial
archives were stored
before the Russian
Revolution. Spacious
interiors with décor
depicting archivists,
busts and frescoes in
the Empire style.
Russian and Western
European cuisine.
Some of the dishes
are cooked in front of*

diners. A very good place for lunch.
🔲 🅲

Stroganovsky Dvor
Nevsky
Prospekt 17 ◆ **A** B4
Tel. 812 315 23 15
Metro Nevsky
Prospekt
Open noon– midnight
A café-restaurant in the glass-roofed courtyard of the Stroganovsky Palace. Noted for its buffet, a touch simple and stodgy but one of the bargains of the city when you happen to be very hungry. Buffet US$5 (open until 10pm).
🔲 🅲

Valhall
Nevsky Pr. 22/24
◆ **A** B4
Tel. 812 571 00 24
www.valhall.ru
Metro Nevsky
Prospekt
Open 10am–3am
In the heart of the city, opposite the Cathedral of Our Lady of Kazan, Valhall has become a renowned and popular restaurant. Russian, Western European and Scandinavian cuisine, in which northern dishes feature prominently: Norwegian salmon, Greenland prawns, steaks served "on a Viking shield". The décor features 9th-century armory, and the waitresses are dressed as Valkyries.
🔲 🅲 🏔

Za Stsenoy (Behind the Scenes)
Teatralnaya
Ploshchad 18/10
◆ **D** F3
Tel. 812 327 05 21
Metro Sennaya
Ploshchad
or Sadovaya
Open noon–2am
This is the restaurant of the Mariinsky Theater, whose very first guest was Placido Domingo.

It has a bohemian atmosphere, and the dining room is pleasingly decorated with theatrical paraphernalia – curtains, mirrors and pointed shoes. Russian and Western European cuisine are served.
🔲

Zolotoi Ostap
Italianskaya Ulitsa 4
◆ **A** D4
Tel. 812 303 88 22
Metro Gostiny Dvor
Open noon– midnight
The entrance to the Zolotoi Ostap, located beside Arts Square, is guarded by a bronze statue of Ostap Bender, the hero of Soviet satirical literature. Within is a suite of dining rooms decorated in the Art Nouveau style.
The menu features not only Russian and Western European dishes but Caucasian and Chinese specialties as well. Zolotoy ostap, the house specialty – veal steak stuffed with smoked salmon – is recommended.
🔲 🅲

Russkaya Rybalka (Russian Fishing)
Iujnaya Doroga 11
Primorsky Victory
Park ◆ **B** B2
Tel. 812 323 98 13
www.russian-fishing.com
Metro Krestovsky
Ostrov
Open noon–9pm
Set amid greenery, this restaurant stands on stilts at the edge of a lake filled with trout and sturgeon. Fishing tackle can be hired on site and guests may catch their own fish, which are then prepared – smoked, grilled or baked in foil – according to individual taste. Guests have included Russian president

Vladimir Putin, who has entertained foreign leaders here. Prices are based on the weight of the fish caught: about US$7 per lb for trout and US$9 for sturgeon. There is no additional charge for cooking the fish.
🔲 🍴 🐕

Podvorie
◆ OUTSIDE MAP AREA
Flitrovskoye Chosse 16
Tel. 812 465 13 99
www.podvorye.ru
Open noon–11pm
Well-known country-style restaurant at the entrance to Pavlovsk Park. A favorite spot for company junkets and the banqueting of visiting VIPs – Vladimir Putin once celebrated a birthday here. Standard Russian dishes, good choice of Crimean wines. Live music. Cossack and gypsy shows. A Russian bear at the entrance offering visitors a shot of vodka sets the tone for a fun place.
🔲 🎵 🐕

Akvarel
Birjevoy Most ◆ **A** A2
Tel. 812 320 86 00
Metro Sportivnaya
Open noon–11pm
"Fusion" cooking with strong Thai and Japanese accents, to a high standard. Modern, light interior. Akvarel occupies a moored boat, with spectacular views of the city. Café above, restaurant below. Bar and dance floor, with DJs on Fridays and Saturdays, add to the lively atmosphere of this trendy new venue.
🔲 🏔

Austeria
Peter and Paul
Fortress ◆ **C** C6
Tel. 812 238 42 62

Metro Gorkovskaya
Open noon–midnight
At the time of Peter the Great "austeria" meant "inn", and the restaurant's interior re-creates a 17th-century Dutch inn. The menu, with a strong emphasis on vodka, caviar and blinis, is typically Russian.
🔲

Flora
Kamennoostrovsky
Prospekt 5 ◆ **A** C1
Tel 812 232 34 00
Metro Gorkovskaya
Open noon–11pm
The depressing modern exterior conceals a delicate Art Nouveau interior where Ilya Lazerson, one of the city's great chefs, holds court. French and Russian dishes. The flower-filled "tropical" setting, complete with a little bridge and a live parrot, make this a fun place to escape on a freezing day. With live ballet shows on Fridays and Saturdays, Flora is one of St Petersburg's most entertaining restaurants. Note also the related café and shop nearby, at Malaya Posadskaya Ulitsa 18.
🔲 🎵

Gorny Oriol
Alexander
Park ◆ **C** B5
Tel. 812 232 32 82
Metro Gorkovskaya
Open noon– midnight
This family restaurant located opposite the zoo is a good place to come to sample a wide variety of Georgian dishes. Especially recommended are the famous shashlyk (skewered meat). House wine is served in pitchers. The terrace, open in summer, looks onto the zoo.
🔲 🏔 🐕

Na Zdorovye
Bolshoy
Prospekt 13 ◆ **D** A5
Tel. 812 232 40 39
Metro Sportivanaya
Open noon–11pm
*Exceptional kitchen.
"The utopia of
Russian cooking"
says one Russian
critic. The décor is a
mix of Soviet retro
and old Russian. The
menu likewise, but
with a few dishes
betraying a French
influence. Duck
breast and fried
goat's cheese jostle
with the salted
salmon and the
pork marinated in
kvass (a popular
Russian drink made
from fermented
bread). A cheerful
atmosphere,
with gypsy
entertainment.*
■ ♫

U Gorchakova
Bolchaya
Monetnaya Ulitsa 19
◆ **C** C4
Tel. 812 233 92 72
Metro Gorkovskaya
Open noon– midnight
*The Gorchakova is
located in the fine
residence of Prince
Gorchakov, the
eminent 19th-century
Russian diplomat
and chancellor.
However, neither
the unusual and
eclectic décor nor
the menu match the
atmosphere of the
state rooms. It's
definitely worth a visit.*
■

STRELNA
Restaurant Strelna
◆ OUTSIDE MAP AREA
(NEAR PETERHOF)
Sankt-
Petersburgskoye
Schosse 58A
Tel. 812 421 41 96
Open 11am–
midnight
*From this restaurant
there is a magnificent
view of the Strelna
Palace. Taste Russian
and Causasian
cuisine, while
listening to the
musical
accompaniment. Be
sure to check out the
fish of the day.*
■ 〽

VASILYEVSKY ISLAND
New Island
Universitetskaya
Nab. (level with
1 Linia) ◆ **D** E1
Tel. 812 963 67 65
Metro
Vasileostrovskaya
*A restaurant on a boat
moored near
Rumiantsevsky ramp
on University*

VIEW OF VASILYEVSKY ISLAND

GRIBOYEDOV CANAL

*Embankment. Enjoy
Russian and Western
European cuisine as
the boat makes its
way along the Neva,
passing a succession
of magnificent
riverside palaces.
The boat trips take
place only between
April and November,
when the river is
navigable; New Island
is ice-bound in winter.
Trips along the Neva
cost US$8, and
dinner about US$35.*
■ 〽

Restoran
Tamozhenny
Per. 2 ◆ **D** F1
Tel. 812 327 89 79
Metro
Vasileostrovskaya
Open noon– midnight
*Opposite the entrance
to Peter the Great's
Kunstkammer on
Vasilyevsky Island.
Smart, restrained
interior by Andrei
Dmitriev, the most
original young
designer in the city –
he also designed the
Mariinsky Theater's
restaurant; spacious
area, with a menu
printed on recycled
banknotes, that will
suit all budgets. Good
service, excellent
atmosphere. The
kitchen attracts mixed
reports for its fancier
dishes, but the open
fire makes this a good
place to retreat for
blinis and dumplings
with tea on a cold
day.*
■

Russkiy Kitsch
Universitetskaya
Nab. 25 ◆ **D** E1
Tel. 812 325 11 22
Open noon–2am
Metro
Vasileostrovskaya
*The décor is
everything the name
suggests – a parody
of nouveau-riche bad
taste. Some of the
joke carries over into
the food: blinis with
asparagus, for
example. But the
French-influenced
cooking is serious,
and for this city is by
no means overpriced.
Six rooms, two
galleries behind glass,
dance hall.*
■ ♫

Staraya Tamozhnaya (Old Customs House)
Tamojenny Per. 1
◆ **D** F1
Tel. 812 327 89 80
Metro
Vasileostrovskaya
Open 1pm–1am
*Exceptional kitchen.
Grand food, even
grander wine list, high
prices, French chef.
The mainly French
menu also salutes
some Russian
classics, including
blinis with black
caviar. Historical
touches to the décor
help to create the
sense of tradition in
this red-brick vaulted
chamber, a customs
point in the 18th
century. Two bars,
jazz in the evening.
An institution.*
■

VYBORG
7–40
Bolshoy
Sampsonievsky Pr.
108 ◆ **C** D1-2
Tel. 812 246 34 44
Metro Lesnaya or
Chyornaya Rechka
Open Mon. 3pm–
11pm, Tue.–Sun.
noon–11pm
*Exceptionally good
Jewish cuisine, with
a wide selection of
traditional dishes,
including tsimes and
forchmak. The food is
served on clay
crockery painted in
the style of Chagall.
Live violin music.*
■ ♫

CAFÉS

Bistro Le Français
Galernaya Ulitsa 20
◆ **D** E2
Tel. 812 315 24 65
Open 11am–1am
*Traditional French
cuisine. Bar with
movie theater and
videos of French
movies for hire.*

Che
Poltavskaya
Ulitsa 3 ◆ **E** D4
Tel. 812 277 76 00
Open daily 24 hrs
Metro Ploshchad
Aleksandra Nevskovo
or Ploshchad
Vosstanya
*A trendy café with
Latin-American and
jazz music in the
background. A huge
choice of teas and
cakes on offer.*

Coffee-Break
Kanala Griboyedova
Nab. 22 ◆ **A** C5
Tel. 812 314 67 29
Open 9am–11pm
*A café with a fine
view of the Cathedral
of Our Lady of Kazan.
Wide selection of
coffees, and black,
green and red tea;
delicious desserts.
Exhibitions
of contemporary
painting.*

Idiot
Nab. Reky
Moyky 82 ◆ **C** A6
Tel. 812 315 16 75
Open daily
11am–1am
*Vegetarian cuisine.
Cluster of noisy, cosily
furnished basement
rooms, a popular
refuge for students
and foreigners.
Overflowing
bookshelves and
bizarre ornaments
help to create the
wonderfully eclectic
atmosphere.
The food is mainly
but not solely
vegetarian.
Complimentary shot
of vodka provided
with each alcoholic
drink. The full bar,
which serves*

*cocktails, makes
this an excellent place
for a late drink as
well as for a
leisurely lunch.*

James Cook
Chvedsky per. 2
◆ **E** A3
Tel. 812 312 32 00
or 812 571 11 51
*Two naval-themed
rooms in this café,
offering a good
choice of teas and
cakes. There's also
a pub with a large
selection of beers
and savory dishes.
Musical flavor: jazz,
blues, country.*

PUBS AND BARS

Mollie's Irish Bar
Ulitsa Rubinstein 36
◆ **A** F6
Tel. 812 319 97 68
Open noon–2am
*An off-the-shelf
Irish pub, and none
the worse for that.
Guinness, some
20 types of beer
and a wide range
of cocktails on offer.
Some hot food, and
hardwood stools.
Friendly atmosphere.
Popular with
foreigners.*

**Podval Brodiatcheï
Sobaki**
Isskusstv pl. 5 (near

Nevsky Pr.) ◆ **E** B3
Tel. 315 77 64
Open daily
11am–11pm
Metro Nevsky
Prospekt
*The name of this
café in a vaulted
cellar literally means
"stray dog". It
opened in 1912 and
numbered among
its regular customers
the poets Anna
Akhmatova and
Vladimir Mayakovsky;
they still preside over
it today, in the form
of portraits hung
along the walls.
A pleasant stopover
for a cup of tea
after a visit to the
Russian Museum.*

Quo Vadis
Nevsky Prospekt 24
◆ **E** A3
Tel. 812 571 80 11
www.quovadis.ru
Metro Nevsky
Prospekt
Open daily 24 hrs
Internet café.

Shamrock
Ulitsa Dekabristov 27
◆ **A** A6
Tel. 812 318 46 25
Open noon–2am
*Another Irish pub,
located opposite
the Mariinsky Theater,
and again a
fashionable place*

*with a bohemian
atmosphere. Beer
from US$2.*
◼ ▭ ◼

Sunduk (Coffee)
Furchtatskaya
Ulitsa 42 ◆ **E** D2
Tel. 812 272 31 00
Open 10am–10pm
*Three small rooms,
one with a stage
where jazz, blues and
rock bands perform.
Friendly, relaxed
atmosphere. Beer
from US$2.50; snacks
from US$1 (cover
charge US$1).*
◼ 🎵

Tinkoff
Kazanskaya
Ulitsa 7 ◆ **A** C5
Tel. 812 314 84 85
www.tinkoff.ru
Open noon–2am
*Microbrewery (the
modern interior with
a glass partition
allows customers to
watch the brewing in
action) with fine beer
and fair food,
including a sushi bar.
A St Petersburg
institution.
Big and often noisy
(quieter at lunch), with
live music and giant
television screen. A
trendy, vibrant place,
popular with students.*

LEISURE

CASINOS

**Premier Casino
Club**
Nevsky Pr. 47 ◆ **A** F5
Tel. 812 315 78 93
Open 24 hours
*Bars and Palkin
restaurant: cozy
atmosphere and
good-quality Western
European cuisine.*

**Taléon Casino
Club**
Reky Moiky
Nab. 59 ◆ **A** B5
Tel. 812 315 76 45
Open 24 hours
*Located in the
former residence
of the Russian
merchant Eliseev,
with many rooms and
a strong gambling
atmosphere.*

NEVSKY PROSPEKT

JAZZ PHILHARMONIA

Restaurants and concerts. Private functions some evenings.

CINEMA

Dom Kino (the Movie House)
Karavannaya Ul. 12
◆ **A** E5
Tel. 812 314 80 36
Open exclusively to members of the film-directors' union during the Soviet era, the Movie House is now a center for cinema enthusiasts. Events include screenings of European movies, retrospectives and film festivals.

CIRCUS

Sankt Peterburgsky Tsirk
Reky Fontanky Naberejnaya 3
◆ **A** E2
Tel. 812 314 84 78
www.circus.spb.ru
Ticket office open 11am–7pm
One of the oldest Russian circuses and one the most beautiful in Europe. Established in 1877, it was the first edifice of stone to be constructed specifically for circus performances.

CONCERTS

Bielosselskikh-Bielozerskikh Dvorets
Nevsky Pr. 41
◆ **A** E5
Tel. 812 315 52 36
Chamber music performed in the Oak Room and Mirror Room of the Beloselsky-Belozersky Palace.

Filarmonia Dmitria Shostakovicha
◆ **A** D5
Home of the fine St Petersburg Philharmonic and of the smaller Glinka recital hall.

OSTROVSKY SQUARE

SMOLNY CATHEDRAL

SHOSTAKOVICH (LARGE) PHILHARMONIC HALL (Bolshoy Zal):
Mikhailovskaya Ul. 2
Tel. 812 110 42 57
Ticket office open 11am–3pm, 4–7.30pm
GLINKA (SMALL) CHAMBER HALL (Maly Zal):
Nevsky Pr. 30
Tel. 812 311 83 33
Ticket office open 11am–3pm, 4–7pm
The Shostakovich Philharmonia's distinguished concert hall has an excellent orchestra. Major international musicians perform here. The Glinka Philharmonia also hosts several festivals, including an early music festival where all the pieces are performed on period instruments.

Kapella
Reky Moiky Nab. 20
◆ **A** C3
Tel. 812 314 11 53 or 812 314 10 58 (ticket office)
Ticket office open noon–7pm
An architectural jewel, St Petersburg's State Kapella is now a concert hall with a wide-ranging musical program.

Oktiabrsky
Ligovsky Prospekt 6 ◆ **E** D3
Tel. 812 275 12 73
Ticket office open 11am–8pm
The largest concert hall in St Petersburg, with a wide-ranging program of musical events.

Smolny Sobor (Smolny Cathedral)
Rastrelli Pl. 3/1 ◆ **E** F1
Tel. 812 271 76 32
Concerts of Russian church music.

JAZZ CLUBS

Filarmonia Djazovoy Muzyki (Jazz Philharmonia)
Zagorodny Pr. 27
◆ **E** B5
Tel. 812 764 85 65
www.jazz-hall.spb.ru
Open: *Great Room* Tue.–Sun. 7–11pm; *Ellington Room* Tue., Fri., Sat. 8–11pm
Established in the 1980s by David Golochtchekin, the renowned jazz musician, this is the oldest jazz club in St Petersburg. Performers from all over the world are invited here, notably for the annual Swing on Summer Nights

festival in June. Smart dress required.

JFC Jazz Club
Chpalernaya Ul. 33
◆ **E** C1
Tel. 812 272 98 50
www.jfc.spb.ru
Open daily 7–10pm
One of the best jazz clubs in the city, where international musicians perform all types of jazz. Knowledgeable audience. Drinks at reasonable prices.

Neo Jazz Club
Solianoy Per. 14
◆ **A** E3
Tel. 812 273 38 30
Open noon–midnight; concerts at 8pm
Soft jazz, duos and trios. Western European and Caucasus cuisine.

NIGHTCLUBS

Fish Fabrique
Ligovsky Prospekt 53 ◆ **E** C5
Tel. 812 764 48 57
www.fishfabrique.spb.ru
Open 4pm–5.30am; concerts start around 10pm
All styles of music. One of the oldest-established underground clubs in St Petersburg, with a bohemian atmosphere. Table soccer and a terrace that's open in summer.

Griboyedov Club
Voronejskaya Ul. 2a
◆ **E** C6
Tel. 812 764 43 55
Open 6pm–6am (Fri., Sat., till 7am)
concerts at 10pm
A fashionable venue located in a disused air-raid shelter hung with Persian carpets. DJ.

Jimi Hendrix Jazz Club
Liteiny Prospekt 33
◆ **A** F4
Tel. 812 279 88 13
Open 24 hours daily

A club by night and a café by day. Blues, rock'n'roll and Latino evenings.
A pleasant place for dinner with friends. Affordable prices. As space is limited, reservations must be made.

Luna (the Moon)
Voznesensky Pr. 46 ◆ **A** A6
Tel. 812 310 16 16
Open 6pm–6am
Two levels, three rooms, restaurants, casino, bars and a dance floor. A varied range of evening performances, with high-class professional choreography. Smart dress required.

Manhattan
Reky Fontanky Nab. 90 ◆ **E** B5
Tel. 812 713 19 45
www.manhattan.by.ru
Open 2pm–5am; concerts at 9pm (except Mon.)
Rock, blues and jazz. Internet café and billiards.

Money Honey and City Club
Sadovaya Ulitsa 13 ◆ **A** E4
Tel. 812 310 05 49
www.moneyhoney.org
Open 11am–6am; concerts at 8pm
Rock music. A club on two floors, with two dance areas and two bars. It has a "saloon" feel, with fireplaces and photographs of rock stars on the walls. A mixed, sometimes lively clientele.

Ostrov
Letenanta Shmidta Nab. 37 ◆ **D** D2
Tel. 812 328 46 49
Open Wed.–Sun. 10pm–6am
Located in a fine restored residence. Unusual décor and a rotating dance floor with special effects and DJ. A relatively wealthy clientele.

Plaza
Nab. Makarova 2 ◆ **C** B6
Tel. 812 323 90 90
Open daily 24 hours
Located in a beautiful old building with a huge dance floor, restaurant and casino. Dancing and concerts in the evening. Fri.–Sat.: concerts. Sun.: DJ.

Port
Antonenko Per. 2 ◆ **A** B6
Tel. 812 314 26 09
www.clubport.spb.ru
Open Wed.–Sat. 10pm–6am
Located next to

STAGE AT THE MARIINSKY THEATER

AUDITORIUM OF THE MARIINSKY THEATER

St Isaac's Square, opposite the Mariinsky Palace. The venue has a high-tech feel. There is a billiard room, several bars and dance floors, including an outsize one. A very mixed clientele and special student evenings.

Red Club
Poltavskaya Ulitsa 7 ◆ **E** D5
Tel. 812 277 13 66
www.redclubonline.com
Open noon–6am; concerts at 8pm
A varied program, with an orientation

toward young rockers. Excellent acoustics. Two floors, with two bars, two stages and a billiard room. A quieter atmosphere than elsewhere.

ENTERTAINMENT CENTERS

Carnaval
Anichkov Palace Nevsky Prospekt 39 ◆ **A** E5
Tel. 812 310 99 88
Russian folk music and dance are performed by top professional companies.

Sankt Petersburg
Lenina Pl. 1 ◆ **C** E5
Tel. 812 542 15 25 or 812 542 09 44
Ticket office open 1–3pm, 4–7pm
Concerts, shows and all sorts of other entertainments are part of a wide-ranging program.

THEATERS

Aleksandrinsky Theater
Ostrovskogo Pl. 2 ◆ **A** E6
Tel. 812 710 41 03
Ticket office open 11am–3pm, 4–7pm; Sat.–Sun. 4–6pm
A classical repertoire

of plays performed in the magnificent setting of a theater designed by the great Carlo Rossi.

Baltisky Dom (Baltic house)
Alexander Park ◆ **C** C5
Tel. 812 232 62 44
Ticket office open noon–3pm, 4–7pm
Having evolved from TRAM (Young Workers' Theater) and LenKom (Komsomol Leninist Theater), this theater is now the home of several small companies that are known for their experimental productions. It also hosts the annual Baltic House international festival, which takes place in October.

G. Tovstonogov's BDT (Grand Dramatic Theater)
Fontanky Nab. 65 ◆ **E** B4
Tel. 812 310 92 42
Ticket office open 1–3pm, 4–7pm
This theater was revived by the eminent director G. Tovstonogov, who brought together the best actors of the Soviet era. The company's repertoire covers the major works of the Russian theater.

Konservatori Rimskogo-Korsakova
Teatralnaya Pl. 3 ◆ **D** E3
Tel. 812 312 25 07
Ticket office open 11am–7pm
The Rimsky-Korsakov Conservatoire's opera and ballet theater is a show-case for its students and teachers. The theater also organizes various Russian and international festivals and competitions.

Maly (Mussorgsky Opera and Ballet Theater)
Iskusstv Pl. 1
(Arts Square) ◆ **A** D4
Tel. 812 595 42 84
or 812 595 43 05
(ticket office)
Ticket office open
11am–3pm, 4–6pm
(6–7pm for that day's
performance only)
*The former
Mihhailovsky Theater
is St Petersburg's
second most
important center of
opera and ballet. It
was once used only
by visiting foreign
companies,
particularly from Italy
and France, but now
puts on a range of
classic works
performed by
Russian singers and
dancers. The building
is worth a visit to see
the architecture and
décor alone.*

Maly Dramatichesky Teatr (Theater of Europe)
Ulitsa Rubinstein 18
◆ **A** F6
Tel.812 713 20 28
or 812 713 20 78
(ticket office)
Ticket office open
noon–7pm
*This theater's artistic
achievements and
innovative
productions have won
it a reputation
of European stature.
Its artistic leader, Lev
Dodin, was voted
Europe's most
outstanding director
three years ago. The
company goes on
frequent foreign
tours.*

Mariinsky Opera and Ballet Theater
Teatralnaya Pl. 1
(Theater Square)
◆ **D** E3
Tel. 812 714 43 44
or 812 714 12 11
Ticket office open
11am–2pm, 3–7pm.
Performances 7pm,
matinees 11.30am.
*The history of this
theater is closely
linked to Russian*

ARTS SQUARE

VIEW OF VASILYEVSKY ISLAND

*musical culture.
Formerly known as
the Kirov Theater, it
has reverted to its
original name and
continues to attract
the most highly
talented actors and
directors. With one of
the best orchestras in
the world, new
productions of the
great classical operas
and ballets are
particularly worth
seeing. As the main
companies have
gained such an
international
reputation they are
more likely to be
away touring in
spring and summer.
Winter is a better
time to find them in
St Petersburg. The
annual White Nights
festival (June)
regularly offers a
highly innovative
program. Note,
however, that ticket
prices are higher at
this time of year, the
high tourist season.*

St Petersburg Opera
Galernaya Ulitsa 33
◆ **D** E2
Tel. 812 312 39 82
or 812 315 67 69
Ticket office open
12–3pm, 4–7pm
*This young opera
company has already*

*won several awards.
Shows take place at
the Yusupov Palace
(Reky Moiky Nab.
94) or at the
Hermitage Theater
(Dvortsovaya Nab.
34). Its productions
have won praise for
their avant-garde,
nonconformist spirit.*

Teatr Muzikalnoy Komedy (Musical Comedy Theater)
Italianskaya Ul. 13
◆ **A** E5
Tel. 812 313 43 16
or 812 313 48 68
Ticket office open
11am–7pm
*This theater,
specializing in
operetta, puts on
magical productions
performed by a
company long
recognized as
distinctive masters of
the genre. The
theater has a
sumptuous interior.*

Zazerkalie (Children's musical theater)
Ulitsa Rubinstein 13
◆ **A** F6
Tel. 812 712 51 35
Ticket office open
noon–3pm, 4–7pm
*Although most of the
repertoire consists of
tales and fables, the
musical shows put on*

*here will appeal to
both children and
their parents.*

SHOPPING

ARMY ACCESSORIES

Soldat Udatchi (Soldier of Fortune)
Nekrassova
Ulitsa 37 ◆ **E** D3
Tel. 812 272 39 78
Open daily
11am–8pm
*Army equipment,
military decorations
and accessories.
Large selection of
knives.*

ART AND ANTIQUES

Antikvarnitsentr
Nalitchnaya
Ulitsa 21 ◆ **D** A2
Tel. 812 355 10 10
Open daily
11am–7pm
*One of the oldest-
established antique
shops in the city.
Large showroom with
a wide variety
of pieces.*

Lavka Stariovchtchika (Bric-a-brac)
9 Linia 26 ◆ **D** D1
Tel. 812 328 56 37
Open Mon.–Fri.11am–
6pm (3pm Sat.)
*All kinds of old
utilitarian objects,
including dinner
services and flatware,
samovars, coffee
mills and furniture.
Affordable prices.*

Panteleimonovsky
Pestelia
Ulitsa 13/15 ◆ **A** F3
Tel. 812 279 72 35
Open Mon.–Sat.
11am–7pm
*A wealth of beautiful
old decorative
objects and fine
porcelain.
Knowledgeable staff.*

Petersburg
Nevsky Prospekt 54
◆ **A** F5
Tel. 812 311 40 20
Open daily
10am–8pm
*A variety of objects
on sale at reasonable
prices.*

When in St Petersburg you do not need to dial the city code 812
before the seven-digit phone number.

KUNSTKAMMER Universitetskaya Nab. 3 Tel. 812 328 14 12/812 328 01 18	*Open Tue.–Sun. 11am–6pm.* *Closed last Tue. of the month.*	▲ *160* ◆ **A** A3
LOMONOSOV MUSEUM Universitetskaya Nab. 3 Tel. 812 328 10 11	*Open Tue.–Sun. 11am–5.30pm.* *Closed last Tue. of the month.*	▲ *160* ◆ **A** A3
MARBLE PALACE Millionaya Ul. 5 Tel. 812 312 91 96	*Open Mon. 10am–6pm, Wed.–Sun. 10am–5pm.*	▲ *184* ◆ **A** D2
MENDELEEV MUSEUM (The Twelve Colleges) Mendeleevskaya Linya 2 Tel. 812 328 97 44	*Open Mon.–Fri. 11am–4pm.*	▲ *159* ◆ **C** E1
MENSHIKOV PALACE ★ Universitetskaya Nab. 15 Tel. 812 323 11 12	*Open Tue.–Sun. 10.30am–4.30pm.* *Guided tours only (call for information).*	▲ *161* ◆ **D** E1
MUSEUM OF DECORATIVE **AND APPLIED ARTS** Solianoi Per. 15 Tel. 812 273 32 58	*Open Tue.–Sun. 11am–5pm.*	▲ *188* ◆ **A** E3
MUSEUM OF LITERATURE (Pushkin House) Naverejnaya Makarova 4 Tel. 812 328 05 02	*Open Mon.–Fri. 10.30am–4.30pm. Guided tours* *only, by appointment (Tel. 812 108 4761).* *A must for Russian literature aficionados.*	▲ *158* ◆ **B** F6
MUSEUM OF THEATER AND MUSIC (Fountains House) Fontanki Nab. 34 Tel. 812 272 44 41	*Open Wed.–Sun. noon–5pm.* *Closed last Wed. of the month.*	▲ *236* ◆ **A** F4-5
MUSEUM OF POLITICAL HISTORY Kubysheva Ul. 2–4 Tel. 812 233 71 13/812 233 70 52	*Open 10am–6pm.* *Closed Thur.*	▲ *150* ◆ **C** D5
MUSEUM OF THE ARCTIC **AND ANTARCTIC** Marata Ul. 24a Tel. 812 117 25 49/813 113 27 81	*Open Wed.–Sat. 10am–5pm, Sun. 10am–6pm.*	▲ *241* ◆ **E** C4
NABOKOV'S HOUSE **AND MUSEUM** Bolshaya Morskaya Ul. 47 Tel. 812 315 47 13	*Open Tues.–Sun. 11am–6pm.*	▲ *198* ◆ **D** F2
NAVAL MUSEUM Birgevaya Pl. 4 Tel. 812 328 25 02	*Open Wed.–Sun. 11am–6pm.* *Closed last Thur. of the month.*	▲ *157* ◆ **A** A3
PETER AND PAUL FORTRESS ★ Revolyutsy Pl. Tel. 812 238 03 29, 812 238 05 11 or 812 232 94 54	*Open 11am–5pm.* *Closed Wed. and last Tue. of the month.*	▲ *146* ◆ **A** B-C1
PHARMACY MUSEUM 16/18 Linaya 7 Tel. 812 323 22 69	*Open Mon.–Sat. 8am–8pm.*	▲ *164* ◆ **D** D1
PORCELAIN MUSEUM Obukhovskoy Oborony Pr. 151 Tel. 812 560 83 00	*Open Tue.–Sat. 10.30am–5pm, Sun.* *10.30am–4pm.* *Department of the Hermitage Museum.*	
PUSHKIN MUSEUM AND HOUSE Reki Moiky Nab. 12 Tel. 812 571 35 31	*Open Wed.–Mon. 11am–5pm.* *Book in advance for guided tours.*	▲ *182* ◆ **A** C3
THE RIDING SCHOOL (The Manège) Isaakievskaya Pl. 1 Tel. 812 314 82 53	*Open for displays Fri.–Wed. 11am–7pm.*	▲ *194* ◆ **A** A5
RIMSKY-KORSAKOV MUSEUM Zagorodny Pr. 28 Tel. 812 315 39 75	*Open Wed.–Sun. 11am–6pm.* *Closed last Fri. of the month.*	▲ *239* ◆ **E** C4-5
RUSSIAN MUSEUM ★ Ingenernaya Ul. 2 Tel. 812 595 42 40/812 314 34 48	*Open Mon. 10am–5pm, Wed.–Sun. 10am–6pm.* *Closed Tue.*	▲ *225* ◆ **A** D4

◆ PLACES TO VISIT

*When in St Petersburg you do not need to dial the city code 812
before the seven-digit phone number.*

RUSSIAN VODKA MUSEUM Konnogvardeisky Bl. 5 Tel. 812 312 34 16/812 312 91 78	*Open daily 11am–10pm.*	◆ **D** F2
ST ISAAC'S CATHEDRAL Isaakievskaya Pl. 1 Tel. 812 315 97 32	*Museum open Thur.–Tue. 11am–6pm.* *Panoramic visit 11am–5pm.*	▲ *195* ◆ **A** A5
ST NICHOLAS' CATHEDRAL ★ Nikolskaya Pl. 1/3	*Open daily 7am–7.30pm.*	▲ *204* ◆ **D** F4
ST PETERSBURG HISTORY MUSEUM (Engineers' Building) Alexandrovsky Park 7 Tel. 812 232 02 96	*Open Wed.–Sun. 11am–5pm.* *Closed last Thur. of the month.*	▲ *149* ◆ **C** C5
SHALYAPIN HOUSE (Museum of Russian Opera) Graftio Ul. 2b Tel. 812 234 10 56	*Open Wed.–Sun. noon–6pm.* *Closed last Fri. of the month.*	▲ *153* ◆ **C** B2
SMOLNY CATHEDRAL AND MONASTERY Rastelli Pl. 3/1 Tel. 812 271 91 82	*Open Fri.–Wed. 11am–5pm.* *Guided tours by appointment (Tel. 812 271 9421).* *Concerts (Tel. 812 271 7632).*	▲ *246* ◆ **E** F1-2
SMOLNY INSTITUTE Proletarskoy Diktatury Pl. Tel. 812 276 14 61	*Open Mon.–Fri. 10am–4pm.* *Guided tours only, by appointment.*	▲ *250* ◆ **E** F2
STROGANOV PALACE 17 Nevsky Pr. Tel. 812 117 23 60	*Open Mon. 10am–5pm, Wed.–Sun. 10am–6pm.* *Waxworks exhibition,'The Romanov Family',* *open Mon.–Fri. 11am–8pm (9pm Sat.–Sun.);* *guided tours (Tel. 812 571 39 44).* *Porcelain gallery (annexed to the Russian* *Museum): open Mon. 10am–5pm, Wed.–Sun.* *10am–6pm.*	▲ *215* ◆ **A** C5
SUMMER GARDEN ★ Kutuzova Nab. 2 Tel. 812 314 03 74/812 314 04 56	*Open May–Oct.: daily 10am–9pm.* *Nov.–March: daily 10am–6pm. Closed the* *last Mon. of the month and in April.*	▲ *186* ◆ **A** E3
SUMMER PALACE Kutuzova Nab. Tel. 812 314 04 56	*Open Wed.–Mon. 10am–5pm.* *Closed last Mon. of the month and* *Nov.–early May.*	▲ *187* ◆ **A** E2
SUVOROV MUSEUM Kirochnaya Ul. 43 Tel. 812 279 39 14	*Open Mon. 10am–4.15pm, Tue. and Fri. 10am–* *5.15pm, Sat.–Sun. 10am–6.15pm. Closed Wed,* *Thur and last Monday of the month.*	▲ *252* ◆ **E** E2
THEATER MUSEUM Ostrovsky Pl. 6 Tel. 812 311 21 95	*Open Thur.–Mon. 11am–6pm, Wed. 1–7pm.* *Closed last Fri. of the month.*	▲ *231* ◆ **A** E6
WATER MUSEUM Chpalernaya Ul. Tel. 326 53 45	*Open Wed.–Sun. 10am–6pm.* *Closed last Sun. of the month.*	▲ *251* ◆ **E** E1
WINTER PALACE see **HERMITAGE**		
WRITERS' WALKWAYS MAUSOLEUM (Literatorskiye Mostki) Rastannya Ul. 30 Tel. 812 766 23 83	*Open April–Oct.: Fri.–Wed. 11am–7pm;* *Nov.–March: Fri.–Wed. 11am–5pm.*	▲ *244* OFF MAP
YUSUPOV PALACE Reki Moiki Nab. 94 Tel. 812 314 98 83	*Open Tue.–Sun. noon–5pm.* *Open daily 12–5pm* *Guided tours obligatory* *Closed first Wed. of the month*	▲ *202* ◆ **D** E-F3
ZOOLOGICAL GARDENS Alexandrovsky Park 1 Tel. 812 232 48 28/812 232 82 60	*Open Tue.–Sun. 10am–7pm.*	▲ *151* ◆ **C** C5
ZOOLOGICAL MUSEUM Universitetskaya Nab. 1 Tel. 812 328 01 12	*Open Sat.–Thur. 11am–6pm.*	▲ *158* ◆ **D** F1

LIST OF ILLUSTRATIONS ◆

◆ INDEX

◆ STREET INDEX

D   E   F

STUDENTCHESKAYA ULITSA

PARGOLOVSKAYA

ULITSA KHARTCHENKO

UL. KAPITANAVORONINA UL.

PROSPEKT MARCHALA BLUKHERA

POLUSTROVSKY PROSPEKT

Ⓜ LESNAYA

ANTEMIROVSKAYA ULITSA

BOLSHOY SAMPSONIEVSKY PROSPEKT

LESNOY PROSPEKT

ALEKSANDRA NEVSKOGO

ULITSA GRIBALIOVOY

ULITSA

1

VYBORG

ULITSA

UL ALEKSANDRA NEVSKOGO

NOVOLITOVSKAYA

LITOVSKAYA ULITSA

LESNOY PROSPEKT

TCHUGURNAYA ULITSA

VYBORGSKAYA NABEREJNAYA

GELSINGFORSKAYA ULITSA

MENDELEIEVSKAYA ULITSA

2

BOLSHAYA NEVKA

OVA

APTEKARSKAYA NABEREJNAYA

PIROGOVSKAYA NABEREJNAYA

BELOVODSKY PER.

TOBOLSKAYA ULITSA

Ⓜ **VYBORGSKAYA**

ZELENKOV PER.

TCHUGURNAYA UL.

ICAL EUM

ANICAL RDENS

LOVIZSKY PEREULOK

ULITSA SMOLIATCHKOVA

UL. SMOLIATCHKOVA

ARSENALNAYA ULITSA

KARPOVKY

GRENADERSKAYA ULITSA

KRAPIVNYI PER.

SAMPSON GARDENS

LESNOY

ARSENALNAYA ULITSA

TCHAPAYEVA

St SAMPSON CATHEDRAL

BOLSHOY SAMPSONIEVSKY PR.

NECHLOTSKY PER.

3

PETROGRADSKAYA NABEREJNAYA

KAZARMENNY PEREULOK

ULITSA FOKINA

PROSPEKT

ULITSA TOTOVSKOGO

VYBORGSKAYA ULITSA

BOBRUSKAYA ULITSA

PINSKY PER.

IEVPATORISKY PEREULOK

VYBORGSKY CULTURAL CENTER

UL. KOMISARA SMIRNOVA

ARSENALNAYA ULITSA

4

TCHAPAYEVA

SADSKAYA UL.

MAL.

ESKY

SAKHARNY PER.

ORENBURGSKAYA ULITSA

ASTRAKHANSKAYA ULITSA

SARATOVSKAYA ULITSA

BOTKINSKAYA

ULITSA AKADEMIKA LEBEDEVA

FINSKY PER.

FINLIANDSKY PR.

St PETERSBURG HOTEL

FLINITCHESKAYA ULITSA

ULITSA MIKHAILOVA

UL. KUBYCHEVA

PENKOVAYA ULITSA

PETER THE GREAT STATE SCHOOL

PLOSHCHAD LENINA

FINLAND STATION

URINSKAYA UL.

INSKAYA

OTEL

CRUISER AURORA

STATUE OF LENIN

Ploshchad Lenina

UL. KOMSOMOLA

THE GREAT'S CABIN

PETROVSKAYA NAB.

ARSENALNAYA NABEREJNAYA

5

skaya chad

NEVA

NABEREJNAYA KUTUZOVA

NABEREJNAYA ROBESPIERA

LITENY PROSPEKT

CHPALERNAYA

ULITSA

PROSPEKT TCHERNYCHEVSKOGO

SPEKT

vorovskaya Ploshchad

PETER THE GREAT'S SUMMER PALACE

GAGARINSKAYA UL.

ZAKHAREVSKAYA

ULITSA

STATUE OF SUVOROV

STATUE OF KRYLOV

UL. ORUJENIKA FIODOROVA

ULITSA

TCHAIKOVSKOGO

POTIOMKINSKAYA UL.

BLE ACE

SUMMER GARDEN

FURCHTATSKAYA

CHERNY-CHEVSKAYA Ⓜ

UL.

D   E   F

6

D

A B C

SMOLENSK CEMETERY
(RUSSIAN ORTHODOX)

ULITSA NAKHIMOVA

UL. NAKHIMOVA

NALITCHNAYA UL.

NALITCHNY PER.

ULITSA BERINGA

GAVANSKAYA ULITSA

OSTUMOVA ULITSA

ULITSA CHEVTCHENKO

MALY PROSPEKT

24 LINIA

MALY PROSPEKT

14 LIN.

16 LINIA

18 LINIA

DONSKAYA ULITSA

NEMAN PER.

GALERNY PROIEZD

CHKIPERSKY MARKET

1

GVANSKAYA ULITSA

CHKIPERSKY PROTO

GAVANSKAYA ULITSA

KARTACHKHINA ULITSA

OPOTCHNINA ULITSA

ULITSA BERINGA

SREDNY PROSPEKT

KIROV ARTS CENTER

28 & 29 LINIA

26 LINIA

24 LINIA

VASILGARDENS

K.LUBN'I PEREULOK

KLUB PROSVETI

22 LINIA

20 LINIA

19 LINIA

BOLS

21

23 LINIA

NALITCHNAYA ULITSA

WOSENNAYA ULITSA

SREDNEGAVANSKY PR.

DETSKAYA ULITSA

KANAREYETCHNAYA

25 LINIA

2

MORSKAYA HOTEL

Ploshchad Morskoy Slavy

BOLSHOY PROSPEKT

KOSAYA LINIA

27 LINIA

KANA

MASLIANY

KOJEVENNAYA LINIA

3

BOLSHAYA NEVA

GALLE ISLAN

4

MEJEVOY KANAL

SEAMEN'S CULTURAL INSTITUTE

DVINSKAYA ULITSA

GAPSALSKAYA ULITSA

RIJSKY PROS

ULITSA STEPANA RAZINA

OB

CHOTLANDSKAYA ULITSA

5

DVINSKAYA ULITSA

DINABURGSKIYE VOROTA

NEVELSKAYA UL.

NAB. REKY IEKATERINGOFKY

IEKATERINGOFKA

LIFLIANDSKAYA ULITSA

IEKATERINGOF PARK

BUMA

GUTUEVSKY ISLAND

MALY REZVY ISLAND

NAB. REKY IEKATERINGOFY

BUMAJNY CANAL

6

A B C